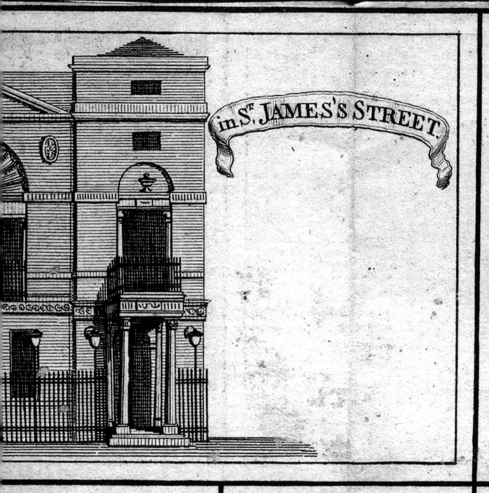

in S.t JAMES'S STREET.

COMMON NOTES
MDCCLXXVII.

Golden Number.....11
Cycle of the Sun.....22
Epact..........20
Dominical Letter....E
Roman Indiction....10
Number of Direction..9

APRIL XXX

☽ Last	1 day 6 morning	
● New	7 day at midnight	
☽ First	14 day 6 afternoon	
○ Full	22 day 8 afternoon	
☽ Last	30 day 5 afternoon	

Easter Tuesd.	9 M 33	
	10 29	
	11 24	
	0 A 20	
Old Lady-day	1 14	
Low Sunday	2 9	
☉ rises 5.19	3 5	
☉ sets 6.44	3 58	
Oxf.& Cam.T.beg.	4 58	
	5 56	
Day inc.5.53	6 54	
	7 51	
2.S.aft.Easter	Qui.Pas.	
Clock with Sun	9 38	
	10 27	
Term begins	11 13	
☉ rises 5.0	11 57	
☉ sets 7.3	Morn	
	0 9	
3.S.aft.Easter	Tre.Pas.	
Day inc.6.31	2 2	
	2 44	
St George	3 28	
☉ rises 4.48	4 13	
St Mark Prs.Mary bo.	5 49	
☉ sets 7.17		
4.S.aft.Easter	Me.Pas.	
	7 34	
Clock slow 3m.	8 27	
Day inc. 7.3	9 21	

MAY XXXI

● New	7 day 8 morning	
☽ First	14 day 8 morning	
○ Full	22 day 11 morning	
☽ Last	30 day 1 morning	

1 S. Phil.& Jac.	10 M 14	
2 ☉ rises 4.34	11 7	
3 ☉ sets 7.29	0 A 7	
E Rogat.Sund.	Qui.Pas.	
5	1 48	
6	2 45	
7 Day inc.7.27	3 43	
8 Ascension Day	4 42	
9 ☉ rises 4.22	Cras.Asc.	
E S.aft Ascen.Day	6 34	
12 Term ends	7 25	
13	8 13	
14 Clock slow 4m.	9 58	
15 Oxf.Term ends	10 41	
16 ☉ rises 4.11	11 23	
17	Morn	
E Whit-Sunday	0 4	
19 Whit-Mond.	Q.Cha.bo.	
20 Whit-Tuesd.	1 27	
21 Ember Week	2 12	
22 Prs.Eliz.born	2 58	
23 ☉ rises 4.2	3 47	
24	4 38	
E Trinity Sund.	5 30	
26	Cras.Tri.	
27	7 16	
28 Oxf.Term beg.	8 9	
29 K.Char.rest.	9 0	
30 Term begins	9 51	
31 Day inc.8.30	10 42	

JUNE XXX

● New	5 day 4 afternoon	
☽ First	12 day 11 at night	
○ Full	21 day 1 morning	
☽ Last	28 day 7 morning	

E 1.S.aft.Trin.	Oct.Tri.	
2 ☉ rises 3.51	0 A 27	
3 ☉ sets 8.10	1 22	
4 K.Geo.III.born	2 20	
5 P.Ern.Aug.born	3 22	
6 Clock slow 2 m.	4 20	
7	5 19	
E 2.S.aft.Trin.	Qui.Tri.	
9 Day inc.8.44	7 8	
10 Prs.Amelia bo.	7 50	
11 St Barnabas	8 34	
12 ☉ rises 3.45	9 16	
13 ☉ sets 8.15	9 57	
14 Clock with Sun	10 38	
E 3.S.aft.Trin.	Tre.Tri.	
16	Morn	
17	0 3	
18 Term ends	0 37	
19	1 28	
20	2 23	
21 Longest Day	3 21	
E 4.S.aft.Trin.	4 14	
23 ☉ rises 3.43	5 8	
24 St John Bapt.	6 1	
25 ☉ sets 8.16	6 58	
26	7 42	
27 Day dec.0.2	8 32	
28 Clock fast 3m.	9 22	
E 5.S.aft.Trin.St Peter		
30	11 6	

BOODLE'S
Celebrating 250 Years

Boodle's in Spring 2012 with the Economist Tower in the background
Previous page: Boodle's: watercolour sketch by Graham Byfield

BOODLE'S
Celebrating 250 Years
1762–2012

MARCUS BINNEY

DAVID MANN

With special assistance from
DANIELLA BEN-ARIE
and contributions from
MICHAEL CLAYTON
DAVID HANCOCK
NEIL HITCHIN
DUNCAN McEUEN

LIBANUS PRESS FOR BOODLE'S

2012

Boodle's in 1916 before the days of parking controls

Contents

Alastair Macpherson of Pitmain, Chairman of Boodle's Club

Foreword

ALASTAIR MACPHERSON

Reaching the milestone of the 250th Anniversary of the founding of Boodle's in 1762 is a propitious moment to publish a book that is both a celebration of a much-loved institution and also a record of some of the highlights that have occurred during the long history of the Club. It is also an occasion to reflect how such an institution has survived for so long. This publication follows on from the excellent history of the Club that was written by Sir Roger Fulford to mark the Club's bicentenary in 1962 and Stephen Hill's *Boodle's Apocrypha* which was published in 2009.

This book is not a history of Boodle's, but a series of pen portraits of the Club, taken at various stages of its existence; from its early days when politics dominated the discussions of the Earl of Shelburne and his fellow founding Members to the Regency era, when magnificent balls and fetes were held by the Club at the Pantheon and in Ranelagh Gardens. The 19th century saw clubland at the heart of London society and Boodle's at the centre of foxhunting which the Club's Foxhunting Committee ran for several decades. The two World Wars in the first half of the 20th century cast a shadow over the Club and its Members, a testament to which is the Roll of Honour outside the Saloon recording the names of those Members who lost their lives in those conflicts. Throughout the Club's long existence, the common threads of good food and fine wine have been at the core of life at Boodle's and we have chapters that give an entertaining insight into some of the Club's more memorable menus and Members' drinking habits.

There are a number of people to whom grateful thanks are due for their contributions to this book. First and foremost it was the late David Mann who initiated the idea of a book about Boodle's to mark the 250th Anniversary and who was supported in the venture by my predecessors Patrick Burgess and Charles Vyvyan. A particular debt of gratitude should go to Daniella Ben-Arie, not only for her fine chapters on St James's Street and Masquerades and Fetes, but for her extensive researches into numerous sources that have produced so much material about the Club's history. We are grateful to all the contributors to the book for their time and scholarly contributions. Above all, we are particularly indebted to Marcus Binney who assumed responsibility for the project from David Mann and who has edited all the extensive material to produce a very fine book that not only adds to our understanding of the Club but also of London society during the past 250 years.

So why is Boodle's in such good health today? Perhaps because in an ever-changing world it has always tried to retain the ethos, principles and traditions that guided the twenty-five young men who founded the Club in 1762. At its heart, it is a place where good food, drink and conversation can be enjoyed in congenial surroundings in the company of like-minded individuals. This book is a tribute to our founding fathers and to the succeeding generations of Members over the decades and centuries that followed who ensured the continuity of our Club and who have left us with such a rich legacy, much of which is captured in the pages of this book.

ALASTAIR MACPHERSON OF PITMAIN
Chairman
December 2012

The Club's Bar hung with paintings of racehorses

Introduction

DAVID MANN

One day I was having a drink with Stephen Hill on the left-hand side of the bar where the most right-wing views are expressed. We started talking about the forthcoming 250th anniversary of the founding of Boodle's in 2012, and that perhaps a book should be written; about how most histories of institutions were unsatisfactory being mere gossip, or self-satisfied pieces of corporate history, usually written as a last hurrah as the entity waned or faded away. In 2009 Stephen published his book *Boodle's Apocrypha: A Story of Men & Their Club in London*.

My continuing curiosity about the history of the Club was kindled again by finding a recipe for Boodle's Grouse in Florence White's cookbook of 1932. Why of all the London clubs was Boodle's the one with so many recipes in its name? And how did they come to be in books written by women?

This got me to thinking about other aspects of the Club's history and what else had been written on the subject. For the 200th anniversary in 1962, Sir Roger Fulford published a short history of Boodle's. Upon rereading Fulford's book, I began to have other questions about the Club's formation and history.

Fulford's literary executor Lord Shuttleworth of Gawthorpe was not able to find Fulford's working papers. And so it was that with the desire to answer some basic questions I found myself fashioning a series of topics about which I would like to know more.

My search for answers evolved into a much larger enterprise. But why a book? Partially it was my own curiosity about subjects that had not been dealt with by Fulford and Hill. But more importantly, the anniversary itself became a compelling incentive to fill in historical gaps and I had the interest and inclination to do so.

I began discussions in January 2005 with the then-chairman Patrick Burgess and continued these discussions with subsequent chairmen Charles Vyvyan and Alastair Macpherson. Of particular help and continuing support was another former chairman and 50-year Boodle's member Sir Richard Brooke, 11th Bt.

Much Club history is passed down by word of mouth, and causes and events once they have become lore are often impossible to verify after the fact. We therefore began the search for answers by going back to the original source material and to information about Boodle's members.

A major challenge was that, apart from the Club books of the first years, there were virtually no Boodle's archives. This meant that, unlike Brooks's and White's, Boodle's did not have a list of members from its founding. A club is about its members. Who were we in 1762 and how could one go about finding out?

For help with this daunting task, I sought the advice of the Honorable Georgina Stonor who recommended Richard Samways, formerly of the London Metropolitan Archive. Richard has provided tireless and invaluable assistance over the past five years of this research. He cannot be thanked enough for his efforts, nor can Georgina who has repeatedly directed me to the right people or resource.

One of the most important accomplishments of our research has been the compilation for the first time of a list of Boodle's members between 1762 and 1896. The new research provides Boodle's with a complete list of members from its founding.

We have also compiled an index of Boodle's Club managers from our founding in 1762 until 1896. Much of the information on proprietors is published here for the first time. We have also examined the proprietor/member relationship, mostly cordial, sometimes fractious, as evidence of court cases herein attest.

Compiling these lists involved many hours of scrutinising signatures with a magnifying glass and heavy use of Debrett's. Copies of these lists are not included in this volume (they were deemed too lengthy) but they are on view in the Club. We learned that in 1782, when we moved to this site, we were 280 men. In this same clubhouse we are now 1,450.

We also tried to find as many extant historical accounts as we could in early English newspapers, journals, diaries, letters and correspondence, trawling archives and record offices for any indications of members' activities at the Club and elsewhere. We even examined auction catalogues and sale advertisements. This allowed us to build an account, slowly, over time of the use of Boodle's by its members.

David Hancock has written a brilliantly perceptive essay that focuses on Boodle's twenty-five founding members and their shared allegencies and politics. Neil Hitchin has written on Boodle's place in eighteenth-century politics looking at our members and their remarkable sphere of influence, from which we can see their extensive political ambitions as well as economic, artistic and literary affiliations.

Boodle's has always been known for its food and wine. These are essential elements in the way Boodle's thinks of itself. My own early questions on food and recipes led to a section on that subject prepared with the helpful assistance of Richard Edmonds, Keith Podmore and Victor Ceserani. On the subject of wine Duncan McEuen has written a wonderful account, despite a dearth of archival material, speculating on what (and how much!) club members were consuming.

Hidden gems also came to light. In the back of an extant club book is a menu created for 'The Attorney General's dinner on April 23rd 1828 for the Kings Counsel' around which we were able to develop an account of the day and our members role in it.

In its early days (particularly during its first fifty years), Boodle's was well-known for the number of fetes and masquerades that the Club organised for its members. One of the highlights of our research was locating a charming watercolour drawing made by Thomas Rowlandson of the magnificent fete organised by Boodle's in 1802, a copy of which now hangs in the clubhouse. Daniella Ben-Arie, an independent scholar who has been instrumental in all of our research, built up the story of these events based on contemporary newspaper and eyewitness accounts.

Foxhunting, which has played an important role in British social history and in the life and times of Boodle's, is also a subject of this narrative. Very little written information exists on hunting. By tradition, most of what is known is passed down by word of mouth. References to hunting appear in personal memoirs and in the novels of Surtees but there is very little recorded information on the subject. As it happens, Boodle's has been heavily involved in foxhunting from its earliest days. The Club began as the political base for country gentlemen, whether as Whig landowners or Royalists at Court with many sportsmen among them. The role of Boodle's in foxhunting was formalised in the 19th century. Between 1856 and 1880 foxhunting in the countryside was administered by a special sub-committee of the Club which was the forerunner of the Masters of Foxhounds Association.

Records from the Boodle's foxhunting committee were uncovered during our research and we enlisted the services of Michael Clayton, highly respected former editor of *Horse and Hound*, to kindly write an essay from this material which provides valuable information for future social historians on the transition of foxhunting from hunts dominated by the great landowners to hunting through subscription

I regret that it was not possible to carry out two projects: the changes in dining habits, and an analysis of the finances of the Members Club since 1896, so one can have an idea of how financial problems were solved and how relative costs, particularly of staff, have changed. Perhaps some younger members will take up the challenge?

I am extremely grateful to all members and others who have answered questions and provided information. Editing a book of this nature, across several subjects and with multiple authors, takes commitment, patience and diligence, and my final thanks are for those who coordinated this process. Marcus Binney, distinguished writer and architectural historian, has overseen the book through its final stages and he has also authored a very interesting chapter on the architecture of our St James's clubhouse. A special thanks also is due to Daniella Ben-Arie, who worked with Marcus on the editing process. Daniella has been involved with the project from its earliest stages and this book has benefitted greatly from her research and scholarship.

Doubtless more information, including reasons for a wind rose on the roof (which cannot be seen from the clubhouse) will emerge in the future to illuminate the 300th Boodle's anniversary in 2062, particularly with the much greater interest of academics in the history of institutions like Boodle's.

Let us hope that Boodle's continues in its agreeable and happy fashion. As Winston Churchill, a distinguished honorary member said – 'The future is unknowable but the past should give us hope.'

DAVID MANN
May 2012

'If Labour get in, would you be "A" Frightened? "B" Horrified? or "C" Terrified?'

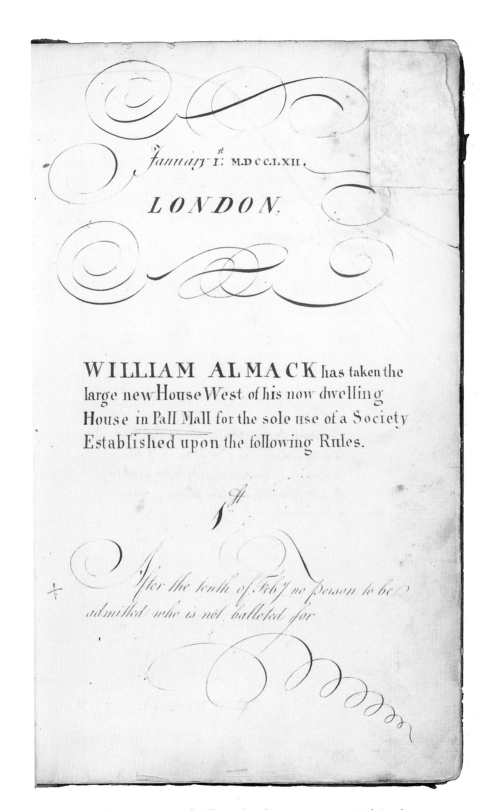

January 1st. M.DCC.LXII.

LONDON.

WILLIAM ALMACK has taken the
large new House West of his now dwelling
House in Pall Mall for the sole use of a Society
Established upon the following Rules.

1st

After the tenth of Feb.y no person to be
admitted who is not balloted for

The opening page of William Almack's 1762 manuscript Rule Book

CHAPTER 1

The Founding Twenty-Five

DAVID HANCOCK

In 1762, the tavern keeper William Almack opened 'the large new House [immediately] West of his … House in Pall Mall for the sole use of a Society', a matter of yards east of today's Pall Mall Place passage. Almack already kept 'a common Alehouse or Victualling-house' at No. 49, in a building recently built by the architect and contractor Henry Holland, Sr, and his imposing two-storey, three-bay, two-door tavern had become a haunt of the *ton* and those who aspired to be near them, famous for its dinners. But either its success was too great or its commonness and conviviality too disconcerting, for in late 1761 twenty-five patrons asked for a more exclusive arrangement. For their 'Society,' Almack set about acquiring and outfitting No. 50.

For their part, the Twenty-Five set about organising. In early January 1762, they agreed on twenty-two 'rules' stipulating who could be a member, how he could be elected, how much he had to pay in dues each year, what food and drink he could expect to find there, what games he would be allowed to play, and what manner of management would prevail. Perhaps realising that twenty-five members alone could not afford to keep an independent clubhouse viable, they expanded the membership, setting 250 as the upper limit. Within their clubhouse, the members could enjoy tea, coffee, chocolate drinks, and wine; dinner and supper; chess, whist, piquet, cribbage, tredrille, quadrille, and ombre; a variety of news sheets, foreign – from Amsterdam, The Hague, and Brussels, though oddly not Paris – and domestic – Dublin (*Faulkner's*), Glasgow (*The Caledonian Mercury*), and 'all the London news papers'; and, above all else, conversation. Appropriate behaviour was prescribed: no healths were to be drunk, nor toasts given; the amount of winnings was regulated and some games, like 'Heads and

Tails,' outlawed; indeed, each member, if he was staying 'in a [fellow member's] private House in London,' was barred from giving money to their servants or, if he had a townhouse, from allowing his servants to accept money from other members.

Inasmuch as No. 50 was under construction and being furnished through August and Almack did not gain the leasehold until September 29, the first nine months of meetings and dinners took place in No. 49's private upper rooms. Only in October did they move next door.

Little is known about day-to-day-life in the house before Edward Boodle enters the historical record. Almack's relationship with the new club is a mystery. He supervised the club when it met under his own roof for the first three-quarters of 1762, but did he continue to manage it after the move next door? Did he hire and supervise the staff? Did he transfer proprietary rights and ownership of the leasehold to Boodle, and if so when?

Indeed, who was Edward Boodle? As best as can be determined from genealogical records, Edward Boodle was one of fifteen children born to John Boodle and his two wives, Margaret Johns and Mary Davies. Boodle Senior was the proprietor of The Three Tuns in Oswestry, Shropshire. Edward was the third son of John and Margaret. Born in St Oswald's Parish, Oswestry in 1722, he married Mary Evans relatively late in life, in 1760, in St Martin's, Shropshire. What he did between 1722 and 1760 is unclear. The historian T H S Escott suggests that he worked at Bowood Park, near Calne, Wiltshire, for either Henry, 1st Earl of Shelburne (of the first creation), John, 1st Earl of Shelburne (of the second creation), or maybe even John's son, 2nd Earl, but no

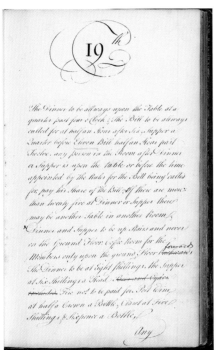

confirming evidence has surfaced in the detailed estate records left by the Shelburnes at Bowood. Escott also states that Boodle found employment doing odd jobs for a waiter at the Chesterfield Street chocolate house, gambling den and ticket office known as Arthur's (or variously White's), but this is surmise. Wherever he worked, he acquired some familiarity with innkeeping at the Three Tuns and perhaps later. The first mention of him in London occurs in an April 1764 newspaper article, which calls the club he manages 'Boodle's.' So he is on the spot at least by early 1764; and he presided over the club until his death in February 1772.

Boodle exhibited considerable entrepreneurial talent, combining social, commercial, benevolent, and political interests, some for the good of members; some for his own. From the start and throughout the heady decade that was the 1760s, he created a space where members went to drink and sup with confederates. Given the rules against gaming, it was never as boisterous as other clubs, especially after 1764 when Almack opened his Assembly Rooms and established Brooks' Club, where gaming reached a fevered pitch, even for London. Boodle's was never crowded; indeed,

throughout the decade, members worried about its viability. The winter of 1764–1765, for instance, was 'not … quite a good one,' given the departure of a number of members to governmental posts overseas. Luckily, though, 'a few active men . . . enter'd some of our seas and entered themselves, [and] the Club' stayed 'upon its legs.' The 2nd Earl of Shelburne, the 4th Earl of Dunmore, and Isaac Barré, to name just three, regularly drank, supped, read, and talked there well into the 1770s, several times a week and often past midnight. Boodle would arrange special meals or stage celebratory dinners, on or off premises, as in 1767 when he managed 'a Treat given to Lord Clare at Black Wall.' He regularly threw balls. He interpreted the rules on gaming loosely; sensing the competition from Brooks's, he began encouraging games, so much so that by 1767 Boodle's had the reputation of a first-rate gaming house. When in London, the horse-and-hounds man John Parker played 'his Game at Whist at Boodles almost every evening,' leaving his young and beautiful wife to fend for herself, and he was 'sometimes tempted to play at Quinze – which sometimes uses him well & sometimes ill'.

Boodle also developed side businesses. He sold tickets to musical soirees, dances, and charitable events around London, and Boodle's became one of the three or four best places in the metropolis to find auction catalogues. He also branched out into supplying members' non-club needs, catering their dinners (he was a regular supplier to Shelburne, when the latter was Secretary of State in 1766–1768, for instance, and hosted diplomatic dinners at his mansion in Berkeley Square), stocking their cellars (Shelburne, again, spent £147 in nine months on three dozen bottles of white wine, three dozen of Madeira, a dozen of Mountain wine, two bottles of sherry, and a bottle of port – and this in 1771–1772 when he was mainly in Europe grieving the death of his first wife), even managing their properties (serving as a go-between in purchase and sale or rental agreements, providing bond for mortgages, and supervising houses while members were in the country). Such services earned him extra money, on top of his wages as club proprietor, in fact more money than the club provided. His vintner's trade was one of the largest to supply fashionable London. To all this work, he added some philanthropy, staging if not encouraging the club's support for members' charities. Boodle created a safe haven in a boisterous town, a place highly regarded by members. Writing from the bug-infested swamp that was his colony of East Florida, Governor James Grant of Ballindalloch articulated general sentiment when in 1768 he admitted to Isaac Barré: 'I often think of the Club & long much to be with them.'

The twenty-five founders were a tight group of restless if elite insiders. They were, in the main, young, well-educated, politically ambitious bachelors who had seen service in the Seven Years' War. They had become friends at college or during war, and the latter experience had made them deeply unhappy with the management of the military and the country. The heart of the Club was their political interests, as their letters indicate. Politics trumped whist from the outset.

The average age of the twenty-four whose identities can be fully ascertained was thirty. Two-thirds of them were younger than that, and George Lord Greville, eldest son of

another member the Earl of Warwick, was only sixteen. All came of age when the power of Britain's military might and the expansiveness of its overseas empire were ascendant, giving them a generational perspective on the new problems of empire. Despite their youth, some of them already had experience dealing with these challenges. One of the older members, the 4th Earl of Shaftesbury, had managed the young colony of Georgia as one of its Trustees. Ten of them helped extend the bounds of empire during the War of Austrian Succession and the Seven Years' War.

When they formed the 'society,' most members were single. Only seven of the twenty-four identifiable members – Lords Boston, Dunmore, Shaftesbury and Warwick, as well as Thomas Bunbury, John Campbell and Paul Methuen – were married in the first year of operation, and even Bunbury only married halfway through the year. Thus, the Club was a home for bachelors. No women were admitted as members, as was the norm in the Georgian era, and few early events included women. (The ones that did were held off-site at places like The Pantheon or Ranelagh Gardens.) The rites of masculinity prevailed at 50 Pall Mall. A club was important for a gentleman about town. It provided him with food and drink away from the *hoi polloi*, and in the absence of a large staff, services he needed because he lived much of the time in the country but maintained a house or rooms in London; an environment to desport himself freely; and the chance to meet others useful to a budding political career. A club like Boodle's perpetuated patterns of male dominance that were endemic to Georgian culture.

By the standards of the day, the members were well educated. Just under a third received some preparatory education at Eton, Westminster, or Winchester. More than half received a university education. Isaac Barré went to Trinity College Dublin; Thomas Fitzmaurice and John Craufurd to the University of Glasgow; and Thomas Bunbury and Robert Smyth to the University of Cambridge's St Catharine's Hall and Trinity College respectively. But it was Oxford that dominated, especially Christ Church, which nearly a third of the founders attended. Christ Church was one of the few colleges to have woken from the doldrums that was early-modern English university education. For most, university, 'was

The Twenty-Five

The twenty-five men who signed the subscription book before balloting began after February 10, 1762 were:[1]

John Parker (1735–1788), of Boringdon, Devon

James Townsend (1737–1787), of Bruce Castle, Tottenham, Middlesex

Robert Bernard (1739–1789), of Brampton, Hampshire

John Aubrey (1739–1826), of Boarstall and Dorton, Buckinghamshire

John Radcliffe (1738–1783), of Hitchin Priory, Hertfordshire

Mr. Bell

John Stepney (1743–1811), of Llanelly, Carmarthenshire

Francis Greville, 1st Earl of Warwick, 1st Earl Brooke (1719–1773), of Warwick Castle, Warwickshire

Lord George Greville, son of 1st Earl of Warwick (1746–1816)

Hon Thomas Fitzmaurice (1742–1793), of Llewenny Hall, Denbighshire

John Murray, 4th Earl of Dunmore (1732–1809)

William Petty, 2nd Earl of Shelburne (1737–1805), of Bowood, Wiltshire

Thomas Charles Bunbury (1740–1821), of Barton, Suffolk, and Bunbury, Cheshire

Lord Charles Spencer (1740–1820), of Wheatfield, Oxfordshire

Clotworthy Upton (1721–1785), of London and Castle Upton, Co. Antrim

William Irby, 1st Baron Boston (1707–1775), of Boston, Lincolnshire

Anthony Ashley Cooper, 4th Earl of Shaftesbury (1711–1771)

Paul Methuen (1723–1795), of Corsham, Wiltshire

General Robert Clerk (1728–1797) of Westminster, Middlesex

Sir Robert Smyth, 5th Bt. of Upton (1744–1802), of Berechurch, near Colchester, Essex

Colonel Sir John Dalling, 1st Bt. (1731–1798), of Bungay, Suffolk

Isaac Barré (1726–1802), of Westminster, Middlesex

Patrick Craufurd (1704–1778) of Auchenames, Renfrew, and Crosbie and Drumsoy, Ayr

John Craufurd (1742–1814), of Errol, Perth and Auchenames, Renfrew and Drumsoy, Ayr

James Campbell (1737–1805) of Tuerechan, Argyll

rather like a fashionable holiday camp, most of their time spent on hunting, drinking, gaming, and feasting.'[2] But four successive deans of Christ Church between 1756 and 1809 instituted a very different regime. They introduced a more varied curriculum and insisted on high standards for teachers and students. They required a classical education of Latin and Greek literature (histories, speeches, plays, and poems), divinity, and philosophy (logic, ethics, and natural science). The number of books students read rose and their range broadened. John Parker, Lord William Fitzmaurice (who became the 2nd Earl of Shelburne on the death of his father in 1761), Lord Charles Spencer, John Aubrey, Robert Bernard, and John Stepney studied there between 1753 and 1760, and Lord George Greville went in the early 1760s. At Oxford

16

and elsewhere, the founders confronted new ideas (in these years, for instance, Blackstone gave the first Vinerian Lectures that shaped *A Discourse on the Study of Law*, with Fitzmaurice and others in attendance), new styles of discourse, and new friends.

The friendships forged at Oxford with landed and wealthy gentlemen distinctly different from those they had grown up with in their own counties and regions were subsequently burnished by war in foreign countries. Indeed, one is tempted to say that wartime experience was the strongest force bringing and keeping the founders together. A quarter – Clerk, Barré, Dalling, Dunmore, Shelburne, and Campbell – saw action in the Seven Years' War. This proved to be the most enduring of bonds, for fellow officers came to the aid of fellow officers, politically and financially, throughout their long and often chaotic careers.

Of their war experiences, the failed Siege of Rochefort of September 1757 was particularly important to the members' shared allegiances and politics. This disastrous operation introduced five of the more active founders of Boodle's to one another; in some sense, it was the crucible of their Club. Their allegiance coalesced around the celebrated James Wolfe and, after his death on the Plains of Abraham, to their memory of him. The siege took place in mid-1757 when *de facto* war minister William Pitt the Elder decided to relieve Frederick the Great's efforts on the eastern front with an offensive on France's western coast ('some action of *éclat*, that might revive our sinking affairs,' Horace Walpole quipped, 'and throw a lustre on the dawn' of Pitt's ministry). The Ministry based its decision in part on an account of 'the condition of some of their fortifications' drawn up by Robert Clerk, who had visited Rochefort in 1754. Clerk had served valiantly in the War of Austrian Succession, and was made 'Chief Engineer' of this expedition, but his 'contribution' to the surprise raid made him relatively infamous for a while.

The Ministry appointed Sir John Mordaunt commander in chief, Generals Henry Conway and Edward Cornwallis deputy commanders, and Lieutenant-Colonel James Wolfe quartermaster general of the planned attack. Notwithstanding the brilliance of its command (which also included Captain Charles Schaw Cathcart, Captain Richard Howe, Captain Samuel Graves, General George Howard, Sir Edward Hawke, and Governor Charles Knowles), bad weather (rain and fog), intense secrecy, and geographical misinformation doomed the mission. Arriving off Rochefort on September 20, the British quickly captured the Île d'Aix. But thereafter the assault disintegrated. Mordaunt and Wolfe disagreed about the strength of mainland defences and preparations, while Conway and Knowles bickered with each other. Wolfe pushed for immediate action, an attack upon Fort Fouras guarding the Charente, and an adjacent raid, but Mordaunt dithered, apparently 'incapable of forming any opinion,' Horace Walpole tells us. Mordaunt finally agreed to attack the fort but, after embarkation, he cancelled the operation based on his reading of the winds and tides. The British then evacuated Aix and departed the Rochefort area, returning to England with nothing to show for it but a large bill for the siege. An inquiry into the failure was held two months later, and court martial proceedings against Mordaunt were commenced before Christmas. During the inquiry, it was intimated (incorrectly, as it happens) that Clerk had passed on faulty information, perhaps knowingly, and thereby contributed to the collapse of the raid.

The connections made during this expedition proved enduring in ways that none of the participants could have expected, notwithstanding the dampening effect it had on Clerk's career. Clerk was present during the attack, as were future club members Isaac Barré, John Dalling, Lord Dunmore and Lord Fitzmaurice (later the 2nd Earl of Shelburne). The young men idolised Wolfe, and despaired when he was overruled by what they saw as uninspired risk-aversion.

Isaac Barré had served in the War of Austrian Succession as an Ensign in the 32nd Foot. In 1755, he returned to active duty in the regiment as a lieutenant. Participating in the Siege of Rochefort, he met Dunmore, Shelburne and, most importantly, Wolfe, falling under the latter's spell, as did many officers of his generation. When Pitt later sent Wolfe to Canada to take Louisbourg in 1758, Wolfe arranged for Barré to transfer to Wolfe's 67th Regiment of Foot. Barré was with Wolfe during the Siege of Québec in 1759, when he lost an eye, and on the Plains of Abraham in late-September when Wolfe fell near him. For his valour, he was given a captaincy in the 28th Foot in 1760 and, on his return to England the following year, a lieutenant colonelcy in the 106th Foot. (Subsequently, he served as Adjutant General and Governor General of Stirling Castle in 1763, the result of Shelburne's support.) Like his comrade Barré, Major John Dalling of the 28th Regiment of Foot also fought alongside Wolfe at Rochefort and later on the Plains of Abraham, but rather than return to England he went on to serve as Governor of Jamaica during the American Revolution.

Dunmore was a more unlikely participant, since he had earlier been a rebel. In 1745, he and his father had participated in the unsuccessful rebellion of Charles Edward Stuart, 'Bonnie Prince Charlie' the Young Pretender, for which they were placed under house arrest. Dunmore's father's brother remained loyal, however, and become a diplomat in Holland; with difficulty, he was eventually able to secure their pardon in 1747. With few opportunities at home in Scotland, John procured a commission as ensign in the 3rd Regiment of Foot Guards in 1749. First as ensign and after 1755 as lieutenant, he served in the early years of the Seven Years' War under Captain Cathcart. He took part in General Mordaunt's 'raid' on Rochefort in September 1757, when he met Clerk, Barré, Dalling, and Shelburne. The following year, Dunmore's battalion participated in the abortive landing at Cancalle Bay in June, the decimating assault on Cherbourg in August, and the humiliating rout at St Cast in September. Like many who saw the uninspired action in France, he petitioned the King to go to Germany and serve under Prince Ferdinand, but for reasons unknown the request was denied. He returned to England in 1759, when he gained a captaincy and married. He retired from service the following year; yet when it came to having his portrait painted by Reynolds in 1765, he chose to be memorialised in the Highlands dress of his 3rd Regiment.

Fitzmaurice (later Shelburne) was Dunmore's closest friend. Tiring of study at Christ Church (where he had matriculated in March 1755 alongside Parker), or perhaps drawn by the adventure of war and the spirit of Wolfe,

Fitzmaurice joined Major General William Kingsley's 20th Regiment of Foot as an ensign in May 1757, which participated in the expedition to Rochefort. (Kingsley had commanded the 3rd Regiment of Foot in the War of Austrian Succession, under Dunmore's father, the 3rd Earl.) After returning to England, Fitzmaurice did not follow Wolfe to North America, despite his infatuation with the man – his parents opposed the move. Instead, he turned to the war's German theatre, was promoted to lieutenant in John Leslie, 10th Earl of Rothes' 3rd Regiment of Foot Guards and served as a Volunteer to Hereditary Prince Karl Wilhelm Ferdinand of Brunswick-Wolfenbuttel-Bevern, Prince Ferdinand of Brunswick, and John Manners, Marquess of Granby. He distinguished himself under Granby at the Battle of Minden (August 1, 1759), and more notably under the Hereditary Prince at the Battle of Kloster Kampen (October 15, 1760), where, with the defeated British and Allied armies in retreat, he came to the aid of the Hereditary Prince. He had, newspapers reported, 'a Horse killed under him, with several Musket Balls, and a great many Shot went through his Cloaths.' The second Horse he mounted was likewise wounded.'[3] For this action, he was praised by Prince Ferdinand and Granby and, on their recommendation, was made an aide-de-camp to George III two months later.

Two other club members served in the Seven Years' War, although not with Wolfe. James Campbell went directly to North America and later fought in the West Indies. He served as an Ensign in the 30th Foot in 1755, was raised to a Lieutenant and transferred to the 60th Foot the following year, and made a Captain of an Independent Company of Foot three years later. The comparatively aged Earl of Warwick saw no active duty but, as Lord Lieutenant of Warwickshire, was heavily involved in recruiting and mustering troops at home.

The founders of Boodle's had gone to war with high hearts and returned disillusioned. Almost to a man, they took up the cause of peace on their return and advocated pacifism throughout their careers. The *annus miserabilis* 1757 was profoundly determinative. Leaders such as Mordaunt were unimaginative, unwilling to break rules, brook obstacles and seize initiatives; the systems on which they depended were faulty, be it the slow transport service, the information network, or the contract provisioning system. Careers had been squandered, and promotions had been bungled. Their heroes 'had borne the dilatoriness of the "chief commanders" with indignation.'[4] At every step, the Government had failed to measure up, even if it had struggled through to the end and won the war. For men of action, the idea of an earlier era which enjoyed balanced powers, great leaders, decisive actions, pure politics, and civic harmonies was compelling.

Initially, they aimed to reinvigorate royal prerogative and thereby re-balance the constitution; ultimately, they hoped to regulate and monitor the quality and performance of politicians. Their understanding of a 'balanced constitution' sprang from Commonwealth and Country ideological writings, especially those of Henry St John, 1st Viscount Bolingbroke. According to this line of thought, political liberty could only be maintained through the independence of the Crown and Commons. Lack of independence would result in corruption. With independence came virtue – not merely opposition to mal-government but civic responsibility. Those who understood the constitution this way thought the Crown had lost much of its prerogative due to an overreaching House of Commons; they believed George III should assert his 'independency' and in doing so 'recover Monarchy from the inveterate Usurpation of Oligarchy.'

They saw George as a young king (as young as themselves) who was so trammelled by tradition that he was unable to lead, much as Wolfe had been unable to break through the hierarchy at Rochefort or Granby had struggled with faulty government contracting in Germany. George III and his tutor, the Earl of Bute, whatever their actual philosophical convictions on mixed government, expressed an exuberant disregard for the Ministry (Pitt was nothing but a 'snake in the grass' and Newcastle a mere 'knave'). This resonated with the club's founders. Idealistic, energetic and ambitions, they entered the political arena dissatisfied with the way things were handled. Out of a desire to institutionalise and operationalise public virtue, they sided with Bute against an old

regime that was, he and they believed, inbred, bureaucratic, sclerotic, and inefficient. They saw Bute as threatening the Whig oligarchs' hard-won authority and power, and at the same time as free of the need for personal fame and aggrandisement. Bute was in all likelihood doing so for his own, more complicated reasons, but the founders saw the similarities, not the differences.

John Stuart, 3rd Earl of Bute, had been a confidante of the Dowager Princess of Wales, George III's mother. Moreover, Bute had been George III's tutor, who instilled in the prince a sense of the importance of virtue in politics. After the accession of his pupil in October 1760, Bute's influence remained strong; he was named to the Cabinet as Secretary of State for the Northern Department in March 1761, where he was an immediately divisive figure. In the Cabinet, he opposed Thomas Pelham-Holles, 1st Duke of Newcastle and William Pitt the Elder. In the Parliament of November 1761, which convened a month after Pitt resigned office, factions and individuals dominated: and the prior strong support for Government disappeared. Bute commanded at least a quarter of the votes in the Commons. Six months later, Newcastle was dismissed, and was replaced by Bute.

Most of the founders of Boodle's owed their promotions and seats in the Commons to Bute and his allies Henry Fox and George Dodington. This was especially true of the Scots in Parliament. Dunmore owed his seat in the Lords to Bute's placing him on the 1761 Court List and arguing successfully for his election as one of Scotland's representative peers with the Duke of Argyll, then the political manager of North Britain. Patrick Craufurd of Auchenames represented Renfrewshire largely because Bute controlled that county's election; highly regarded by Fox, he was always unabashedly supportive of Bute in the Commons, even years after Bute fell from power.

Bute came to the aid of English members of Boodle's, as well. At Bute's suggestion, Clotworthy Upton was appointed Comptroller to the Dowager Princess of Wales's household, and he held this office until her death. Bute and Shelburne obtained the post of Surveyor of the Ordnance for Barré, which the latter refused as he would have had to give up his position in the army; ultimately, Bute named him Governor of Stirling Castle, a very sweet sinecure. Lord Spencer was technically a member of the Bedford faction, but he voted with Bute in 1761–1762, if for no other reason than that Bute was the fount of his many high-paying sinecures. And then there was Thomas Charles Bunbury, perhaps the most independent of the founders. He intended, he announced in 1762, 'speaking for Lord Bute,' not as Bute's 'creature,' but as a supporter, 'on condition he may speak as he please.' His brother-in-law Henry Fox tried to coax him into greater attachment to the prime minister. But while he wished 'to be of Lord Bute's side in everything he approves of,' he did not want 'to be tied to him or anybody else.'[5] Bunbury, according to Shelburne, had 'such notions of independency' that 'he would not take a place for the world.' He never asked for a place, and the post he wanted – Secretary to the Lord Lieutenant of Ireland – was the choice of the Lord Lieutenant, not Bute. Eventually, with the help of Bute's men and over the opposition of the ambassador, Bunbury became Secretary to the Paris Embassy.

But it was the Irish-born Lord Shelburne who was most intertwined with the Favorite in 1761 and 1762. Bute had helped him become an aide-de-camp to George III for his service in Germany, gaining that honorific ahead of a more senior and decorated officer-friend, Lord George Lennox, younger brother of the 3rd Duke of Richmond, a member of Arthur's. Shelburne did not join Bute's Cabinet in 1762, probably because the King and Bute were annoyed that Shelburne had called for the removal of troops before Bute. According to Lady Caroline Fox, 'Lord Bute was particularly hurt with Lord Shelburne's speech, and the turn it took in the world was as if Lord Shelburne was setting himself at the head of a faction against the Court, and which, after the marks of favour he had received from the Court, was not talked of in an advantageous light for him. He, seeing the turn it took, grew very uneasy.'[6] Somewhat chastened, he thereafter vigorously promoted Bute's plan for peace in the Lords. In addition, Shelburne controlled two seats in the Commons. He appointed Barré to Chipping Wycombe and Fitzmaurice to Calne, and saw that they reliably voted for Bute's bills. Plus, he arranged with Lord Boston to seat John Parker at Boston's Bodmin

in 1761; when Parker left Bodmin for a seat in Devon the next year, he did so with Shelburne's and Bute's approval. In return, Parker voted for Bute's peace preliminaries.

'The little knot of young orators' – Horace Walpole's term for the young men who came into the Commons in November 1761 and gathered around Shelburne – were drawn into the high-stakes political skirmish between the of Newcastle–Pitt administration, and the growing Bute faction. They repudiated the Great Commoner Pitt, whose primary cause as Leader of the House of Commons since 1756 and Secretary of State for the Southern Department since 1751 had been the successful prosecution of war. They attacked his procedures as minister and his principles as politician and supported Bute's own peace program, even if some of them differed on the timing of its implementation.

Bute's increasing differences with Government – already latent in the Summer of 1761 – became manifest when the young Barré rose to give his maiden speech in the Commons on December 10, 1761. A first speech is seldom noteworthy, but this one – by the son of a Huguenot refugee in Ireland who had served with Wolfe at Rochefort, Louisbourg and Québec – was different. He was 'a black, robust man . . . rather hard-favoured, with a peculiar distortion on one side of his face' due to a gunshot wound to an eye, yet he spoke with 'very classic and eloquent diction, and as determined boldness,' and mesmerized listeners on all sides.[7] Barré was probably induced to speak by the Paymaster-General Henry Fox (Barré admitted as much) but, as Barré had recently received Shelburne's safe seat of Chipping Wycombe, Shelburne, who in various ways was tied to Fox, must have been complicit in the vituperative attack and its reiteration the following day. The abuse Barré heaped upon the Newcastle Ministry in general and Pitt in particular revealed the direction the factions were moving. He attacked not just Pitt's mismanagement of the war but also his 'political principles,' describing them as riddled by 'change and contradiction.' Several months later, on February 5, the 4th Duke of Bedford, again probably with Shelburne's encouragement (for 'Shelburne spoke very finely on that side'), turned from Pitt's mismanagement of the war to the matter of peace itself, moving for an immediate

Triple portrait by Sir Joshua Reynolds. The Earl of Shelburne (right) is portrayed with two early members of Boodle's, the barrister John Dunning (later 1st Baron Ashburton) and the soldier Isaac Barré both elected in 1762 and both close friends and political associates of Shelburne

end to the war in Germany and the recall of the troops. Even Bute was not yet ready to take that step; nor was he willing to concede that Parliament should lead on the matter.

At the same time many of the Twenty-Five were attacking Pitt, Newcastle, the Ministry and a war in which they had fought and friends had died and were rallying around Bute, they gathered in Pall Mall in 1762 to create a 'society' for themselves. Clubs were part of 'the wider development of public sociability' during the eighteenth century, which in turn 'promoted 'a more modern, integrated and city-centred national society',' the historian Peter Clark tells us. Club membership became 'an essential part of the social and cultural language of urban life.' Between 1688 and 1760, clubs and societies as institutions matured: penetrated the counties, widened their reach to increasingly diverse groups, grew more established and formal, and met more frequently. With new money commanding attention and dominating the English-speaking market, 'traditional status indicators lost much of their meaning or became ambiguous.' The selection processes for club admittance and the opportunity to gain a familiarity on a small, intimate club scale with those so selected helped minimise the tensions that arose from modernisation. Boodle's in this sense was at the crest of a social and cultural wave that engulfed the English-speaking world.[8]

In Boodle's case, the immediate impetus for the new club was rejection by another club on political grounds. According to a newspaper account published in March 1762, 'several of the . . . Quality' were excluded 'by a Black Ball' from membership in Arthur's. In response, they decided to form their own 'society' at Almacks' and call it 'The Virtue Club.'[9] Subsequent notice of The Virtue Club at Almack's occurred in contemporary newspapers. Its first mention in print appeared on April 3, 1762, when a gentleman in Ireland writing to a friend in London noticed that men were vying to get into something called 'The Virtue Club.'[10] If the word 'virtue' was not suggestive enough, the 1764 pamphlet entitled *Letter to a Noble Member of the Club in Albemarle-Street, from John Wilkes, Esq.; at Paris*, which was reprinted in *The St James's Chronicle or The British Evening Post*, clarified the political nature of the society. 'In the same Manner, Wilkes explained 'it is necessary that political Societies, public or private, dining at home or at Wildman's, should found their conduct on some system.' 'The Virtue Club at Boodle's was, in its primary Institution, intended for the Support of the Earl of Bute.'[11] Since Arthur's was the haunt of Administration oligarchs such as the 2nd Marquess of Rockingham and the 4th Duke of Devonshire who aligned themselves with Newcastle and Pitt, Boodle's would be the haunt of anti-Administration Whigs.

So it was that Shelburne could observe to Dunmore in May 1762 that 'whist has given way to politics.' The principal *raison d'être* for the club was not dinner, drinks, and cards, as at Almack's – but politics and particularly supporting Bute's leadership and program. From the sanctity of their clubhouse, members devised attacks on opponents (as in later years they organised elections and mobilised voters). They rallied round the cause of virtue; its precepts were enshrined in their speeches and letters. Not coincidentally did Shelburne take *Virtu Non Verbis* as his motto, and he and his political allies decried the supposedly amoral practices of the Whig oligarchs. Perhaps uncharitably but not without perception, Richard Rigby, a member of Arthur's, characterised Shelburne as one 'who always laments that virtue does not govern, and who always thinks that she is possessed only by his own friends.'[12] Six months

later, Henry Fox's wife Caroline, who was more partial to Shelburne, made much the same observation: Shelburne 'thinks all the goodness, virtue and honour in this country are confined to' her future brother-in-law, founder Thomas Bunbury, 'and two or three other friends of his Lordship, *cela c'est penser en jeune homme.*'[13]

In the heady days of late 1761 and early 1762, before peace was assured and Bute ruled supreme, a group of young men who had been educated together and fought together created a space for discussion among like-minded politicians free from rancour and eavesdropping. In their own house in Pall Mall, they could dream dreams of reforming the government and returning to a more virtuous arrangement perfected and practiced in some time and place immemorial, along the lines they imagined the King espoused. The club that emerged was wholeheartedly dedicated to the promotion and preservation of virtue in governance. With Bute's elevation to Prime Minister, less reason existed to band together or to need secrecy, and the founders opened up the membership to 250. The need to pay rent, wages, and provisions may have contributed heavily to their decision, of course. But the 'society' remained dedicated to 'virtue' and, not surprisingly, their club became a nursery for reform.

WE *whose names are underwritten Subscribe to the Society according to the above rules and regulations.*

One of the Club's 10 surviving ballot boxes restored in 2007. Committee members take a ball from the cup at the top and place it unseen in one or other side of the box. The candidate's name is displayed on a card set in the slit at the top. At each election between 10 and 25 candidates may be proposed for election. Despite appearances the No drawer is likely to be empty

William Almack, the founder of a series of fashionable clubs and assembly rooms in London, provided Boodle's with its first clubhouse in Pall Mall. This mezzotint by Richard Josey is after a painting by Thomas Gainsborough

CHAPTER 2

Edward Boodle and his Successors

DAVID MANN

On the night of Sunday, 9 April 1769, a fragrant, powdered, well-coiffed monkey escaped from one of the rooms in Boodle's Subscription House at number 50 Pall Mall. The monkey scampered across the rooftops before disappearing down the chimney of a nearby house. This was no wild animal on the loose but rather a trained pet, known as Pug, who belonged to Edward Boodle and who lived with the proprietor at the Club. It had been just one year since Boodle took on sole ownership of the Club that had previously been run as a partnership with the Yorkshire-born impresario, William Almack.

Boodle was said to have had 'a remarkably cheerful disposition' as well as 'a good constitution', both advantageous traits when running a Club. One hopes he also had a good sense of humour as it was his waiters who were responsible for dressing up the monkey 'belonging to their master . . . in a sailor's habit, [who] then rubbed his head with pomatum and powdered it'. The prank ended badly – the room into which the monkey escaped was occupied by a man attending to a corpse. *The New York Gazette and Weekly Mercury* (5 June 1769), a Colonial newspaper, reported that 'upon the man's seeing him and his dress, and hearing him begin to chatter, he ran out greatly frightened, crying out, "the Devil is come down the chimney," and left poor Pug in his uniform to dance about the room at his Pleasure.'

Edward Boodle was born in Oswestry, Shropshire on 14 May 1722. As a youngster he became an apprentice to his father, John Boodle, who ran an inn called The Three Tuns. Boodle subsequently became a servant to Sir Robert Grosvenor, 6th Bt at Eaton Hall and by 1754 he was made a freeman of Chester in the Grosvenor interest. Shortly thereafter he left for London where he started to work

for Almack who was the proprietor of the premises at 50 Pall Mall, which became the first location of the Club after its founding in January of 1762.

The Club's original rules refer to Almack as the contractor and state that he then 'delivered over the concern to his principal waiter Edward Boodle'. This occurred in 1764 when Almack decided to open his own club at number 49 Pall Mall. A notice of Almack's new club was published in *The Gentleman's Magazine* in August 1764 proclaiming that Almack's at 49 Pall Mall was 'no longer to be used as a public tavern but is to be set apart for the reception of a set of gentlemen, who are to meet after the manner of the minority of *Wildman's.*'

Boodle and Almack would remain partners in Boodle's for another four years after this. In 1778, Almack's Club moved to new premises in St James's Street and became Brooks's. Thus were two of London's oldest clubs established, and, in 1782 when Boodle's moved from Pall Mall to the Savoir Vivre's Club premises on St James's Street, they became permanent neighbours.

The Proprietors

Edward Boodle was the cousin of another Edward Boodle, founder of the well-known solicitors Boodle Hatfield. Contemporary accounts suggest that he had a gregarious personality. Boodle left a deep impression on William Hickey, who was then just a young man preparing for his work as a lawyer in India, and who would posthumously be remembered as a memoirist. Hickey described Boodle as living 'very freely . . . He was never happy unless he had a parcel of young people about him . . . Nothing delighted him more than sitting out the boys, as he called it. Indeed, his head was so strong that he generally succeeded in so doing, and when he perceived his young guests began to flag, or become drowsy, he would get up, lock the door of the room, and putting the key in his pocket, strike up the song of "'Tis not yet day" &c. His companionable qualities were extraordinary.' It was under Boodle's management that Edward Gibbon was elected (1767) and where he could be found 'writing at Boodle's in a fine Velvet Coat with ruffles of My Lady's chusing'. Gibbon would eventually be elected Manager twice (in 1770 and 1773). When Boodle died on 8 February 1772 the Club was still in Pall Mall. He was buried in Ongar Church, in Essex, where his family's tomb is situated.

Following Boodle's death the Club was taken over by Benjamin Harding both 'in the house and business'. Harding had been born in 1739 and had originally worked as a vintner. For a time Boodle's was referred to as 'Harding's Club' but the name did not stick and ultimately reverted to the name of the original proprietor.

In June 1782 Harding decided to move Boodle's to its present premises on St James's Street, into a building whose original occupants had been the Savoir Vivre (also known as the Scavoir Vivre) Club.

The building at the new location was designed by John Crunden (c.1741–1835) and commissioned by Nicholas Kenney, the owner of the Savoir Vivre. Crunden's building, strongly influenced by Robert Adam, was built between 1775 and 1776 for £10,000 according to Roger Fulford. It is not surprising that Harding desired these premises. They were recently built, and Boodle's and the Savoir Vivre had a good working relationship having collaborated on events such as a Regatta on the Thames in June 1775.

Harding presided over the Club's only move. He also brought in Richard Cuddington as a new partner in 1796. When Harding died aged sixty-nine on 13 September 1808 Cuddington became the sole proprietor. Cuddington himself was born in 1761. Relatively little else is known of his private life, or indeed his proprietorship other than that John George Fuller joined him in 1817/18 to run the Club jointly.

The elegantly carved inscription on the handsome Boodle family chest tomb in Ongar Parish, Essex

Cuddington died on 1 August 1829 aged sixty-eight. His will left the Boodle's assets to his niece Margaret Toms as well as to Fuller, in trust, to be offered to the latter at a 'fair price' – a note on the will specifies this as £4,068. Margaret had married a Charles Middleton at Streatham in December 1830 and one can speculate if this is the same Charles Middleton who was elected as a member in 1849. (There are memorials in Charlwood Church, Surrey to the Cuddington and Middleton families.) A poem mentioning the partnership of Cuddington and Fuller, and continuing the tradition of the Boodle's name being lampooned was published in *Blackwood's Edinburgh Magazine* in 1825:

'Beam, bum, boodle, loodle, loodle
Beam, bum, boodle, loodle, loo.'

Pretty writing that – . . . But is it Irish? *Negatur*. I deny it poz! Boodle's! Why, Boodle's is a Club of good humdrum gentlemen, kept by Cuddington and Fuller, at 31, St James's Street; but not particularly Hibernian. A chorus in the same taste concerning them, would run thus,

'Bow, wow, boodle, noodle, doodle
Bow, wow, boodle, noodle, pooh!'

John George Fuller ran Boodle's as its sole proprietor until 1849. Described as a wine merchant, Fuller was a friend of

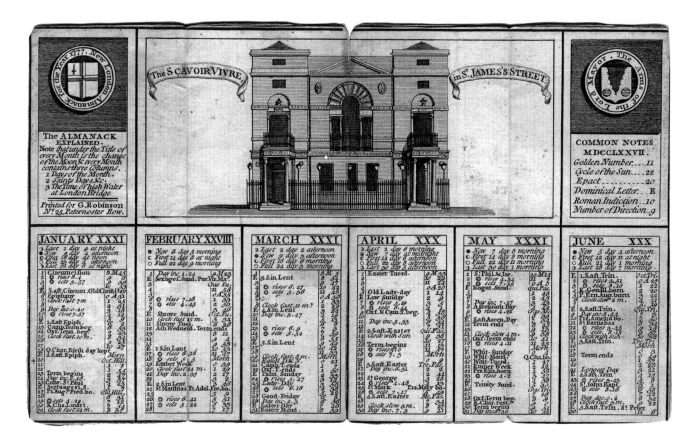

The newly completed front of the Savoir Vivre formed the centrepiece of the *London Almanack* in 1777. This shows the Club before the bow window was added. The right hand door then served a separate narrow house

John Buonarotti Papworth, one of the founders of the Royal Institute of British Architects and Surveyor-General to Wilhelm I, King of Württemberg. In the 1820s and 1830s Papworth was commissioned by Fuller to draw up architectural alterations for the Club, as well as a private residence for Fuller at Leigham Court, Streatham. An article in *The Builder* in 1844 describes Fuller as having been 'formerly a waiter there, and passed through all the degrees to the possession of wealth; contrary to the general usage in these cases, he is a good master, and bears his fortune with humility.'

By 1849 this aforementioned fortune had dissipated and 'having fallen on hard times' Fuller was declared a bankrupt. In May 1851 Fuller, by now an 'elderly gentleman', was back in court as an insolvent debtor, after being chastised by the Judge 'on the folly of man who after they were discharged by bankruptcy or insolvency, resumed their debts'. The

bankruptcy court hearing laid out his parlous position: unsecured creditors for £21,947; creditors holding security £40,140, being the freehold estate in Streatham and the clubhouse in St James Street, together with furniture and fixtures; overall deficiency £5,465 (paying crippling rates of interest of 20 per cent and 30 per cent).

Debtors included the George Douglas Campbell, 8th Duke of Argyll and Francis D'Arcy Osborne, 7th Duke of Leeds, and other members of Boodle's, possibly as payment for the wine supplied to members, as well as Mary, Lady Combermere, 3rd wife of the 1st Viscount, reason unknown. Ultimately Leigham Court had to be sold. Fuller died on 9 December 1860 of 'natural decay', aged eighty-three, in Brixton.

William Gainer took over ownership of Boodle's the year of Fuller's bankruptcy. Often mistakenly referred to as a

John Buonarotti Papworth, pencil drawing by William Brockedon

lated from Pembroke College, Oxford and migrated to St Mary Hall (later Oriel College) before graduating with a degree, below fourth class, in an unknown subject. He achieved a BA in 1850 and a MA in 1851.

While at Oxford, William Charles changed the spelling of his name to Gayner. Although he became proprietor of Boodle's upon his father's death in 1866, he was called to the Bar at the Inner Temple in 1872. Nothing is known about his legal career, but it is conceivable that he might have thought it was helpful to have some knowledge of the Law (in particular how it related to the quasi-judicial proceedings of the Master of Foxhounds (MFH) sub-committee).

William Charles died on 27 January 1893 when his estate was valued at £65,029. His obituary, published in *The Daily Telegraph* on 1 February, reported:

> Today the funeral of the late Mr C. (sic) Gayner, 'the Master of Boodle's' takes place in Kensal Green Cemetery. The deceased gentleman died suddenly from heart disease, and his demise will be a great loss to the oldest club in England. With Mr Gayner one of the familiar landmarks of Boodle's disappears. He was a survival of the old club days, before huge caravanserais took the place of a social house, and when the members of a club knew each other instead of merely being a gathering of strangers. His courteous manner, peculiar old fashioned dress of the last century, and strong disapprobation of any attempt to modernise the club were part of Boodle's itself, which still retains its interior as it was a century ago, even to the old moderator lamps [a type of lamp that burnt colza or rape oil, the flow of which was regulated to maintain an even supply] and candles. Notwithstanding Mr Gayner's decease, it is stated that the club will be carried in exactly the same manner.

William Charles had no children and his estate was bequeathed to his unmarried sister Georgina Elizabeth Gainer. Her acumen was held in high regard, having said to possess 'considerable knowledge of business'. During a long illness it was said that 'the old butler of Boodle's' –

single person, references to 'Gainer' being proprietor are actually to two people, a father and a son. The elder Gainer was William (1789–1866) who referred to himself in a letter to *The Times* on 5 October 1837 as the 'House-steward of Arthur's Club', of 69 St James's Street. He had this same title at Boodle's in the 1841 census before becoming the Club's proprietor and was later described as a wine merchant. William Gainer lived in the clubhouse with wife and four children.

The elder Gainer died in 1866 and was succeeded by his only son William Charles Gainer (1831–93). William Charles was admitted to St Paul's School in 1838. In 1844 he matricu-

The Gainer family tombstone

who may have been Frederic Powell, the butler recorded in the 1891 census – 'practically managed the club'. Her death on 7 July 1896 left members 'somewhat anxious' at their uncertain fate. It appears that they had good cause for concern as one paper reported that 'it still has to be decided whether the sisters of the late Miss Gayner (sic) will carry on the concern or whether they will close the Club. Should they decide to do the latter, it is almost certain that a syndicate will be found to acquire the clubhouse, in which case the Club will be re-organised and a new Boodle's arise to replace the old.'

One possible purchaser, in October 1896, was rumoured to be the Royal Yacht Squadron, which held a meeting each year at the Club. They denied this claiming that a London clubhouse would be superfluous as 'every member belongs to more clubs in town than he can make use of'.

The third of the sisters, Charlotte Sarah Greenhill, married Charles Frederick Greenhill, a wax chandler in Bury Street, and who presumably supplied candles to the Club. She died a wealthy widow at her home 35 Norfolk Square on 29 April 1909, and left an estate valued at £162,737 (over £9 million today). Her bequests included the Gainer Greenhill bequest to St James's Church on Piccadilly to support Sunday schools; to provide food, fuel and clothing for the poor of the Parish; and a Gainer scholarship for classics or Eastern languages at Pembroke College, Oxford, to be competed for by the boys of St Paul's School.

The Gainer's would be the last proprietors of Boodle's. Following the example of Brooks's and White's, which had converted from proprietor to membership-ownership in 1880 and 1888 respectively, on 1 January 1897 Boodle's was run by a managing committee of twenty-six members with Thomas Kynnersley as the first Chairman. The list of members was sifted and the revived Club started with 350 members.

Changes in Membership

In 1783, a year after Boodle's moved to the present building, there were 281 members; throughout the nineteenth century the Club had six hundred members, approximately the same number as at Brooks's and White's. Both of these Clubs massively expanded their buildings in the nineteenth century and also changed from proprietor's clubs to members' clubs.

Richard Samways, formerly of the London Metropolitan Archives, has done a remarkable service to Boodle's in preparing lists of members: one of the Proprietor's Club, 1762 to 1896 and the other of the Members' Club, 1896 to 2000. He estimates that up to 1896, there were 4,000 members, with six hundred to seven hundred names as well as twenty-six years missing as, for example, William Wilberforce.

Even though his sons state in their biography that Wilberforce was a member and who wrote that 'the very first time I went to Boodle's, I won twenty-five guineas of the Duke of Norfolk', he is not recorded in the books. This is also true for George 'Beau' Brummell, who only appeared on the list of members in 1814 (there were 570 members in that year), but in the betting book in 1806. Both Brummell and Wilberforce were also members of Brooks's and White's. While William Petty, 2nd Earl of Shelburne was a founding member, subsequent generations were not, joining Brooks's or White's and were involved with the founding of the Athenaeum.

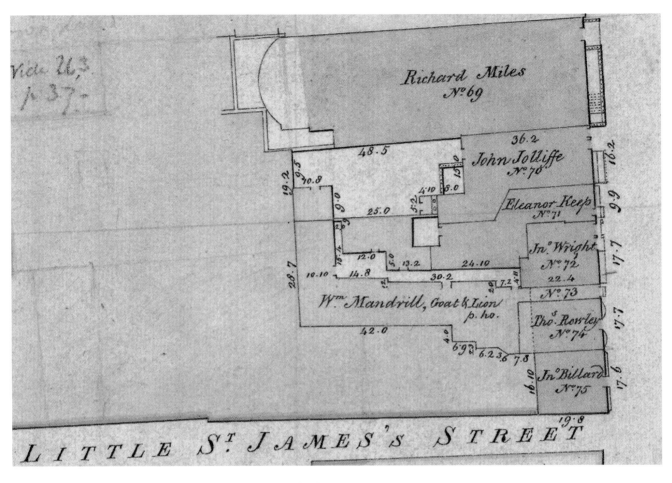

Plan of properties on the west of St James's Street showing Richard Miles's premises

The annual average of elections in the 1840s was thirty-five; while the 1850s and 1860s were the peak years. In 1853 there were forty-six members elected, in 1857 there were sixty-four, in 1859, forty members, in 1862 there were sixty-two members, and 1868, sixty members. The increase in the election of members implied that there was an informal hunting committee before 1857 and shows the extent to which foxhunting must have dominated the Club. The Masters of Foxhounds were particularly entitled to hold an annual dinner in June each year.

After the fracas at Boodle's in 1880 (which was the result of a dispute between William Charles Gainer and the Club's members) there were eighty new members elected suggesting a determined effort to make up numbers. There are no numbers for resignations but with membership maintained at 600 it suggests that there must have been a massive turnover during this period, with the implication being that Gainer may have been running the Club as a commercial enterprise for the foxhunting crowd.

As an indication of the decline of Boodle's in the last years of Gainer's proprietorship, after the resignation of Henry Somerset, 8th Duke of Beaufort and the hunting set (as a result of the above mentioned dispute), there were six hundred members elected between 1868 and 1881; between 1883 and 1895, fifteen were elected, with none in the years 1892 and 1895.

Right: Letter from William Gainer the Elder to Sir John Nettlethorpe informing him of his election to the Club, and (*above*) the receipt from Gainer for the 11 guinea subscription. Though Gainer was the proprietor, the Club continued to be called Boodle's with the name now set in a splendidly Victorian ornamental cartouche

A Club of Country Gentlemen?

By 1815 Sir George Onesiphorous Paul, 2nd Bt (1770) would write of a clear distinction between the Court Party at White's and the country gentlemen at Boodle's. The question must be when and how Boodle's changed from being the Club for a political group to becoming the Club of country gentlemen, whether or not members of Parliament. If one sets the figures in Bateman's *Great Landowners of Great Britain*, 1889, against the number of members of the clubs, 24 per cent of the members of Boodle's were so described, compared to 28 per cent at White's. Of the Clubs classified as 'political', 39 per cent of the members of the Carlton Club and 36 per cent of Brooks's were great landowners.

Early in its history Boodle's, like the other clubs of its era, was essentially a meeting place for political groups, adjacent to the Palace of Westminster, particularly the House of Commons. Following the Act of Union with Scotland in 1707, the Commons had 558 members and after the Act of Union with Ireland in 1800, the size increased to 658. The House in 1832 had space for 250 on the floor and twenty-five

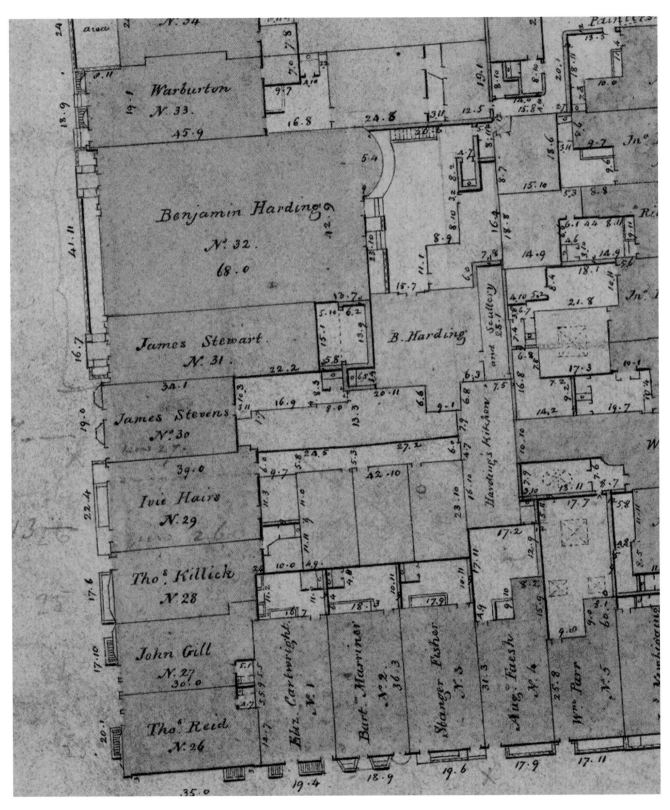

Warburton
Nº 33.

Benjamin Harding
Nº 32.
68.0

B. Harding

James Stewart.
Nº 31.

James Stevens
Nº 30

Ivie Hairs
Nº 29

Thoˢ. Killick
Nº 28

John Gill
Nº 27

Thoˢ. Reid
Nº 26

Harding's Kitchen

Eliz. Cartwright
Nº 1

Bartʰ Mariner
Nº 2

Stanger Fisher
Nº 3

Augˢ. Fuesh
Nº 4

Wᵐ Parr
Nº 5

in each gallery, in total 300 plus 120 strangers. With space for roughly half the members, limited facilities for comfort and extremely poor ventilation, members of parliament probably only attended the House for the great occasions, major speeches or significant decisions.

Dod's Parliamentary Guide, started in 1838, indicated a member's London address as well as his club, where he could be found. The well-connected Charles Greville (1794–1865), whose diary gives a full accounting of British political and social life, shows just how the Club functioned for its members as a meeting place and point of call, and just how integrated Club and political life had become. He mentions being summoned so 'accordingly I went to Boodle's, where I fond him, and he immediately began his case' or bumping into the Home Secretary by accident at Boodle's 'so I took the opportunity of talking to him about these Bills'.

Indeed the Carlton Club, founded in 1832 and the Reform Club, founded in 1836, were clearly political in purpose and the first rules of each Club stated that the Club should remain open for an hour after Parliament had risen. It was only by the 1860s that the House of Commons could be described as the 'best Club in the world', having followed the Carlton and Reform Clubs for developments in facilities.

Much politicking, in the course of discussing '*dans les couloirs*', probably occurred in the clubs, where members must have spent most of their days when in London for the parliamentary season, February to August. Even as late as the first rules of a reconstructed Boodle's in 1897, there are references to the sessions of Parliament. So many advantages were associated with belonging to a club that Theodore Hook, a writer (and notorious practical-joker) asked in 1839 exactly 'how men about town [ever] existed without them.'

Above: Watercolour by Dugald Graham-Campbell (2012). The one tree in St James's Street marks the front of Boodle's Club
Opposite: Plan of St James's Street when Benjamin Harding was proprietor. At this stage the southern porch opened into a separate narrow house

A Whist_er at Boodles _ or a _
_ choice peice of double milled Yorkshire Broad cloth _

Pub.d July 1820 by Fores Panton St Hay market

I.R. Cruikshank fecit.

July. 1820

An 1820 hand-coloured etching by Isaac Cruikshank satirising a country member looking forward to a good meal

CHAPTER 3

The Early Members of Boodle's

NEIL HITCHIN

Boodle's was founded in 1762. But how and why did the Club come into being, and why did it survive? It is not a simple story, for there were many personalities and groups who came together to form what is now Boodle's. Among the most important of their interests was politics. An earlier historian of the Club, Roger Fulford, says that William Fitz-maurice-Petty, 2nd Earl Shelburne (and later 1st Marquess Lansdowne), was the founder of Boodle's, and that it was initially a political club. This was partly true, but the Club was not founded with solely politics in mind. There were far more varied political and other interests at work in the emergence of Boodle's than this implies. In order to understand Boodle's in its first twenty-five years, we need to see the club as a part of the increasingly organised electoral politics of the later Georgian age, as well as a sociable venue for wealthy men.

Boodle's started life under that great entrepreneur of clubs, William Almack, on the site of numbers 49–51 in Pall Mall, in the same set of buildings where Almack started Brooks's, at the same time. Because of this cohabitation some historians of clubland have wondered if the two clubs were initially the same, dividing in 1764 for unknown reasons, perhaps relating to rules about excess in gambling. However, the club subscription list seems to be conclusive: the clubs were always separate.[1] Almack and Edward Boodle established a reputation for organising fashionable dinners between 1759 and 1762, and in January 1762 an unnamed private society was 'established in the house adjoining the tavern'.[2] Although the record survives in the Boodle's archive, this does not prove that Boodle's was that society – only that the record was in the possession of Edward Boodle. The property records of the site, however,

show that Col John Scott (elected 1763) had a pivotal role in the emergence of the Club, for he acquired the lease in September 1762, which he then let to Almack for 21 years. Scott himself lived next door.[3]

It is all a bit murky. Scott was the greatest gambler of all in the age of 'deep play', accumulating a vast fortune of £500,000, much of it through the gaming table, but also through the purchase of East India stock. It was proverbial to describe someone as 'rich as Scott', and it was news worth recording on those rare occasions when he lost at the table. When he died, George Selwyn wrote to Frederick Howard, 5th Earl of Carlisle (elected 1765, aged 17), who had been his protégé upon his entry to the fashionable world: 'General Scott is dead . . . The place of Nickster which is in the Devil's gift and vacated by John Scott is not dispos'd of. We go into mourning on Thursday. The waiters are to have crepes round their arms and the dice to be black and the spots white, during the time of wearing weepers, and the dice box muffled.' He suggested a motto: '*Sic Dice placuit*'.[4] As Selwyn was not a member of Boodle's, he would not have been describing mourning at the Club. But great characters are always mourned. Boodle's may well have done something similar. Scott was, after all, on the Management Committee in 1763 and 1766, and controlled the Club's site.

If Scott was indeed lurking behind Almack and Boodle, he was not the only gambling soldier to underwrite the formation of a club; nor was he the only one to have some connection with Boodle's. General Richard Smith made his fortune in India as the commander of the East India Company's army in Bengal, but bounced in and out of great wealth and poverty over the years.[5] Returning to England, he stood for parliament in 1774, won his seat (Hindon), but was stripped of it for electoral corruption (a real feat, considering the norms of the time). He later stood again for the same seat, in 1776, but this time there were 'such gross Instances of Bribery and Corruption' that he was fined 1,000 marks and imprisoned for six months. He was also a powerful figure behind the Savoir Vivre club, setting it up with others to make a fortune out of the wealthy young men, or, as Horace Walpole put it: Smith 'and a set of sharpers' then 'formed a plan for a new club, which, by the excess of play, should draw all the young extravagants thither. They built a magnificent house in St James's Street, furnished it gorgeously, and enrolled both the clubs at White's, and that of Almack's. The titular master of the house the first night acquainted the richest and most wasteful of the members that they might be furnished in the house with loans of ready money, even as far as forty thousand pounds.'[6] He was never elected to Almack's or Boodle's, though he was elected to Brooks's. But he does seem to have invested in the building which Boodle's has lived in since the demise of the Savoir Vivre club.

Gambling impresarios and chancers are hardly the main reason for the founding of broad bottomed clubs, however. The interest and support of noblemen was needed to make Boodle's into something more than a dining society and gambling den. Almack had married a woman whose father was factor to James, 5th Duke of Hamilton, and her brother was the Duke's physician. She might also have been waiting maid to the Duchess. The Duke's son, Lord Archibald, later the 9th Duke of Hamilton, who 'cared more for racing than politics', was one of the original members of Boodle's.[7] Edward Boodle was a protégé of the Grosvenor family, a number of whom were early members of the club, too. It is hard to know what to make of William Hickey's story that Boodle 'squandered away a handsome fortune' and was 'reduced to the necessity of accepting the management of one of the fashionable gaming houses in Pall Mall which bore his name', but his source was Captain John Mitford, who had married Boodle's niece; so, prima facie, it seems likely. Boodle's easy manner with wealthy young men seems to attest to his having money behind him when young.

Like Almack, Boodle appears to have run more than one

club at the same time. John Wilkes, the politically divisive City alderman, rake and politician, described a club under Boodle's management from 1761–64 as having the character of a 'Virtue Club', as 'in its primary institution, intended for the support of the Earl of Bute'.[8] Was it the same club established by Almack in January 1762? Was it, in fact, Boodle's? It isn't clear, although David Hancock makes a compelling case that Boodle's and the Virtue Club were the same, in this volume. Also unclear is whether it was called the Virtue Club, or whether Wilkes was referring to a kind of reformation of manners club in order to mock them, since he had, by the time he wrote this, already become a scandalous public figure. There is an unmistakable imprint of support for Bute among those early members of Boodle's who were members of parliament, lending credibility to Boodle's as Wilkes' 'Virtue Club'. This shouldn't surprise us if Shelburne was indeed a significant figure in founding Boodle's since, having returned from the wars in June 1760 he was working closely with Bute to organise the election of 1761, analysing the seats and recommending candidates. Shelburne first entered the Cabinet under Bute. They seem to have known each other even before 1759.[9]

Shelburne and Boodle's

When George III ascended the throne in 1760, it was a moment of great political change. The King depended on his former tutor and 'dear friend', Lord Bute, as his Prime Minister and confidante. Sir Robert Walpole's political manager, Thomas Pelham-Holles, the Duke of Newcastle, was gradually losing his power after decades of control, and the elder Pitt, the great war leader, was undecided about whether to return to the Cabinet. The decadent ministry of the Pelhams was lurking in the shadows, and Henry Fox was being courted but holding out for more money. Shelburne, barely back from his military service in the Rhineland, and finding himself appointed aide de camp to the new king, aligned himself with Bute.

Shelburne, or Lord Fitzmaurice as he then was, had grown up in his grandfather's military minded, feudal and decidedly unintellectual household in a remote part of Ireland.[10] On his mother's side, however, Shelburne descended from Sir William Petty, the statistician and political economist, his great grandfather. Shelburne attended Christ Church, Oxford, a place dominated by Westminster men, of whom he was not one; although his father was a Whig and was created an earl, the Petty-Fitzmaurices were not among the Old Whig families. Snobberies at the highest levels of society are sharper than anywhere, and in many ways, however much he was at the centre of public life for decades, Shelburne was and remained a political and social outsider who needed to build both reputation and support.

He hardly had the time to build a power base for himself in the Commons, for he was no sooner elected to parliament than his father died, and instead of taking his seat in the Commons to learn the political craft, he entered the House of Lords and was catapulted into the centre of government at a fractious political moment. It was an opportunity to learn from men with the best and the worst of traits, but a danger to his future reputation. He was not without some friends before he entered parliament, however.

In the early 1760s 'a little knot of young orators' gathered in various small clubs and in Hill Street, London, at Shelburne's home where they 'mixed with literary men older in years and of various political opinions'.[11] It was a remarkable constellation of talented people, most of whom went on to make names for themselves as political figures, and many of whom were also early members of Boodle's.

In a letter to Lady Kildare (30 Sept 1762), Lady Bunbury[12] wrote: Mr [Henry] Fox is trying to persuade Mr Bunbury to be quite attached to Lord Bute, and has a notion that [he] is one of the wrong-headed, prating people that were in a set last winter – you heard of them, I don't doubt; Lord Shelburne is at the head of them – but he is vastly mistaken, for, to do my poor husband justice, he is the most right-headed person I ever saw ... He has told me that his intentions are to be of Lord Bute's side in everything he approves of; but not to be tied to him or anybody else. He wishes to be independent as much as possible'.[13] At the centre of this set was Isaac Barré, Shelburne's closest political ally and friend. The previous autumn, on 10 December 1761, two speeches by

new MPs were widely condemned for their fierce attacks on Pitt and the German war. Barré is better remembered for this attack; but Bunbury spoke first, and in the same vein. Both were considered to be flashy, theatrical and immoderate in their speeches. Lady Bunbury refers to 'a set' of people, and she was in a position to know. She had married Sir Thomas in June 1762, and he was a founding member of Boodle's, as was 'F Bunbury'.[14] Furthermore, Lady Caroline Fox informed her correspondent that 'Mr Bunbury is very attached to Lord Shelburne'.[15]

The Hill Street Circle

Much has been made of the 'Bowood Circle', a group of Enlightened people who lived at or visited Bowood often.[16] But Shelburne's first circle of intellectual friends was convened at his London home on Hill Street, Berkeley Square.

On returning from the wars, where he had demonstrated bravery in battle, Shelburne had set about improving himself by finding men who were both worldly and intellectual. This was surely the reason for the gathering of the 'little knot' of men around his home at Hill Street.[17] A number of the names of the men mentioned in Fitzmaurice's *Life of Shelburne* are among these earliest members of Boodle's. Heading the list are Shelburne (1762), Barré (1762) and John Dunning (1762) (later 1st Baron Ashburton), whose close relationship was recorded in a triple portrait, George Dempster (1762), the future patron of Robert Burns, and John Calcraft (1763). 'Captain Howe' (1762), who had been a Royal Navy Captain since 1746, and who was appointed Lord of the Admiralty in 1763, was Richard, the 4th Viscount Howe, who succeeded to an Irish peerage in 1758.

Like Barré, Howe was somewhat older, aged thirty-six in 1762; but he was not the eldest of the group. 'Sergeant Glynn', John Glynn (1722–79), was older still. He was sergeant at law (1763) recorder of London (1772–79) and MP for Middlesex (1768–79), was counsel for the printers of the *North Briton*, during their trial in 1764, and for John Wilkes in 1768. But he was never a member of Boodle's. He was defeated at the election for the parliamentary seat

View of the HOUSE OF COMMONS *from the River Thames.*

View of the Office of Ordnance with the Entrance of the HOUSE OF LORDS

Views of House of Commons and House of Lords in 1777 when there the facilities were extremely restricted

at Newtown, Isle of Wight, in 1768, and encouraged to petition against the result by Shelburne and Dunning; but a vacancy occurred in Middlesex before he could do so, which he won, backed by John Wilkes. James Townsend, on the other hand, was a founding Committee member of the club. An MP and leading member of the Bill of Rights Society formed in 1769 to support the campaign to reinstate John Wilkes as an MP, he was also an Alderman in the City, where he and Wilkes led the radical party and were the only two aldermen unconnected with business or banking.[18]

Another man close to Shelburne at this time was Laurence Sulivan, director of the East India Company, and the rival of Robert Clive, 1st Baron, at India House. He was not a member of Boodle's, but his and Shelburne's collaborator Laughlin Macleane was elected to the club in 1768. Macleane worked closely with Sulivan and John Calcraft to capture the board of the East India Company in that year, but their success was short-lived, for the East India stock bubble burst in 1769 leading to a falling out between Macleane and Shelburne, and considerable losses for Shelburne and those around him. Would Maclaine have remained a member or resigned? We don't know.

38

Two eminent lawyers, Charles Pratt (1714–94), later Lord Camden and Chief Justice, and William Blackstone, whose lectures Shelburne heard as an undergraduate, and who was introduced to the King by Shelburne, were also part of this circle in the early 1760s. Hans Stanley (elected 1766), who made a study of the law of nations and international relations, was said by Grenville to have written 'the first dispatch in which I ever saw metaphysical reasoning.' It was meat and drink for philosophers, but one can hardly imagine David Hume (1762), a member of both the Hill Street circle and Boodle's, one of the greatest metaphysicians of the age, including such things in his dispatches from Paris when he followed Lord Hertford there as his secretary in 1763.

About half of the men known to have been part of Shelburne's Hill Street circle were early members of Boodle's, and a number of them were somewhat older; but even those who did not join the Club had political and social connections with many other Boodle's members. They continued to meet at Shelburne's London home from 1761–65 (at least). We don't know what this group of lively and intellectual men discussed in detail but their ideas about political and administrative reform was consistent with the character of Boodle's in its first generation, and their conversation might have helped to shape the views of other Boodle's members. More than most clubs, perhaps more than any of the time, Boodle's was a club in which, for many members, big ideas mattered.

Shelburne himself only appears on the original Management Committee, in 1762, but those around him continued to serve on the Committe over a number of years. His brother Thomas Fitzmaurice was on the founding committee as were James Townshend, Sir John Aubrey (a school friend of Willoughby Bertie, 4th Earl of Abingdon and close to Shelburne), Sir Robert Bernard (who set up the Constitutional Society with Townsend), John Parker (at Oxford with Shelburne), Francis Greville, 1st Earl of Warwick and his sixteen-year-old son Lord Greville. The next year Isaac Barré, George Dempster, Townsend, Parker and Col John Scott, all known friends of Shelburne, were on the committee, as were Anthony Ashley Cooper, 4th Earl of Shaftesbury and

the Earl of Warwick (for a second year), John Hall Stevenson, George Montagu, 4th Duke of Manchester, and Sir John Rushout. The pattern continues of Shelburne's friends sitting on the Committee in 1764 with Thomas Fitzmaurice and Sir John Hort (both family), and other loyal friends.

Boodle's records

The list of members provides the foundation of this essay, for without it we simply could not make the detailed family, social and political connections to show, or at least suggest, how the club worked as a private institution for public figures. In 1762, it was simply a matter of signing up to become a member. After 1762, the members had to be proposed and elected. This fact helps to explain the co-existence of a number of families and factions whom we should be most surprised to find in a club which had, as one element, political organisation for electoral and parliamentary purposes. According to the traditions of Boodle's history, we are not surprised to find Lord Shelburne and his brother Thomas, a number of Grosvenors, various known supporters of Bute's ministry, including many Scots MPs, and several leading Scottish intellectuals; we also find friends of Shelburne from his military career joining or elected in the first few years, especially those who served under General Wolfe. But to find members of the Fitzwilliam family and other followers of the Marquess of Rockingham among the original and later members, who were Whigs with whom Shelburne did not get along politically or, in some cases socially, is startling.

Also striking is the number of peers and baronets who clearly signed up and then demurred in 1762: the earls of Thanet and Talbot,[19] Lord Titchfield[20] and Viscount Torrington, Barons Romney and Leigh, Sir William Knatchbull, Sir Henry Grey, Col George Gray,[21] Lords Folkestone and Foley, Lord Brome,[22] and a sprinkling of others, are all recorded in the records as crossed out. Very few men who resigned or simply did not take up the Club were not peers. This has to tell us something: but what if anything did they have in common? Many of these noblemen were followers of the Marquess of Rockingham, who had a well-organised

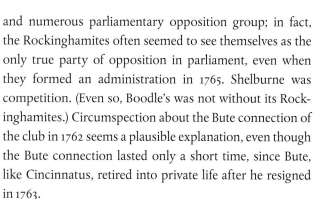

Almack's Rule Book. Second and third Rules inscribed in a fine copperplate hand. Further examples of pages from the Rule Book follow in this chapter

and numerous parliamentary opposition group; in fact, the Rockinghamites often seemed to see themselves as the only true party of opposition in parliament, even when they formed an administration in 1765. Shelburne was competition. (Even so, Boodle's was not without its Rockinghamites.) Circumspection about the Bute connection of the club in 1762 seems a plausible explanation, even though the Bute connection lasted only a short time, since Bute, like Cincinnatus, retired into private life after he resigned in 1763.

The original members

In 1762, Boodle's did not elect members. The Club was a business, and Boodle and Almack needed to bring people into the Club to make it viable. So the initial list of members is a unique cohort in the history of the club, because they chose to join, rather than being selected by existing members. Of course, whether by invitation or suggestion,

the profile of the first members reflects the social relationships of the smaller group of people who were responsible for initiating the Club. It is not possible, except by educated guessing, to confidently identify which of the first members were the prime movers, even with the list of original club managers in hand. Like any committee, some members will have been more active than others. But close inspection of the details of the early members' lives suggests some social patterns underlying initial and early recruitment. Several groups stand out: country gentlemen, intellectuals, politicians, military men, aesthetes, sportsmen, Irish and Scots. Inevitably, there is overlap between them.

Youth and age

Shelburne was aged twenty-five in 1762. Of original members whose ages are known, 43/91 (47%) were thirty years old or less. In fact, 17 of them were less than twenty-one and another 19 were between twenty and twenty-five years old.

(A further 7 were between twenty-six and thirty.) Boodle's was a very young club. Many of them had either been elected to parliament in 1761, stood as parliamentary candidates in 1761, or became MPs by the next general election in 1768.[23]

But the profile of new members in 1763 was already starting to be older than that of the original members. There was only 1 new member under twenty-one, 4 members between twenty-one and twenty-five, and 3 between twenty-six and thirty years of age – 8 out of 31 – whereas 19 out of 31, almost two thirds, were over thirty-six.

The early 1770s were a low recruitment period for the Club, sometimes with no new elections at all. This followed the death of Edward Boodle in 1772, and hints that there was some disarray in the Club; but it may simply be that the club had reached its physical limit in the Pall Mall building. The low number of new elections continued until 1781. The new clubhouse, and probably the political cycle, had most to do with the 1781 expansion. There were only 8 new members in 1779–80. In 1781, 135 new members joined, and 26 more were elected in 1782; but only 6 in 1783, none in 1784 and only 2 in 1785.

Regional connections

As Boodle's was in London, it seems reasonable to assume that the members lived in London. But this is not so. London, especially political London, in the 18th century, was a seasonal city; people would migrate to and from the capital and their homes in the provinces. This was not the only geographical aspect of membership. London was a meeting place, and in the later 18th century and early 19th century frequent and increasingly rapid travel was facilitated by the growing number of turnpike roads. Whereas it might take a week to travel from London to Bristol in 1700, by 1780 it could take two days. The greater ease of movement around the country was a spur to the economy, but it also had an effect on social life. The expense of rapid travel could be high, but it was at least possible for the wealthy, and this brought them together more easily and frequently, so a club in London would have a role which was more national than local.

Nevertheless, locality still mattered, and we can see clear regional groupings among the members. These are partly due to family connections, but it is obvious that neighbours were invited to join too. The Club members from the West Country, and Wiltshire especially, were friends, relations and neighbours of Shelburne. Shropshire and Cheshire provided many members, relations and neighbours of the Grosvenors and the Egertons of Tatton Hall, families who were devoted to field sports as well as being connoisseurs. Suffolk gentry were nearer to London, and Bury St Edmunds was an important town of fashion. Sir Thomas Bunbury and Lord Archibald Hamilton were early and influential members and Sir Charles Davers, 6th Bt, 'a gentleman of a very ancient family and independent fortune' was 'esteemed in the truest sense of the word, a respectable country gentleman', whose family represented Bury St Edmunds from 1689 to 1767.[24] Similar examples can be found in many other counties.

When we consider the range of geographical regions from which the members of Boodle's were drawn, two things stand out: that it encompassed the whole of the British Isles, including Ireland, and that if Shelburne had hoped to use the Club to extend his range of political support, the Club could have become the origin of a national parliamentary Whig Party organisation, superseding the Rockingham organisation easily, which was concentrated in Yorkshire and the north. But Shelburne, unlike Rockingham and his successors, was unwilling to impose his will as a matter of party discipline, because as an Enlightenment man of ideas he was determined that intellectual liberty must not be compromised. This was good for the club, but weakened his own political legacy.

Ireland

Initially, there were only seven members who could be clearly described as Irish, although the number might be higher if we include the Irish estates, business interest and other properties of various members. The proportion of Irish members neither rises nor falls much over time, but there was a healthy number of Irish peers, and this, together

There must be present at Balloting at least Fifteen Members & every one of these must give in his Ball otherwise it is no Ballot.

with commercial interests, meant that Boodle's members maintained a steady connection with Dublin and its hinterland, at least. Shelburne was Irish by birth and upbringing, and had estates there. Simon Luttrell, later the Earl of Carhampton, was the son of Henry Luttrell, a commander in James II's army, who came over to the Williamite side at the siege of Limerick, and received his brother's estates in Ireland as a reward. He was later shot in his sedan chair in Dublin, and the culprits were never found. Simon was known as the King of Hell, and had the reputation of starting the courtesan and spy Mary Nesbitt on her career by seducing her. His son Henry was John Wilkes's opponent at the Middlesex election, which would surely have created some tense moments in the Club.

The Caribbean

The empire was not only a world of commercial enterprise or military expedition, although these were two of the most common ways of experiencing the wider world. A number

of members grew up in colonies, and their families often had a cosmopolitan tone. St Kitts seems to have provided an unusual share of members, however. Patrick Blake (1762) was from St Kitts, and had an Irish mother (Sir Thomas Bunbury was his brother in law). James Farrel Phipps (1762), cock breeder, fighter and hard drinker, was from St Kitts and the Hon. Charles Marsham's (1769) mother, the Baroness Romney, was as well. William MacDowall Colhoun (1779) and his wife were both born and raised there, where he owned plantations, as well as two estates in Norfolk. According to his biographer, he was a promise-breaking rogue with no sense of decency, but he was supported by Wilkes as a candidate for Dover in 1773.[25]

The Scots

John Wilkes observed that a club, 'intended for the support of the Earl of Bute; though now . . . more agreeable to the idea of a Virtue Club', had as 'one of the principal rules and orders that no Scot shall be admitted into that society'.[26] An earlier historian of clubland appears to think the Virtue Club was an actual club.[27] But this is a tricky passage to interpret. Three things stand out. The first is that anti-Scots sentiment was widespread in the capital at the time, and Bute, being a Scots nobleman named Stuart, was a specific focus for it. The second is the capricious idea that a club to support him would have a rule barring Scots from membership. Thirdly, the word virtue had a particular philosophical resonance within Scottish Enlightenment moral and political thought, contrasting with the English preference for utility as the foundation of ethics. Why does any of this matter? A surprising number of Scots were among the early Boodle's members: at least 21 out of 122 of the original members can be certainly identified as Scottish. Many of them were famous men of letters or highly respected political figures. And all of them seem to have been friends of Shelburne.

The British Coffee House in Cockspur Street, off Charing Cross, redesigned in the 1770s by Robert Adam, was the centre of Scottish social life in London, and not a great distance from Pall Mall. It would be easy to see the Scots presence in the club as a consequence of Shelburne's early connection with Bute, but there is another angle. Shelburne was introduced to Edinburgh society as the guest of Colonel John Scott when he visited in the winter of 1759–60; and Scott became a close ally, as well as controlling the property on which the club met. He even travelled to the American colonies in 1769, and wrote to Shelburne that he thought the commercial regulations were 'absurd and injurious to both countries'. Scott worked for their repeal in parliament thereafter, but at least within Boodle's, he was working with the grain, and was a Committee member. Earlier, in the controversy over the Scottish Militia Bill in 1757, he was one of the six Scots personally lobbied by Newcastle and was almost certainly among the six who walked out before the division.[28]

David Hume (1762) wrote to Shelburne on 12 December 1761, upon leaving London, of his recollections of the Hill Street coterie and regret at having to return to Scotland and leave behind 'such an active and sprightly society as that of which your Lordship invited me to partake'.[29] It was not the last Shelburne, or London, saw of Hume, for he appears at Bowood in autumn 1768 'reading state papers' with Shelburne, according to Lady Shelburne's diary.[30] At about the same time Hume left London Benjamin Franklin appeared in the city. He and Shelburne recalled years later when trying to end the American war amicably, that they 'talked upon the means of promoting the happiness of mankind, a subject far more agreeable to their natures than the best concerted plans for spreading misery and ruin.'[31]

Shelburne's biographer and descendant Lord Edmond Fitzmaurice does not mention Adam Smith (private tutor to Shelburne's younger brother Thomas Fitzmaurice at Glasgow University), William Robertson (to whom Bute was a patron, and who was subsequently the tutor of Lord Greville, also elected to Boodle's in 1762),[32] or Adam Ferguson in his list of the Hill Street circle; but then, neither does he record Thomas Bunbury, and we know from other sources that he attended the evenings. It seems inconceivable that these Scots thinkers, also original Boodle's members, did not attend Hill Street too. Smith was famous at the time, across Europe, for his *The Theory of Moral Sentiments* (1759)

James Gillray's 1797 caricature of Francis Cunningham, Captain in the Coldstream Guards

rather than *The Wealth of Nations*, though he was already teaching the ideas which Shelburne gradually adopted and which would later be published in Smith's famous book. Smith was a family friend, and not Shelburne's 'discovery'; his father was one of the few to be graced with a courtesy copy of *The Theory of Moral Sentiments*.

Adam Smith had long standing friendships with a number of early members of Boodle's, among whom was James Oswald, one of the most respected MPs of his time, whose opinions on economics, philosophy, history, and law were valued by Shelburne and Hume; his practical knowledge of government and economics were a profound influence on Smith, whose own interest in economics he seems to have stimulated. The fathers of Smith and Oswald had been close friends as well, and Oswald represented both the county of Fife and Dysart Boroughs at different times in the Commons, over many years.[33] Oswald's son later represented Shelburne in the secret negotiations to end the war with America.[34]

Military connections

Shelburne was one of a number of men who had returned from service in the Seven Years' War, some of whom were elected to, or at least stood for Parliament in the 1760s. The role of that war in shaping the early club was significant. Shelburne had met Isaac Barré, with whom he worked closely in politics for the next thirty years, when they were both serving with James Wolfe on the continent. Shelburne later wrote that his friendship with Wolfe had been his true education. Literature and philosophy, correct social form, and the determination always to seek improvement of his character were all gifts he received under Wolfe's tutelage, and he remained grateful for it throughout his life. The nation hero-worshipped the idea of Wolfe; Shelburne honoured the man. Barré, some years older than Shelburne, served with Wolfe and Shelburne on the Rochfort Expedition and was Wolfe's Adjutant General in Canada, where he lost an eye in battle, an injury which led to his blindness, eventually ending his political career.

It was almost entirely the older original members who had military experience, and it is surely due to Shelburne and Barré that they joined. Like Shelburne, they had served with General James Wolfe, either at Quebec or Rochfort, or had been in the same regiments as Wolfe in the years before. Wolfe was a pioneer of combined naval and land operations, and this helps explain the presence of naval officers in the club, who had come to know him during campaigns. In later years, a number of the new members were con-temporaries of this first group, some of them joining as they returned or retired from naval or regimental postings abroad. Among them were men who achieved public prominence, such as General John Dalling, Richard

Howe, RN,[35] Colonel Sir Jeffrey Amherst,[36] who was Commander in Chief in Quebec, General Daniel Webb, Major General Robert Monckton, Wolfe's 2nd in Command in Quebec, General Robert Clarke, Colonel Hamilton Lambert, Colonel George Scott[37] and Captain Henry Smyth.[38] John Wetham (whose maternal uncle in law was Wolfe) joined in 1762. Shelburne and Charles Grey[39] both knew Wolfe on the continent.

As late as the 1780s these early connections with Wolfe continued to shape the club. John Jervis, the great naval reformer, was elected to Boodle's in 1781. He had served on the coast of America during the Seven Years' War, was friendly with Wolfe and Barré, and would later be connected with Shelburne and Barré politically. Indeed, it was Shelburne who arranged for his entry to parliament in 1783, and probably for his appointment to the Order of the Bath in 1782. General Charles Grey's late election in 1789, after a long career encompassing the Seven Years' War and the American revolutionary war, suggests that he then anticipated remaining in London. But in 1794 he and Jervis, now Lord St Vincent, commanded the expedition which captured Martinique.

Had Wolfe not died on the Plains of Abraham outside the Quebec citadel, he would surely have been one of the first and foremost members of Boodle's. It is probably significant that Lord Grosvenor, an original member and former employer of Edward Boodle, purchased the original painting of the 'Death of Wolfe' by Benjamin West when it was first displayed at the Royal Academy in 1771. General Robert Monckton, the only person in West's painting known to have been at Wolfe's side as he died, was also an original member of Boodle's.[40]

The City and Boodle's

Shelburne had already gained political experience at the Board of Trade under Bute, and his friendship with men like Adam Smith and David Hume had attuned him to the larger philosophical questions of how people live and work together, how wealth is created and distributed, and its role in increasing the happiness of people. It was all very well to grow food and extract other natural bounties – but what was it for? To provide for people's needs. And to do that, commerce and transport were also basic needs. Cities and their links, across the land or across the sea, and the role of money in all of this wealth creation and distribution, needed to be understood. Governments had a role, as did large business enterprises; but how large a role ought they to have? In the 1760s, these questions were beginning to congeal around two major issues: the role of taxation and colonial commerce in America and India, and the proper relationship between the government and private corporate enterprises, such as the East India Company. In America, the challenge was a directly political one about the constitution; in India it was about the balance of private enterprise versus government. Who should pay for things like security and what is the purpose of a colonial system, in America; and was the East India Company rapaciously out of control? Had too much power become concentrated in too few hands? Was there a danger that Crown intervention into the affairs of powerful companies could create even greater corruption?

Boodle's members with City and commercial connections make up a striking set in their own right, for City wealth was not insignificant among them. Shelburne and his close colleagues, several of whom were members of Boodle's, made great efforts to reform the East India Company from within, by working to get their own people elected as directors. John Calcraft (1763) divided some of his stock into further shares to create new electors within the Company, a tactic which was also sometimes used in parliamentary elections. But, as Shelburne later wrote: 'I interfered a great deal at one time in the affairs of the Company, but upon its taking a very corrupt turn, I scrupulously shut my door against them.'[41] In order to try and reform the Company, he and his associates who were senior figures in the Company attempted to get reformers elected to the Court in 1767–68, and tried to rebalance the internal finances. But, as so often happens, a broader financial crisis hit the economy in the midst of these changes, which precipitated massive losses in the share price. Government intervention looked essential, but Lord North, who became Prime Minister at this point,

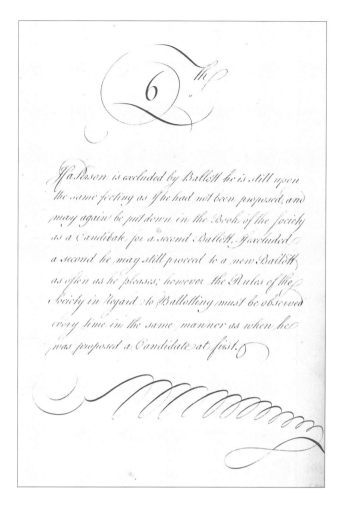

seems to have cleverly played for time, believing that Government control of the East India Company would be a disaster. Shelburne's efforts were not viewed in a kindly light by everyone, and he was accused of trying to manipulate the stocks for self-interested reasons. He was later accused of profiting from the end of the American war, just as Bute had been accused twenty years before over the conclusion of the Seven Years' War. It is probably true that Shelburne was secretive about the East India Company negotiations, and he had certainly allied himself with some shady characters in order to reform the Company; but the secrecy was at least in part to ensure that there was not a financial crisis in the markets. That is what a good statesman ought to have done. *Sapiens acts hac.*

Other Boodle's members were senior figures in the

Bank of England, the South Sea Company, the Sun Fire Insurance Company, in commerce ventures with continental countries and with the American colonies. Among the early City figures elected to Boodle's were: Benjamin Lethieullier (1766; MP 1768–97), whose father was a director of the Bank of England, and who owned substantial stock in government debt; John Drummond (1765; MP 1768–74; Director, Sun Fire Office, 1763–74); Peter Burrell (1765; Director South Sea Company, 1763–75; Sun Fire Office, 1773–96); and Nicholas Linwood (1763; MP 1761; Director, East India Company, 1749–51, 1752–4; Director, South Sea Company, 1758–64; Director, Sun Fire Office, 1760–death) whose chief connections with politicians before entering the House were with another close Shelburne associate, John Calcraft, and with Henry Fox. Calcraft asked friends in Germany for contracts for Linwood repeatedly. Another figure of real significance was the Assay Master of the Mint, Joseph Harris, who wrote on economics and finance, and seems to have been an important early figure in the practical management of Boodle's, though he was not a Committee Member. His presence in the Club is a small mystery, since he had no obvious family or political connections with other members, and does not seem to have come from a substantial family. But it could be that Shelburne came to know him during his time at the Board of Trade, or that he was already known to the Scots economic thinkers who were early members.[42]

There were many members with West Indian connections, whether as planters, plantation owners, active managers of plantations, traders, judges or politicians. Henry Dawkins was an MP from 1760 to 1784, (twice for a Shelburne borough, Chippenham), an owner of 20,000 acres in Jamaica, and of estates in Wiltshire and Oxfordshire. The father of his descendant, Professor Richard Dawkins, inherited the Over Norton estate in 1949, whence he returned from colonial service in Nyasaland. Henry Dawkins was another of those independent minded MPs, who are often described as Tory. The Lascelles family, later earls of Harewood, whose fortune included West Indian trade and plantations, were also well represented in the club from the 1760s onwards. Sir William Codrington, 2nd Bt, owned

plantations in Barbados and Antigua. These are but a few examples. The overlap between the Caribbean, the City and politics was considerable among members.

Some Savoir Vivre elections?

A large number of members of the Savoir Vivre club seem to have been elected to Boodle's, which would account for a notable rise in elections to the club in 1781–82.[43] Since there does not seem to be a surviving list of members of the Savoir Vivre, the best guess we can make about who they were must be based on the Boodle's members who were elected in this year. Two Boodle's members stand out as Savoir Vivre types. John Pratt, son of Lord Camden, one of Shelburne's Hill Street circle, was a young man about town, and elected to Boodle's in 1781. He had entered parliament in 1780 and with his friends, his father recorded, went 'to bed about 3 in the morning: rise at eleven, breakfast, ride to the park, till it is time to dress – then dinner, and the evening of course dedicated to amusement . . . They talk a little politics at their clubs . . . but with respect to the real state of the country they neither know nor care about it.' Pratt was a man whose 'modesty, reserve and diffidence are the leading peculiarities of his disposition, and all conspire with the natural turn of his endowments to make him rather an interesting companion in private life than a conspicuous figure in the senate.'[44] Richard Payne Knight was educated at home, and from 1767 toured Italy and the continent for several years. He was an MP from 1780 to 1806 and was elected to Boodle's in 1782. He wrote books and articles on sculpture, gems, coins, and other antiquities and, as a connoisseur and a member of the Society of Dilettanti, he was regarded as an arbiter of taste. His theories of the picturesque, and his interest in ancient phallic imagery were two of his more notable intellectual hobby-horses. Un-married, he left his extensive collections to the British Museum. Payne Knight was also one of a substantial body of club members who were described by contemporaries as Country Gentlemen.

Country Gentlemen

It was a convention of 18th-century belief that the best political constitutions maintained a balance of power between monarchy, aristocracy and democracy. Each had its virtue and failings; each expressing different forms of political power. In combination they could act as a check on each other, with independent lawyers and judges mediating specific conflicts over, say, the outcome of an election. The 18th century has been called the age of aristocracy, and with reason, since the political, economic and cultural power of the nobility had reached a peak in the British Isles. But some thought it had gone too far and become an oligarchy which was marginalising the Crown and controlled the Commons, creating an imbalance in the constitution.[45] The oligarchy needed to be restrained, even in the eyes of some of their own.

This aristocratic power was a legacy of the Whig revolution of 1688–89: the Stuart monarchs had tried to impose their wills on the nation, and the great Whig families had saved the nation from despotism. It was true enough to sustain and enhance the power of the nobility throughout the first half of the century, especially with the (admittedly decreasing) threat of a restoration of the Stuarts to the throne. After the defeated rebellion of 1745, the Jacobite threat was ended, and by 1760 many of the constitutional arguments of 1688 ceased to relate to the problems of the day. The constitutional battles of the age used the rhetoric of 1688 and of the balanced constitution, but the substance of those battles was different. The main problem from 1760 onwards was the imbalancing influence of public debt and vast accumulations of wealth and power in few hands. The Bank of England had been created by the Whig grandees to enable the state to finance its wars through debt, with the promise of tax revenues later to pay it off. The strongest opponents of this oligarchic debt financing were the independent Country Gentlemen.

Shelburne seems to have adhered to this analysis of the constitution, that the oligarchy needed restraining, because it was encroaching on the Crown, and that the Crown needed strengthening. This was consistent with Bute and in many ways with Chatham, who saw the Crown's role as providing support for the independent Minister. (It fits oddly with John Dunning's later motion (1780) that the 'influence of the Crown has increased, is increasing and ought to be diminished'; but circumstances change quickly in politics.)

The Country Gentleman element of parliament, and of Boodle's, were generally supportive of the Crown, and strongly independent of party. The 'Country' tradition in parliament, as opposed to the 'Court' element, was easily caricatured by government Whig apologists as Tory buffoonery, not to say Jacobitism: Joseph Addison's Sir Roger de Coverley being the archetype. But independence of opinion, political or otherwise, was a foundation of Enlightenment thought. Dependence undermined liberty, and the public debt created a form of national slavery. Parliamentary disputes over the debts and financing of the Royal household were actually disputes over the liberty of the King, with the Whig courtiers and Ministers as the men threatening the independence of the Crown. This helps explain how the independent Country Gentlemen could be both supportive and suspicious of the Crown: they were not blindly loyal to the Crown or the King's ministers.

But there were Whigs and Whigs. The Country Whigs were as touchy about their political independence as the Tories, and both forms of Country politics were suspicious of, and even hostile to the oligarchic Court Whigs and their policy of debt financing for the State. In this respect, the Country Gentlemen were a coherent group, whatever their family traditions or personal convictions about the constitutional rightness of the Glorious Revolution. (This Country tradition continues to inform political discourse about taxation, the role of banks and public debt, because even after 300 years it is still the right question to pose.) But organising the votes of these back bench MPs was like herding cats; they expected to be consulted, and would take offence if they felt taken for granted or otherwise ignored by the Government, whether 'Whig' or 'Tory'.

This Country tradition helps make better sense of what seems an incoherent political profile among many of the Boodle's members. Shelburne, 'the greatest enigma in

If any alterations in the Rules or any new proposal is to be made it must be put down in the Book of the Society three months before it can be agreed to & the alteration or proposal must be Balloted Yes or No by at least Thirty Members on a Thursday between twelve & one in the forenoon, one Black Ball is a Negative & stops the Alteration or Proposal.

18th-century British politics' makes more sense as a representative figure with this in mind.[46] He seems inconsistent, being both Chathamite populist and a Bute monarchist; he seemed so to his contemporaries, who resented his lack of collegiality in Cabinet when he was Prime Minister. But it was his determination to remain above Party, a Chathamite idea, which made him seem imperious. This ideal of independence was consistent with the liberty he gave to his protégés in parliament, and with the Country political traditions. 'Measures, not men' was his principle, adopted from Chatham. But where men are concerned, measures for the public good have their limits, since men want things for themselves, too. Shelburne, like most intellectuals, does not seem to have instinctively understood this, although he could accommodate it. Boodle's, to the degree that he was a

prime mover in its formation, was not, despite Wilkes's comment, a Party club, but a club through which independently minded people could meet, discuss public questions, and organise in ways which would preserve that political independence in public life. Political controversies could make this a difficult balance to maintain at times.

The first Rockingham ministry (July 1765–July 1766) was the only government ever to be made up almost entirely of members of the Jockey Club.[47] It was a party which was guided by some of the greatest Whig names, and yet was able to attract and retain the loyalties of many independent Country MPs, perhaps because they were genuinely devoted to breeding and racing horses. Lord North, Prime Minister from 1770 to 1782 was a natural ally of the Country Gentlemen, being by temperament and conviction one of their number.[48] He was relatively successful in positioning himself above party, something that Shelburne tried to do, though with little success. North's wit and amiable ease enabled him to attract affection even from opponents, where the more serious minded and intellectual Shelburne had loyalty from his friends, but suspicion from everyone else. And yet, Shelburne, for all his intellectual habits and City connections, was by temperament a Country Gentleman too. Boodle's has always had the reputation of being a club for Country Gentlemen and military men, hunting, shooting, fishing and racing their way throgh life. In fact, if we rightly understand the political meaning of the Country Gentleman in the Georgian age, the reputation is well founded, and reflects a tradition of independence and liberty.

Political connections

Evidence of connections to Bute, Prime Minister at the time, is abundant among the early members, although, as is hinted at in Lady Bunbury's letter, quoted earlier, there were tensions. Likewise, there are many who were connected to the Duke of Newcastle, whose star was on the wane but who remained a figure to reckon with. A small contingent of seven members of Wildman's Club, a Newcastle group, were elected in the first five years, and two others were elected as late as 1781: George Harry Grey, 5th Earl of Stamford and Humfrey Sturt (who was ejected almost as soon as he was elected for belonging to another, proscribed, club, and re-elected the following year). But an added explanation for apparent connections to Bute is the role of the Opposition group around Augusta, the Dowager Princess of Wales. This is more difficult to trace, but it was under Prince Frederick, the Prince of Wales, and eldest son of George II, at Leicester House that opposition became acceptable again, since his followers were Whigs rather than Jacobites. The Prince's death in 1751 caused political convulsions, as his heir, later George III, was only twelve; the opposition Court retained some continuity through the 1750s owing to his mother, who was firmly behind Bute as his mentor, so there must always be a suspicion that those whom Bute advanced to office, and who had opposition on their minds, had the approval of Leicester House. Clotworthy Upton, later Lord Templetown, was Clerk Comptroller to the Princess, and a Committee Member of Boodle's in 1763 and Hector Munro (1767) owed his early military promotions to her influence, and he later became a General. There were others. Although there may have been a Bute connection in 1761–62, Bute had lost influence by 1766 and he had been in absolute retirement since 1763. And he was never a member of the club.

The election of men who were associated closely with Lord Rockingham into Boodle's is something of a surprise. The parliamentary reformers, the Opposition as they became for many years, were divided into several coalitions of noble factions. The dominant group were followers of Rockingham, (the patron of Edmund Burke), with his regional power centred in Yorkshire and extending across the north and into the midlands, through family and followers. Both the 6th and 7th Viscounts Fitzwilliam, father and son, became members of Boodle's in 1762, and Lord Tichfield, who succeeded as the 3rd Duke of Portland in 1762 had placed his name on the original list, though he did not remain a member. Portland, to whom the Rockingham mantle of leadership fell, later headed up the Fox-North coalition in 1783, following Shelburne's departure from office. Portland's daughter, Lady Elizabeth Bentinck, later married another original member, Thomas, 3rd Viscount

Weymouth, later the 1st Marquess of Bath, who was a cousin of the Earl of Warwick (yet another original member). Such evidence supports the view that the club was initially intended to provide a new focus for Opposition politics. Indeed, over time Rockinghamites continued to be elected to the club, including members of the extended family and many candidates and MPs from Yorkshire, in particular. William Wentworth, the 4th Earl Fitzwilliam, and the heir to Rockingham's estate, was elected to Boodle's in 1789. This election took place seven years after Rockingham's death, upon which Shelburne had become Prime Minister. This suggests that by 1789 whatever factional interest Shelburne's people had was now superseded by a new generation of Whigs at Boodle's, who were content to see leading Rockinghamites elected to the club. Even Lionel Damer, the nephew of Lord George Sackville (later Germain), who Shelburne loathed, was elected a member of Boodle's in 1771, as were a number of other men of the extended Sackville family.

Boodle's, clubs and politics

Boodle's was established as a business, providing dining, a place to meet with friends and for gambling and many members used the Club for these things alone. But where there is money there is power, and political and business interests intersected at Boodle's from the beginning. For peers, with their established places in the House of Lords, there was no need to manage their own elections. If they had a particular area of interest, they could raise it in the House at any time; but speaking to an issue would only have an effect if the power to marshall votes in the House of Commons could be brought to bear, and so it was necessary to engage in electoral politics as well. Money and position had their limits, however. For all that has been said and believed about rotten boroughs in the unreformed system, very few individuals could expect to control more than one or two seats, if even that many, so that they could, in effect, appoint an MP. It is difficult to determine how absolute this power was even in an age when there were seats which could be bought and sold, as they were attached to specific pieces of land. (Similarly, the right to appoint a cleric to a parish living could be bought, sold or inherited as property.) Even Lewis Namier, who made a careful study of the subject and concluded that ideas and policies had little place in 18th-century politics compared to the tribalism of family and friends, thought that 'no two men will from the same data reach identical conclusions' about the ability of an individual to nominate or influence the election of a candidate.[49] With this caveat in mind, the number of parliamentary seats into which Club members could potentially place friends, family and protégés, or sell to either the ministry or someone else who wanted a seat, is impressive. Similarly, the capacity to make deals with people who were not members, but who might have family or other connections with members, has to be considered as another way in which members of the club could advance the interests of those whom they wished to see in the Commons.

But Boodle's was not simply a political club like others of the time, which were often explicitly named for the nobleman who was the leader of a 'party' in Parliament, such as the Rockingham Club, or later, the Fox and Pitt Clubs. (Admittedly, these were the sons of noblemen, but by their time, politics was taking on a more populist image.) Charles Turner, MP for York, 1768–83 (1770) wrote to Charles Wentworth, 2nd Marquess of Rockingham that he refused to join the Rockingham Club (the society of York Whigs) in 1767, because its name sanctioned the interference of a peer in elections, and [he] did not wish Rockingham to share the election expenses. He wrote on 1 March 1768: 'Surely, my Lord, there is a very material difference as well in argument as fact between a club retaining its general name, let who will be its president. In the first case the principles of the club determine the choice of its president, in the last the partiality to the president influences the principles of the club.' Turner's observation surely tells us something important about Boodle's, and implicitly about the way in which Boodle's was run. It was not a specifically partisan club. Shelburne was not that sort of man, and he does not ever seem to have sought to control the Club. But Boodle's was a club that had a role as a political career maker, even if it did

50

not have the formal structure of a political party machine.

The Whig Club, members of which supported the Rockingham party, was the first club to begin organising extra parliamentary support, widening the political hinterland; but it was not really until the late 1780s that something like an organised modern Party, with finance and a systematic approach to electioneering, came into being.[50] The change from 'personal' to 'political' parties was beginning to take place in the 1770s, and has generally been associated with the Rockinghamites and their successors after the death of Rockingham in 1782; this is partly due to the role of Edmund Burke, Rockingham's secretary, a propagandist for his party and a great theorist of Party. But for all the importance of Rockingham and his national political reach, the story of Boodle's has some things to teach us about this early history of political organisation.

Shelburne had a smaller political footprint; but he seems to have been experimenting with the idea of political party as a vehicle for ideas in the early 1760s, before the Wilkes controversy of that decade was even a small cloud on the horizon. Family and local connections had a profound role in shaping the club from its early years, but it began as a place where political ideas mattered and as a means of organising and recruiting prospective members of parliament.

Lord Grosvenor, for whom Edward Boodle was steward before going into business with Almack, shifted his allegiances between 1757 and 1784, and it is worth bearing his changes in mind when considering the political dimension of Boodle's during the first generation. He followed the Elder Pitt and Newcastle in the late 1750s, and switched to Bute in 1761 (in which year he was created Baron Grosvenor). He joined Boodle's in 1762. He then changed again in 1766, when Pitt, now Chatham, formed a Ministry. But when Lord North formed his long lasting Ministry, he transferred his loyalty to him and remained pro North and supported the war effort until North fell; he voted against Charles James Fox's India Bill and was created Earl Grosvenor in 1784 under the Younger Pitt. It would be easy to see him as an opportunist, but this would be a shallow interpretation. He was an archetype of the Country Gentlemen in parliament; he might be better understood as a man whose opinions changed with changing political problems, rather than with changes in political leaders.

Election of new members and the political machinery

The founding of a club is one thing; decisions about who to admit thereafter are less straightforward. Elections to Boodle's often followed quickly after a man inherited wealth, whether it was a title or simply an estate. In the first few years it was desirable to elect new members who had the power or influence to return candidates to parliament.

In 1762 Boodle's members had at least fifteen and perhaps twenty seats either in control or under influence. Five peers are noted as 'crossed out' in the list of members. Their apparent unwillingness to take up membership reduces the number of seats by five, to fifteen. But it makes a strong point: whether they were invited or persuaded to put their names down as members, it was partly because they were patrons of parliamentary seats. They might have decided not to join the Club because they felt that the aims were partisan and they did not wish to lend their support to a faction which they perceived was being created through this means. Perhaps they valued their independence; maybe they objected to Bute. The fact that Shelburne soon became a convert to the Elder Pitt's ideal that party should have no place in government did not draw them back to the Club.

Almost all of these twenty seats had peers as patrons. However, between 1763 and 1767 another twenty parliamentary seats were brought into the Club, and the majority of these seats were owned or influenced by commoners. The circumstances of John Buller's election are revealing. In 1765 Shelburne had backed James Townsend for the bye-election at West Looe, on the Trelawny interest. But his opponent was a government candidate on the Buller interest, and he lost. (The returning officer was not impartial, being a Buller supporter.) But two years later, Townsend stood again for West Looe and won the seat. What had changed? Was it because Shelburne was in office again and had used his

influence, as has been suggested, or was it because Buller was elected to Boodle's in 1767? *Quid pro quo*.

Whatever else can be said about family connections, friendships and so forth, this single statistic of Club members who were members of parliament tells us what we need to know. Boodle's was founded, partly, to push a political agenda. The evident dominance of independent Country Gentlemen as MPs among the members, together with the generally Chathamite tendency of the Club, is not inconsistent with ideology. Rather, it is the ideology of political independence that is visible in the behaviour of the members. The power to allocate or influence 35–40 parliamentary seats was electorally significant. In his path breaking work on the 18th-century House of Commons, Lewis Namier estimated 205 seats were under patrons in 1760. So the club members had close to twenty per cent of the available patronage,

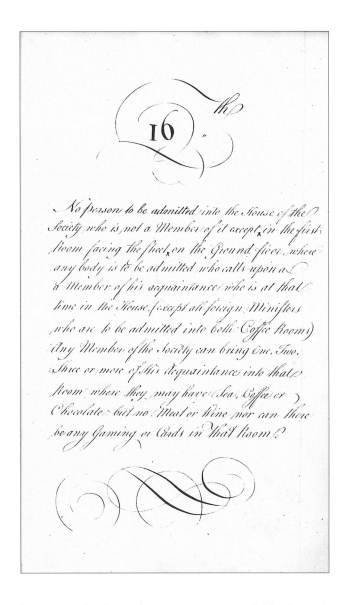

No person to be admitted into the House of the Society who is not a Member of it except in the first Room facing the Street on the Ground floor where any body is to be admitted who calls upon a Member of his acquaintance who is at that time in the House (except all foreign Ministers who are to be admitted into both Coffee Rooms) Any Member of the Society can bring One, Two, Three or more of his Acquaintance into that Room where they may have Tea, Coffee or Chocolate but no Meal or Wine nor can there be any Gaming or Cards in that Room.

parliament at some point. The number is certainly far higher, probably well over half.

By the end of 1762, Boodle's had 122 members: 25 had entered the Commons in the years 1754–60, five of whom were members of Wildman's Club. Of the 122 original Club members 18 had become MPs before 1761. At least seven had been in the House for at least one term before the 1754 election; five were elected in 1754; and another six between 1754 and 1760. That is, around fifteen per cent of the original Boodle's members were or had been MPs before the election of 1761. Another 12 members were elected to parliament in 1761. So, in 1762, 30 of the members had been or were currently, members of parliament. But this does not include those who stood for election and were not elected, so it may be that a good half, or more, intended to go into parliament. Of those who joined the club in 1762, 47 served as MPs at some point.

Looked at from another angle, 31 men became Club members after they were first elected to parliament in 1761: 12 of them joined Boodle's in 1762, another five became MPs in 1763 and six more by the next election in 1768. Thus, 24 out of 31 MPs who joined or were elected to Boodle's by the next parliamentary election became Club members during the 1761–67 parliament. Altogether, then, of the 81 Boodle's members who were already MPs in 1762, 66 (81.5 per cent) joined the Club by 1767, and 15 in 1767 or later.

These numbers do not fully reflect those members who stood for election to parliament unsuccessfully in 1761 but there are hints that no small number of those who were among the earliest members of Boodle's intended to stand at the next available opportunity. If we look at the number of years between a man's election to Boodle's and his election as an MP we can get an impression of the extent to which Boodle's was in part a recruiting ground and, an electoral machine.

Organisation of candidates and seats generally began two or three years before a general election, so if Boodle's was indeed operating as a club for electoral management, we would expect to see evidence that the election of new members relates to their return to parliament within two to three years. Some 30 MPs were elected to Boodle's three

leaving aside the wider connections available through extended family and friends who also had boroughs available to them. If you wanted to be an MP (or even if, like Edward Gibbon, you didn't), Boodle's was not a bad place to find a patron.

Looking in closer detail at who was elected to Boodle's, and when, does seem to suggest that the elections of individual members relate to planning and organisation for parliamentary elections, or to the admission of new MPs to the club. Incomplete data reveals that of over 800 club members between 1762 and 1800, over 230 were elected to

years or less before entering parliament; another 25 were elected to Boodle's within a year of becoming MPs, and 20 more were elected within two years of becoming MPs. Not a few were elected to the Club in 1765–7 who went on to stand for election in 1768.

If Boodle's was in part a machine for political organisation, we might also expect to see new members elected in relation to the times of major political events. General elections provide a particularly good test; but so does a slightly more subtle comparison between how many years before or after someone was elected to Boodle's and their election to the Commons. The question is whether election to Boodle's was a means to getting a seat in the House, or whether getting a seat in the House was a reason for being elected to Boodle's. It is also possible that they do not relate at all.

My analysis of the membership is incomplete, and much more detailed for the first decade, so the real numbers of Boodle's members who were MPs are undoubtedly higher, and probably much higher. But of the members between 1762 and 1800 who entered parliament at some point, 76 were members of Boodle's before their election to parliament, of whom 31 joined the Club three years or less before election to parliament and 13 six years before, which implies that they may have stood for parliament without being elected, initially. Only seven were elected in the doldrums of the electoral cycle, four to five years after an election. A further 25 were elected to the Club more than seven years before entering parliament. But 131 were elected to Boodle's after election to parliament. Of them, half (62) were elected to the Club within three years of their election as MPs. A further ten MPs were elected to the Club in the same year as their entering parliament, and it is not possible to say whether this took place before or after. The larger numbers who were elected to the Club after entering parliament takes some explaining, if the Club is to be understood as a vehicle for elections and the organisation of parliamentary influence, rather than a club for those who were already MPs. If you want to influence the next election, you need people who are within the system already. They might have pocket boroughs available as patrons; they might have

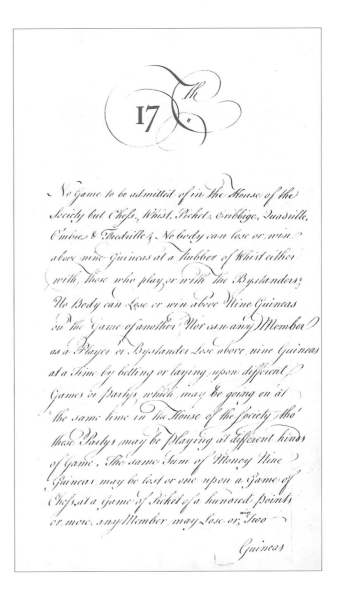

influential relations, or simply be people who are sympathetic to the aims of influential men within the Club. Their reputations and friendships could persuade other potential candidates to stand. And as sitting MPs, they had votes, and could be appointed to select committees. In either role, they could play a part in determining the outcome of policy decisions within the House.

The most powerful 'borough mongers', the Eliots, controlled six parliamentary seats, and they were commoners rather than peers. Edward Eliot, later Baron Eliot, was almost certainly elected to Boodle's in 1766, though the records only give the name Eliot. His control of these seats enabled him to nominate candidates with certainty that they would be elected and this made him a substantial figure in politics, for it meant he was in a position to sell positions in parliament. A 'high flyer conscious of his own merits', he was disappointed by the Duke of Newcastle and turned to Bute in 1760–61.[51] This would have brought him into the circles of Bute supporters who provided an important impetus behind the Club in the first few years. His election in 1766 is suggestive: he was not a member at the time the Club was most closely associated with the Bute interest, but he was elected later in good time for managing the 1768 election. He was, for all this association with elections in rotten boroughs and corrupt elections, described by Burke in 1790 as 'one of the most upright, able and industrious members of the House'. Eliot's intriguing observation, to Newcastle on 5 October 1756, that if he was appointed to the Board of Trade he would be able 'to get such information as may enable some of us young people who act together to put in execution the resolution we have formed, of endeavouring to speak in the House of Commons on points of business' resonates strongly with what we have already seen of the ideological aspects of the origin of Boodle's.[52]

Eliot certainly seems to have made use of Boodle's to recruit and promote new MPs, though he did not simply put his seats at the disposal of the Club. The date of his election suggests that there was such a purpose. Eliot was MP for St Germans (one of his own seats), 1748–68, and then for Cornwall, 1775–84. He returned George Jennings in the interim, 1768–74. He returned Edward Gibbon, his relation, for Liskeard 1774–80, and Wilbraham Tollemache (Shelburne's nephew) for Liskeard, 1780–84. Two other club members, elected in 1781, had been MPs elected in his interest in the 1760s.

Another member who was a political manager was John Calcraft, who acted as the whip of a group of leading soldiers in parliament and was an election monger in his own right, like Eliot. He returned his brother Thomas for Poole in 1761 and 1768–74; he captured control of Wareham by buying the Drax interest by 1768, but was unable to lay hold of Corfe Castle. Similarly, Shelburne bought out his neighbours

interests at Calne by 1765, one of whom, Northey, was elected to Boodle's in 1778. Shelburne then returned Calcraft for Calne in 1766.

Boodle's and ideas

In the spirit of General Wolfe, Boodle's was not all drums and muskets, even with its military contingent. Shelburne is remembered as a Prime Minister; but he was perhaps even more important as a patron of men of ideas, like Joseph Priestley, Jeremy Bentham and Richard Price, and it is no surprise to find some of the leading intellectuals of the age were founding members of the Club. Upon returning to Britain from Germany, Shelburne travelled to Edinburgh for the winter of 1759–60, as we have seen, and one of those who introduced him to Edinburgh society was Col John Scott, who 'maintained in the fashionable world the character of a bluff soldier'. Shelburne, ever the self-improver, gained the friendship of the moral philosophers Adam Smith, Adam Ferguson and David Hume, and of William Robertson, the historian and Principal of Edinburgh University (1762–93), and each of them were elected members in 1762.

The election of the historian Edward Gibbon in 1767 displays several of the usual connections which brought members to the Club. His grandfather had been an army contractor, and a director of the South Sea Company. His father had intended him to enter parliament at the next election, in 1761, when he returned from the Grand Tour in 1758. Gibbon did not wish to do so, but dutifully stood, and met Shelburne to discuss the matter. More importantly, two months after the election (he declined the poll on the day) he attended Shelburne again to present him with a copy of his *Essai sur l'Etude de la Litterature*, published the previous day, and asked Shelburne to present a second copy to Lord Bute. He did not enter parliament until 1774, but in light of the frequency with which members were elected to the Club in the year or so before a general election, it is conceivable that there were plans to find Gibbon a seat in 1768. But the point is, Gibbon was a writer, he was young, and Shelburne was a friend. When Gibbon did enter parliament, he became MP for Liskeard, a seat controlled by his cousin's husband, Edward Eliot.

The concern with excessive wealth and concentration of power in government hands was also reflected in a pamphlet written by two other members, Sir John Rous, Bt, and William Johnstone on the *Effects to be Expected from the East India Bill*, which argued that the Bill would be an incursion on private property by government and the start of tyranny.

Policy: implementing ideas

Shelburne later wrote in a memoir that persuading people that a new idea is right is hard enough, but that you are only a third of the way to success at this point: a whole raft of self-interest, factionalism and pride get in the way of actually implementing new policies based on the ideas. He referred to Adam Smith, saying that after thirty years, his ideas were still resisted, even though all agreed on the rightness of them.[53]

Shelburne's brother attended Glasgow University specifically to be taught by Adam Smith, and Smith received £100 a year to provide specific tuition for Thomas Fitzmaurice. Shelburne said to Dugald Stewart that his own journey from Edinburgh to London in 1761 with Smith in a carriage changed his life:

> I owe to a journey I made with Mr Smith from Edinburgh to London, the difference between light and darkness through the best part of my life. The novelty of his principles, added to my youth and prejudices, made me unable to comprehend them at the time, but he urged them with so much benevolence, as well as eloquence, that they took a certain hold, which though it did not develop itself so as to arrive at full conviction for some few years after, I can fairly say, has constituted, ever since, the happiness of my life, as well as any little consideration I may have enjoyed in it.[54]

Did the club retain some degree of coherence in political aims and action over the early decades? Boodle's was not a party machine in the modern sense of the word; the Rockinghamites remain the first to have an identifiable party finance machine. But there is an undoubted consistency to the votes of the members on key parliamentary votes which are generally understood to indicate a kind of party allegiance. It has not been possible to properly analyse the voting patterns of members, but a strong impression of consistency comes across when reading the parliamentary biographies of those who were Boodle's members and MPs.

Wilkes and liberty

The controversy over John Wilkes generated a varied range of votes on several important constitutional issues. Should parliament have the right to bar someone from taking their seat in the House when he has been properly elected by his constituents, on the grounds that he was an outlaw, having been convicted of seditious blasphemy? Should General Warrants be legally permissible?

Wilkes was a supporter of the Elder Pitt, the great War Minister in the Seven Years' War. The peace negotiations with France, under Bute's ministry, were controversial, because many, including Wilkes, felt that they were too generous. The rhetoric deployed by Wilkes and other opponents of the peace terms argued that it was a betrayal of Protestant Britain, implying that Bute, John Stuart, was a covert Jacobite, that King George III was his puppet, and that England was under threat from a restoration of a Catholic monarchy, or, just as bad, a despotic system of 'popery'. (Popery being a shorthand for political despotism.) Shelburne, as a minister allied to Bute in 1762, was associated with these charges, and the later attacks on him as 'the Jesuit of Berkeley Square' had as much to do with this political memory as it had to do with his secretive manner. But, with the irony that only political conflict seems to be able to generate, Shelburne was a Protestant, and on the radical end of the spectrum, at that; he was an Anglican *philosophe*.

But Shelburne soon allied himself to the Elder Pitt, and has been convincingly interpreted as a politician whose aim was to perpetuate Pitt's legacy.[55] With this in mind, we should expect to see Boodle's MPs voting against General

Warrants and broadly to be supportive of Wilkes, if the club was a bastion of the ideas of Whig liberty, in their varied forms, during its early years. And this is, in fact, what we see. Of those whose votes we know about, no one voted for General Warrants. Some, finding Wilkes personally repugnant, or because their understanding of the constitution was that the Commons had an absolute right to reject an elected member, voted for his expulsion from the House to express their support for the sovereignty of parliament. But the general tone of known votes over the course of a generation is in favour of the liberties which the various controversies over John Wilkes brought to the considered attention of parliament.

Shelburne retired to Bowood from December 1763 until early 1765, to retrench his outlying estate at Wycombe, to read, and collect manuscripts, entertain friends, make a lake at Bowood, and to marry, in 1764. Shaftesbury wrote to ask when he would be done with his 'silly manuscripts', and sent him a lion for the menagerie at Wycombe. In the end, Shelburne did not stay away from London for very long, and the group resumed meeting up to the time Bute sold him his unfinished new house in Berkeley Square in 1765. (It seems likely that Shelburne's Hill Street group was gradually diluted by an expansion of the number of visitors to the new house, later known as Lansdowne House.)

By the time Shelburne returned to London the legal and constitutional battle over John Wilkes was intensifying. The Wilkes issue appears to have been at the centre of concern for many Club members, not least because so many of the men who were most responsible for founding and running Boodle's had friendships with Wilkes and close interest in the goings-on in the City. But Wilkes was a difficult character, and not one who could be described as a virtuous martyr to liberty. Charming and funny, but arrogant and contemptuous of his followers, he became the cause célèbre of his generation when the ministry mishandled his prosecution for seditious libel, after his attack on the King's speech in 1763, in his paper the *North Briton*. It was apposite that the particular issue was No. 45 (a reference to the Jacobite uprising of 1745) for it resonated strongly with the anti-Scottish, anti-Jacobite tone of the *North Briton*, and played on the

fact that Bute, a Scot, named Stuart, had written the speech. The King ordered a General Warrant for the arrest of those responsible. Wilkes defended himself on the grounds of parliamentary privilege from arrest for libel, with which the Chief Justice agreed. But after he returned to the attack, MPs voted the change the law, enabling Wilkes to be arrested again for seditious libel. He escaped to France, where he stayed until the election of 1768 (he returned partly to flee his French creditors), and he was elected MP for Middlesex. He was arrested and barred from taking his seat, which provoked riots.

Many Club members are known to have voted against the government over the Wilkes issue; some knew him and liked him; some disliked him but voted to support the principle of liberty which had been violated by his expulsion from the House and arrest; and some eventually voted with the Government because they found him personally repellent. Thomas Scrope (a madman, admittedly) campaigned in 1764 at the Aylesbury bye-election caused by the expulsion of Wilkes from the House. One of the items in his accounts is 'for banners, with his own arms emblazoned on one side and Wilkes and Liberty on the other'.[56]

More drama over Wilkes would follow, this time in St James's. Hervey Redmond Morres, 2nd Viscount Mountmorres was described by Philip Dormer Stanhope, 4th Earl of Chesterfield, in October 1768, as having recently distinguished himself in the Irish Parliament, and as being a 'very hopeful young man' and by his friend, the memoirist Nathaniel Wraxall, as 'active, and always on his feet, to so great a degree as to convey an idea of ubiquity personified; – for, he seemed to be in many places at the same time'.[57] He certainly showed some spirit during the Wilkes riots in 1769.

'Of all the outrages perpetrated on this eventful day, the most scandalous and audacious was one offered personally to the Sovereign. Immediately before the rioting had commenced at St James's, and while the King was closeted with his Ministers, a hearse, drawn by four horses, two black and two white, was drawn up to the principal entrance of the palace, accompanied by every offensive circumstance of intimidation and insult. On one of the panels of the hearse was a picture of the soldiers shooting young Allen in St George's Fields, while another panel represented the tragical death of one Clarke, who, during one of the recent elections for Middlesex, had been killed by some chairmen in the pay of the Government candidate. On the roof of the hearse stood a man habited so as to represent an executioner, having an axe in his hand, and his features concealed by crape. This person, as well as the driver of the hearse, were generally supposed at the time to have been gentlemen.'[58] According to Wraxall, who had known Mountmorres well for many years, the 'daring individual was a young nobleman of considerable notoriety in his day, Harvey Redmond, second Viscount Mountmorres'. Mountmorres had some genius and literary ability, writing, among other things, *The history of the principal transaction of the Irish Parliament* (1792), and was a recognised figure in fashionable circles and on the streets of London. He had not long been a member of Boodle's at the time of the event; what the members must have thought of this drama is hard to say, but if they knew it does not seem to have counted against him: he sat on the Management Committee in 1771 and 1776. Despite the theatricality, the action expressed an idea. Wilkes had support at Boodle's.

Country Gentlemen: their finest hour?

The overthrow of Lord North in 1782, after more than a decade as Prime Minister, had not a little to do with Boodle's members.

Boodle's moved from Pall Mall into the former Savoir Vivre building, with its swaggering fan shaped window, in 1782. The Club had clearly reached its limit of expansion by the late 1770s, and required new premises. But the timing of this move was remarkable, for it coincided with the closing stages of the American war and the crisis in government. Shelburne was at the centre of these dramatic events, both as secret negotiator with the Americans and then as Prime Minster (July 1782–April 1783); a number of other members were, predictably, similarly involved.

The Country Gentlemen were not MPs because they wanted to be politicians; it was a duty, to represent their

Bust of Lord Shelburne who by tradition is held to be the founder of the Club

local community and its interests – their 'Country'. Independent in their views, they could be led by persuasion, but not by party or patronage. This made them difficult to manage when important votes arose, and if the estimate that there were around two hundred such independent MPs is to be relied on the potential for trouble managing the House was no small concern. On the other hand, their independent mindedness often resulted in their votes cancelling one another.

As a class of MPs, they were not keen on the Court, but

were loyal to the Crown. They were critical of wasteful government expense and, being farmers, averse to risk, even if some wealthier ones also had interests in manufacturing, mining and other speculative ventures like turnpikes and canals. There was a strong tradition among them of suspicion toward the City and the great Whig families, due to their memory of the creation of the Bank of England and the creation of public debt to finance wars. It is difficult to estimate what proportion of Boodle's members were such Country Gentlemen, but there can be no doubt that they formed a substantial body of the Club, whether they were members of parliament or not: perhaps as many as half of the members might be described this way. But Boodle's also had a substantial number of members with

interests in the City and banking, and a number of courtiers, too. Perhaps they needed a larger building to keep away from one another.

The acknowledged leader of the Country Gentlemen in parliament was Thomas Grosvenor. Like his cousin, Richard, the first Baron (and later Earl) Grosvenor, he supported the Crown, and supported the government of Lord North over the American war. Although Lord Grosvenor was one of the founding members of Boodle's, and several family members were elected in the 1780s, Thomas was never a member. But his parliamentary role would have influenced many in the Club, and the decision taken by this group of backbenchers to withdraw their support for North in March 1782, over his conduct of the war, precipitated the fall of the government and a subsequent constitutional crisis. It was Sir John Rous, a former Committee member, who moved the vote of no confidence in the Government.

St Alban's Tavern

A number of Club members joined the St Albans Tavern group in January 1784, 'the most important attempt of the country gentlemen to act as a group during this period'.[59] Their aim was 'to conciliate differences and to forward a union of the contending parties in Parliament' in the wake of the collapse of the Fox-North coalition; in particular, they sought to reconcile Charles James Fox and William Pitt. Of these seventy-eight MPs (listed in *The Annual Register* of 1784), one-quarter (around twenty) were members of Boodle's; Richard Wilbraham Bootle, Sir George Cornwall, Filmer Honeywood, Benjamin Keene, Sir John Trevelyan, the Hon George Berkeley, Ambrose Goddard, William Hussey, Sir Robert Lawley, Sir James Tylney Long, Francis Annesley, Richard Payne Knight, the Hon Charles Marsham (later Lord Romney) and Sir Robert Smythe, Sir Horace (or Horatio?) Mann, Sir Matthew White Ridley, Sir George Shuckburgh, Sir Thomas G Skipwith, Robert Smith, John Tempest (probable), Robert Thistlethwaite, Beilby Thompson (1787), and possibly Glynn Wynn, supported the St Albans group. Most had been elected in 1781 or 1782, and the rest in the 1760s (Trevelyan in 1774). Marsham, MP for Kent and a member of Boodle's since 1769, was joint chairman of the group, and an advocate of 'measures not men', that distinctly Shelburnian phrase. The failure of the group to bring about the much desired reconciliation of parties forced them to choose sides, and they divided fairly evenly between Fox and Pitt, one more demonstration of the variability of the country gentlemen as a political group.

Sir Robert Smythe was one of the more colourful Boodle's characters. He was an original member, aged eighteen, but appears to have resigned at some point, for he was elected again in 1781. He was chairman of the Essex Committee of Association, a Rockinghamite parliamentary reform group, in the early 1780s, and was strongly attached to Fox. He seems to have been a member of Brooks's, and yet we find

A Suffragette demonstration passing up St James's Street 9 June 1910

him on the Management Committee of Boodle's in 1784 and 1788. Over the several years between 1784 and 1789 he had become 'a violent democrat' and settled in Paris as a banker in 1790 after withdrawing from Parliament. 'Intimately connected with some of the leading republicans', he was a close friend of Thomas Paine and a member of the British revolutionary club in Paris. Nevertheless, like many, he was imprisoned during the Terror. He was able to get a passport in 1796, with Paine's help, to travel to Hamburg to collect money from England. Liking 'neither the government nor the climate' of England, he died in Paris in 1802.

Boodle's influence on culture

Shelburne came to know Samuel Johnson through Bute, and through Johnson to know Oliver Goldsmith and Joshua Reynolds. He sat for a portrait by Reynolds in March 1764 and again in 1766. (We also see payments to Reynolds in the accounts at Bowood, years later.) After leaving office for the last time in 1783 he travelled on the continent, collecting sculpture and other antiquities which formed the superb collection at Lansdowne House, which he reordered to accommodate them. Shelburne had left his Grand Tour rather late but, predictably, many other members had made the Grand Tour, usually shortly after leaving Oxford or Cambridge.

Some early members were notable figures in country sports, like foxhunting. Sir Simeon Stuart (1767), of whom Gibbon, who liked him and knew him well, said: 'Take him out of foxhunting and country affairs he has nothing left to recommend him but his good nature'. Sir Peter Beckford (1770), nephew of the immensely wealthy Jamaican plantation owner and City Alderman Beckford, and cousin of William Beckford, a collector and the builder of Fonthill Abbey, was more interested in hunting than politics, but his book *Thoughts upon Hare and Fox Hunting* (1781) is still one of the classics of field sports. Sir John Whalley Smythe Gardiner (1781) was prominent in hunting and racing circles, and a member of the club Management Committee in 1783.

The Earl of Abingdon, an original member, was educated at Westminster, Oxford and Geneva, and succeeded to his title in 1760, not long before Shelburne in 1761. He was an unusual character, 'sentenced in the King's Bench to some month's imprisonment for libelling an attorney named Sermon' when young. Horace Walpole describes him as 'a singular young man, not quite devoid of parts, but rough and wrong-headed, extremely underbred but warmly honest'. Lord Charlemont writes of him, 'a man of genius, but eccentric and irregular almost to madness'.[60]

He was a music patron and composer; political writer; brother in law of Giovanni Gallini (through his older sister Elizabeth), who brought him into contact with J C Bach and Carl Friedrich Abel, and he was much involved in their careers; he was also a friend of Haydn, who may have encouraged him to compose. At the same time, he was a keen racehorse owner, and in 1770 he started the Earl of Abingdon's Hunt.

He funded Swinford Toll Bridge, built across Thames near Eynsham. He lived at Rycote, Oxfordshire, the family's Tudor palace. Capability Brown landscaped the site in 1778, clearly part of the rebuilding after the fire in 1745, which killed the 10 year old heir in his bed. But the house does not seem to have quite been finished. In 1779 Abingdon held an auction of all the interior goods at Rycote. All the plans to renovate and refurbish had come to naught, and shortly after his death the entire building was sold off in lots; only the Tudor front remained, either because it could not be

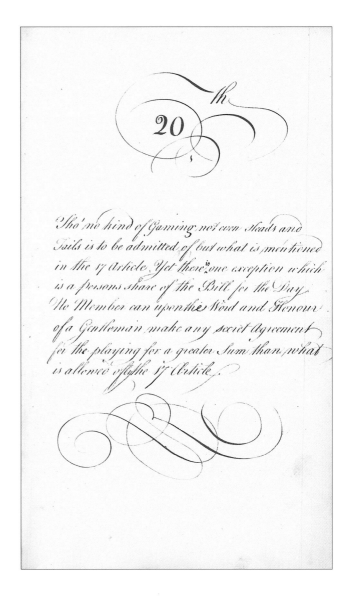

sold or in order to keep it as a folly.

He was also a friend of Shelburne, and applied to him to get a place for his protégé Samuel Estwick. Estwick had come to his attention for a pamphlet he wrote in 1776 which argued against the war with the 13 American colonies, and that Britain could not defend West India without America. Estwick had intimate knowledge of Barbados since the start of his series of administrative appointments in 1763. This chimed with Abingdon's views, and Abingdon put him into parliament for Westbury, 1779–95. Estwick was elected to Boodle's in 1781, and Abingdon applied to Shelburne on his behalf in March 1782, owing to the depletion of Estwick's fortune through natural disaster, to get him appointed an under secretary of state. Shelburne, who must have known Estwick already, since he lived on Berkeley Square, offered him a place abroad, which he declined. But when Barré became Paymaster General he appointed Estwick his deputy. Shelburne provided further for him shortly before leaving office.

And then there was John Hall Stevenson, the old Hell Fire Club man, with his rather strange poems about sex, social morality and religion, which have an almost Byronic lightness, despite their forthright language.

Politics, letters, the fine arts, sports and economic improvement all came together at Boodle's. We have mentioned little of the intermarriage of members' families; but it probably does not need to be said: friendships around the Club were sometimes hard to distinguish from meetings of extended family.

The mad, the bad and the dangerous

Ideas can have funny consequences, at times. Was it the ongoing political dispute about the role of militias which unhinged the mind of Thomas Wynne (1763)? Born in 1736, he became auditor of land revenue in Wales and Monmouth in 1756, aged twenty (presumably a sinecure arranged by his father to pay for his Grand Tour) which he retained until 1781. He went on his Grand Tour 1758–60. Upon his return he became MP for Caermarthenshire in 1761, and immediately added the Lord Lieutenancy of Caernarvon and was appointed Constable of Caernav Castle, both of which he held until 1781. He married the daughter of the 2nd Earl of Egmont in 1766. He succeeded his father as 3rd Baronet in 1773 and was created Baron Newborough, an Irish peerage, in 1776. It was all fairly conventional, on the surface. But Thomas Wynne was a very odd character, who was not well liked in the Commons. On the day of the Coronation of George III, he set up a secret society at Fort Williamsburg in Wales, following this a few years later with a Holy Order of Sisterhood, United Connected and regulated with the Free, Firm and Friendly Garrison of Williamsburg. And

with martial tastes to go with the esoteric ones, he later raised his own private militia, 'to defend the coast', and built fully equipped fortifications.

Namier and Brooke described the militia 'with their oaths, secret proceedings, and quaint ceremonial, . . . [as being] characteristic of the man and his time'. Wynne wrote against the American war. He was defeated by his brother, with whom he had quarrelled, in the borough. He left for Tuscany in 1782 on losing his local offices and honours, and on the death of his wife. He married Maria Stella Petronilla, aged thirteen, daughter of Lorenzo Chiappini, an innkeeper of Modigliana in 1786, but his time in Italy was marred by battles with in-laws, and he was imprisoned over debts which he had apparently incurred through promises to his wife's father. He was extracted from the situation in 1792, the debts being settled through the assistance of friends in the government and diplomatic service, among whom, it seems, was Sir Horace Mann.

Gambling

The Club was a home away from home for some very rich men in an age when gambling to the point of destruction was beginning to replace duelling, and some of the deepest players of the age were members of Boodle's. The Club was not founded as a gambling hell; Shelburne was not a man who sought his danger at the gaming table. But others did.

Not everyone had the goddess Fortuna covering their heads like Colonel John Scott, the greatest gambler of the age, but Henry Fox Strangways, Lord Stavordale, came close. He was as passionate a gambler as his cousins, Charles James and Stephen Fox, and Horace Walpole recorded one of the greatest gambling quotes ever, when he wrote to Horace Mann on 2 February 1770: 'Lord Stavordale, not one and twenty, lost eleven thousand . . . last Tuesday, but recovered it by one great hand at hazard: he swore a great oath – "Now if I had been playing deep I might have won millions."'

One of the reasons the stakes were high over a seat in the House was that it insured you against imprisonment for debt. The Hon William Hanger (1767), a rake and gambler, may have obtained his seat 'to avoid his creditors'. When

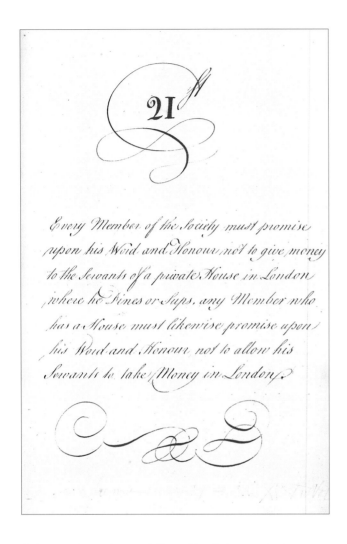

Every Member of the Society must promise upon his Word and Honour not to give money to the Servants of a private House in London where he Dines or Sups, any Member who has a House must likewise promise upon his Word and Honour not to allow his Servants to take Money in London.

failure at the table was followed by failure at the hustings, there were few options. The Hogarthian conclusion to the spectacular disintegration of an estate of an evening would be suicide. And yet, the gamblers don't seem to have done this, preferring to try and gamble their way out or simply to leave for the Continent. Another way out was tried by Edward and Thomas Foley, brothers who became overwhelmed by gambling debts and attempted to upset their fathers will in 1777. The younger, steadier, brother, also a member of Boodle's, held the estate in trust according to the will. Whether the habits of civility were able to restrain the passions within the club is not known.

Conclusion

A number of different groups of men formed the earliest cadre of Boodle's membership, and Shelburne, with his background, interests and reforming aims, was connected to all of them. The overwhelming impression is that the conscious role of the Club, in its first generation, was to recruit and promote men who appeared to be the sorts of independent minded and reforming people the Opposition wished to see returned to the Commons.

The political dimension of Boodle's in its first twenty-five years could easily fill a book of its own, for the devil is in the detail with political history. The Club was founded at the start of the reign of a young king, and a new political generation was just beginning to take power. Although reform was in the air, and about half of the founding members of the Club were 'young men about town' with ambition and new ideas, Boodle's also had a practical and traditional purpose: to organise electoral campaigns, recruit new candidates and win seats. Other Opposition clubs of the time, which have not survived, had the same aim. The Rockinghamites, more closely associated with Brooks's, were better organised, their reach was wider, and they were better at promoting their ideas and gaining adherents. They seem, too, to have been the first party to begin the difficult process of changing from a personal party, where MPs adhered to a nobleman, to a political party, where the ideas and policies rather than the person are the organising principle in the competition for power, although they found it difficult to accept the realities of popular political participation, despite years of pressing for this very thing. And yet, it is Shelburne and his followers who pressed the cause of 'measures, not men' in politics. Brief as we have had to be here, some of the things we have found suggest that the organisation of modern political parties might owe more to Shelburne, and Boodle's, than meets the eye.

Boodle's had a number of political roles; perhaps starting as a society to support Bute, perhaps as an early way of attempting to organise the return of MPs who, through conviction or connection, would vote reliably; and as events transpired, members may have used the club as a place to organise over particular issues. But these political activities threaded their way through the varieties of friendships, business relationships, personal and family entanglements, gambling and dining, conversation, fetes, and other pleasures which made the club work. As Shelburne himself wrote, in later years, 'It suits the pedantry of historians, who are ever making everything into a system, and it saves others the trouble of combining and thinking. But no great river arises from one source, but on examination will be found to come from the accidental junction of a number of small streams.'[61]

Clubs, if they are to survive, need to have some lasting purpose and a sound footing – buying the freehold, as the Duke of Wellington told the Oriental Club men, is usually pretty important too. But in the 1760s there were few such clubs, most (including even the freemasons' lodges) meeting in taverns rather than in their own buildings. It was not until the 1890s and the passing of laws relating to the management of clubs and societies that clubs were owned by the members. Instead, they were owned by the proprietors as businesses: hence the names of the older clubs, like White's, Brooks's and Boodle's, and those which have passed on into the Elysium of clubland memory such as Almack's, Arthur's and the legendary may-fly Watier's at 81 Picadilly (established 1807, disbanded 1819, where hard drinking, heavy dining and deep play seems to have carried off most of the members within five years). The great expansion of clubs in the Victorian age was more purposeful, on the surface: Reform, Carlton, Army, Oriental, Oxford and Cambridge, Public Schools – the name and the aim were the same. But this is not to say that clubs like Boodle's were not purposeful. Like the Rockingham, the Fox, or the later Pitt clubs, Boodle's had politics as an origin and aim. The constraints of time and space have meant that only a sample of the first generation of Boodle's political activity has been possible to analyse in any detail here. But it seems likely that the Club remained politically engaged in a serious way until, probably, the Reform Act of 1832, at which point the new politics of the reforming age, with more formalised party machinery at the centre of

political life rather than noble patrons and followers, began to drain away the traditional role of such clubs, after which they became, if never purely social, much less political.

63

The beautiful Madame Récamier (1777–1849) attended a 'most brilliant' fete organised by Boodle's in Ranelagh pleasure gardens to celebrate the Peace of Amiens in 1802. This 1805 portrait by François Gérard in the Musée Carnavalet, Paris shows her reclining in an Empire style dress

CHAPTER 4

Masquerades and Fetes

DANIELLA BEN-ARIE

On the evening of 2 June 1802 the 'celebrated Parisian belle' Madame Récamier, born Jeanne Françoise Julie Adélaïde but known as Juliette, could be found milling among hundreds of exquisitely dressed guests at a ball held at Ranelagh's pleasure gardens in the London suburb of Chelsea. This 'most brilliant' fete had been arranged by Boodle's Club to celebrate the Peace of Amiens between Britain and France, a treaty that effectively ended war between the two countries.

While the peace would last just one year, the exuberant celebrations that June night gave no indication that this would be a temporary ending to the war. Just as many Britons took the reprieve in fighting as an opportunity to explore the sights of Paris, the socialite Madame Récamier travelled in the opposite direction. Her reputation for wit, intelligence, charm and beauty, and as having one of the finest salons in Paris had preceded her arrival. She visited the most fashionable haunts of London, was entertained by the Prince of Wales, and strolled through Kensington Gardens, in a dress '*à l'antique*'. Fitting the highly anticipated Boodle's fete into this itinerary would have been considered most appropriate.

English society was clearly fascinated with the beautiful, elegant French woman and her daily activities were followed and recorded by both the gossip-loving English and French papers. As a young girl Lady Emma Sophia Edgcumbe, later Countess Brownlow, recalled seeing Madame Récamier at Kensington Gardens wearing a 'muslin gown clinging to her form like the folds of drapery on a statue; her hair in a plait at the back, and falling in small ringlets round her face, and greasy with *huile antique*; a large veil thrown over her head completed her attire, which not unnaturally caused her to be followed and stared at.' She 'created a sensation, partly by her beauty, but still more by her dress.' As Britain's political, economic and artistic elite danced and dined that June night at the Boodle's Ball, Madame Récamier, wearing 'white and silver, her beautiful tresses confined by four diamond daggers, a diamond bandeau, and in front a brilliant star of great splendour' was in her element.

Situated on the River Thames in Chelsea, Ranelagh pleasure gardens was created in 1741 on the old grounds of Ranelagh House. A wooden rotunda, 555 feet in circumference, stood in the gardens and was enclosed within a formal garden of yew and elm trees. The gardens had for over sixty years been hosting masquerades and balls and by the time of the Boodle's fete in 1802 Ranelagh had long-passed its fashionable heyday; it would permanently shutter the following year. Yet despite this decline, the London papers could barely contain themselves. *The Morning Post* reported on the fete over successive days: 'the Fashionable world, scarcely recovered from the fatigue of the grand Masquerade at Cumberland House, last night thronged to the Dress Ball [at Boodle's]' which would 'long be remembered as one of the most brilliant ever seen in this country'.

Three members were responsible for organising the ball that night. Sir Willoughby Aston, 6th Bt, who had been elected to Boodle's in 1783; the Hon Charles Herbert, a member since 1771 (and presumably the grandson of the 8th Earl of Pembroke and brother of the 1st Earl Carnarvon), and a young William Lamb already having developed a reputation for both intellect and charm, and who would eventually be styled Viscount Melbourne and become prime minister. These three stewards had to ensure that the ball went off without any hitches – the club's reputation, along with the expectation of their members, required

This 1802 watercolour by Thomas Rowlandson records the splendid throng at the Boodle's Fete in Ranelagh gardens held in an enormous tent

nothing less. Among their many responsibilities was preventing the admission of guests with forged tickets (a real possibility as demand had been so high). As one wit in *The Morning Chronicle* commented, 'A bank note does not pass through half so severe a scrutiny'.

Those who had been lucky enough to obtain tickets thronged to Ranelagh gardens to partake in the elaborate dinner and drinks, to marvel at the magnificent set decorations, and to watch the parade of wealthy, beautiful and elegant women compete for prizes even though many of their carriages 'were two hours from the time of reaching the line' before their occupants could be set down. The tickets were checked twice upon arrival, 'at the outer door,

and afterwards at an inner door, by two confidential persons of the Club.' People began arriving at around half past nine in the evening having made their way through the throngs outside.

Boodle's had commissioned John Marks, a builder based in Edward Street, Cavendish Square, to erect a temporary structure in the gardens. An extant watercolour by the caricaturist Thomas Rowlandson fully captures the setting that June night. Marks's canvas saloon is seen over-flowing with people, the ladies wearing white and silver and 'diamonds in profusion blazed on almost every head. Tall white ostrich feathers were general, and many paradise plumes appeared'. The men wore court dress, regimentals (military uniform), or club dress (a plain green frock with a black collar). Rowlandson was not a member of Boodle's, and was not mentioned in any of the guest lists that were published after the fete but, according to James Payne, a Rowlandson scholar, the artist was almost certainly present, making his sketches for the finished drawing. The provenance of the watercolour has not been fully established (its earliest known owner was Sir John Crampton, 2nd Bt who died in 1886) but it is likely to have been commissioned by a principal member of the Club, perhaps one of the three organisers.

Marks had designed the temporary room to enclose many of the large elm trees in the garden. He also covered the gravel walk and grass with a baize, in green, to imitate the grass it was covering. As contemporary accounts described, and as the Rowlandson drawing attests, the covered saloon was 'as wide as Pall Mall, and nearly twice as long as it was wide. On descending the steps, the pillars on each side were covered with lamps, and the four trees formed a beautiful alcove to pass through, lighted up with variegated lamps, scattered amongst the branches.'

Marks installed a wooden floor for dancing, with benches and chairs on each side, and a place for the music band to play. This marvelous sight prompted the poet Mary Elizabeth Pye to write: 'Fill'd with delight and wonder, while we rove/thro' the bright mazes of the enchanting grove.' A ballet performance choreographed by the dancer James Harvey D'Egville from the King's Theatre in London, and probably the one indicated on the right side of the drawing, had also been arranged for the guests. Two large transparencies were also erected and celebrated the recent treaty with France. One showed Britannia personified, pointing to her ships on the Thames; the other illustrated a figure representing Peace. These were flanked by medallions containing images of George III and his consort.

The supper that evening was served in the Rotunda, reached by a wooden platform installed in the temporary saloon. The tables, laid with fine linen, china and silver plate, and decorated with an abundance of flower-filled pots, were expected to serve 2,000 people 'every delicacy, warm soups, green peas, cold lamb, poultry of various kinds, jellies,

blancmanges, craw fish, fruits the rarest, and the very choicest wines'. This sumptuous feast was prepared by Charles Waud, cook and confectioner, of New Bond Street.

The Prince of Wales (later George IV), dressed in a scarlet regimental uniform, arrived alone at half past eleven. He was met by Boodle's member and steward of the fete Sir Willoughby Aston who escorted him for the evening. The prince's brother, the arch-conservative, Ernst Augustus, Duke of Cumberland, entered with Sir Sidney Smith, Member of Parliament, and Gentleman Usher to Queen Charlotte. Each of the two princes was allotted his own box for dinner.

'Such a crowd of beautiful women was never seen before' proclaimed *The Sun* while *The Morning Chronicle* said of Madame Récamier that 'we are inclined to think that Fashion has deputed [her] to London to introduce the costume of the French Ladies, and to effect this species of Revolution!' was in excellent company. The 'two Duchesses of Rutland' were in attendance: The formidable dowager Duchess, Mary Isabell, political hostess, and described as 'the most beautiful woman in England', then at the height of her influence, was accompanied by her daughter in law, Elizabeth Howard, wife of the 5th Duke. That night they were said to rival 'each other in beauty, each dressed in white and silver, with a profusion of diamonds.'

Elizabeth Billington, the celebrated singer who, having achieved success on the Continent, was now being feted in the theatres of London, arrived with Diana Sturt, Lady Milner, wife of Sir William Mordaunt Milner, 3rd Bt. The Countess of Shaftesbury, Barbara Ashley Cooper, wife of the 5th Earl arrived looking 'charming, and elegantly dressed'. These ladies were joined in the celebrations by what seemed to be all of Society: the Beauforts, Buccleuchs, Devonshires, Leeds', Gordons, Abercorns, Baths, Salisburys, Cawdors, Yarboroughs, and the Williams-Wynns. The festivities continued well past midnight with many guests still remaining at daylight.

The costs to host this fete must have been enormous but the Club's funds were sufficient enough for Boodle's to donate the remaining subscription fees to a variety of charities in the amount of £824 [approximately £26,500 today].

A Masquerade held in 1773 in James Wyatt's Pantheon in Oxford Street which opened in 1772, and immediately became the most fashionable Assembly Room in London

The 1802 ball was lauded but was not the first that the Club had hosted. Rather it appears to have been the pinnacle of a series of masquerades and fetes that had been organised during the last quarter of the eighteenth century.

Nearly thirty years earlier, on 3 May 1774, between thirteen hundred and fourteen hundred people thronged to a grand masquerade hosted by Boodle's. It was held at the Pantheon which stood on the south side of Oxford Street, just west of Poland Street. The Pantheon had been open just a few years, designed by James Wyatt and completed in 1772. The popularity of holding costumed masked balls was at its height and as a locale the club could have done no better. Horace Walpole called it the 'the new winter Ranelagh' and praised

it as the 'most beautiful building in all of England'. He continued, 'Imagine Balbec in all its glory!'. The Pantheon, along with Ranelagh, would host some of the most magnificent masquerades in London.

By 1802 the vogue for costume balls had diminished. By contrast the 1774 celebration was a masquerade and the invitation stipulated that guests should wear fancy-dress. In anticipation of the forthcoming ball, costumers such as Brackstone's, of York Street, Covent Garden widely advertised their wares: 'The Nobility and Gentry are hereby acquainted that their Wardrobe of elegant Dresses is opened for the ensuing Grand Subscription Masked Balls'.

Boodle's member William Wentworth Fitzwilliam, 2nd

Earl Fitzwilliam wrote to Thomas Robinson, 2nd Baron Grantham from his home in Stratton Street, observing that at first 'nobody thought of going to it, so it was blown upon – but within these three days, it is become the fashion, and of consequence there is fuss enough about tickets – luckily I am provided for, which I was not so clear about last night'.

The nobility and gentry who attended the Pantheon that night were 'the greatest Croud that ever met there on the like Occasion' and 'dressed in the richest manner; and jewels shone through every part of the house'. Lady Almeira Carpenter, considered by the well-known memoirist Sir Nathaniel William Wraxall to be 'one of the most beautiful women of her time but to whom nature had been sparing of intellectual attractions', arrived at the ball 'very beautifully and very richly dressed'. Lady Almeira would soon embark on a long-lasting affair with William Henry, 1st Duke of Gloucester, brother of George III.

The most novel costumes were 'Mile Stone, 45 from London' and a pair of walking breeches being 'a strange sight for the Ladies; the Button-holes of the Waistband were opposite his Eyes'. Katherine Lowther, Duchess of Bolton wore pink and blue. Henrietta Vernon, Lady Grosvenor came dressed as a vestal virgin. This may have been wryly amusing to the other guests as she had been engaged in an affair that ended rather sordidly when she was discovered *in flagrante delicto* with Henry Frederick, Duke of Cumberland, another brother of George III.

'The beautiful, gay, and fascinating' Elizabeth, Lady Craven came as a Virgin of the Sun and had herself just survived a scandal the previous year involving the duc de Guines, French Ambassador to London. Frederick Howard, 5th Earl Carlisle and William Douglas, 3rd Earl of March came as 'Dominos', a commonly-worn costume for masquerades. The 'domino' comprised a gown of sleeves and a cape, often in black, that covered the entire body.

The historian Edward Gibbon, who had a home in London (but who spent many hours at Boodle's, still then at 50 Pall Mall, living in what he called his 'usual manner') described in a letter to his wife Dorothea the forthcoming masquerade with which his 'attention is now very much taken up.' He added that the Club 'have a great deal of Money and consequently of taste. Flying Bridges, transparent temples and eighteen thousand lamps in the Dome are the general subject of conversation.' The transparent temple cost the club £450 to construct, and 'the platform erected at the north end of the room, the disposition and brilliance of the lamps, . . . is impossible to describe' such was its magnificence.

According to one account in *The Public Advertiser* some of the night's festivities did not go according to plan: 'The Black Hole at Calcutta is the only Place I remember the Description of to bear any resemblance to the suffocating Heat of this infernal Place; many of us ascended as quickly as possible, and thought ourselves in Heaven, tho' half stripped and half starved. In the Confusion several Things were overturned; a Basket of Champaign being broke, many were almost drowned in it. . . . Not half of the Company could get either Eating or Drinking' and the costumes 'betrayed a great Poverty of Taste and Invention, they did not produce ten new Characters.'

Despite such pointed criticism Gibbon believed the ball to have been triumphant. It 'cost two thousand Guineas [£126,000 today], and a sum that might have fertilized a Province, [and which] vanished in a few hours; but not without leaving behind it the fame of the most splendid and elegant Fête, that was perhaps ever given in a seat of the Arts and Opulence. It would [be] as difficult to describe the magnificence of the Scene, as it would be easy to record the humour of the night.' Others saw it being 'much more brilliant and agreeable than has ever yet been, both for the splendour of its illuminations, and the variety of good characters.'

On the 26 May 1789, fifteen years after the Pantheon masquerade, Boodle's held a ball at Ranelagh to celebrate the recovery of George III. A severe illness had afflicted the King and had provoked the Regency Crisis of 1788. Now believed to have been caused by porphyria, his illness was then attributed to a 'madness' and it was expected that the Prince of Wales would be made Regent, *de facto* head of state, if the King failed to recover. A few days prior to the Regency bill becoming law it was announced that the King was in recovery. Boodle's decision to hold a grand ball in his honour must have been intended to show their loyalty to the crown.

The Boodle's ball, at which members were expected to wear club uniform, green edged with white, was just one of many intended to honour the King. Brooks's and White's held their celebrations at the Pantheon on Oxford Street. Foreign governments joined in wishing the King well through their embassies in London that threw lavish parties on their behalf. The French Ambassador, the Marquis de la Luzerne, held a gala for the King at his residence in Portman Square (which coincided with continuing unrest in France and the outbreak of the Revolution) while the Spanish Ambassador, the Marquis del Campo, hosted one at Ranelagh.

According to *The London Chronicle* however Boodle's ball although 'last in point of time, in point of magnificence, of order, of management, we will venture to speak as not even equaled, much less surpassed, by any of those public rejoicings, for the celebration of the Royal Recovery, which have preceded it.' Horace Walpole described it as the 'most splendid ball' celebrating the King's recovery [that] cost Boodle's £5,000 [£280,000 today].

That May night the celebrations were spread through three separate buildings in the grounds at Ranelagh. A sumptuous dinner was served in the rotunda where private boxes, ornamented with festoons of roses, had been set up for the royal party. The Prince of Wales, as well as the Dukes of York, Clarence, Gloucester and Cumberland, were in attendance. The Prince was served his supper on gilt plate and feasted on 'peas, strawberries, cherries, and every other delicacy' as a report in *The Times* explained. Included in his entourage was his morganatic wife, Maria Anne Fitzherbert, whom he had married in secret in 1785, and William Cavendish, 5th Duke of Devonshire with his Duchess Georgiana, who had been with Fitzherbert when the prince proposed.

Dancing took place in the ballroom, a temporary building constructed of white painted canvas with a domed-roof supported by pillars with intertwining festoons and lights. A third building, the Temple of Flora, was reserved for the Cotillion, a dance of French origin. This was 'the most

beautiful building that can be imagined' according to *The London Chronicle* and was decorated with orange trees placed between honeysuckle and rose festooned-pillars. A statue of the goddess at the top-end of the temple watched over the floral abundance.

A highlight of the evening appears to have been the behaviour, or rather misbehaviour, of the Prince of Wales who, as Horace Walpole observed, 'got exceedingly drunk there, got on a table, talked irreligiously, indecently, and abused the Queen. Women got on tables to see and hear him, his friends made the music play louder to drown his voice, and at last he was carried out speechless.'

Lady Susan Leveson Gower, Marchioness of Stafford, adds to Walpole's account that 'at Boodle's the Prince after supper was as drunk as possible, and behaved very ill. Your friend Bruhl [presumably the diplomat, John Maurice, Count von Bruhl, minister-plenipotentiary from the elector of Saxony] *ne lui cédait pas dans aucun de ces deux points* [does not concede either of these two points]; Mr Sturt was also very drunk. They were all three obliged to be dragged out of Ranelagh; what a humiliating state man is then thrown into! I might moralize a great deal upon that Supper, but it would be thrown away, as I think (and hope) you will never require it.' Despite this small hiccup, or perhaps even because of it, the notoriety of Boodle's ball was ensured and proclaimed as 'elegant' and 'extremely splendid' in the following day's papers.

Having already held a ball at Ranelagh to celebrate Peace in 1802 (only to see the Treaty revoked in 1803), Boodle's again decided to hold a ball in 1814 celebrating Napoleon's abdication and his retreat to the island of Elba. Unfortunately the intended fete was not held due to interference by the Prince of Wales in determining who should be invited. Club member Sir George Onesiphorous Paul, 2nd Bt, described it as 'the many extraordinary warlike circumstances attending this intended compliment to peace.' His observations on the behind-the-scenes machinations are worth quoting in full:

It appears that the most noble managers of White's ball [in honour of three monarchs, Emperor of Russia, King

'Mute not blind' a cupid gazes intently at a damsel removing her mask, with a pair of amorous doves below. One of the exquisitely engraved admission tickets to the Savoir Vivre masquerade held at the Pantheon on 18 May 1775 engraved by Francesco Bartolozzi after a design by Giovanni Battista Cipriani

MVTO, NON CIECHO

SÇAVOIR=VIVRE
MASQVERADE
MAY. XVIII. MDCCLXXV

G.B.Cipriani inv·   F.Bartolozzi sculp.

of Prussia and Prince Regent, 20 June 1814], in order to oblige the Prince by excluding his dear wife, had agreed to refer to the Prince Regent himself the power to invite the members of the Royal Family. This excluding principle was (it seems) by certain courtiers proposed in the club at Boodle's; it was objected to, and a ballot demanded on a question, and that question was negatived by three balls to one. It was then balloted – 'That the *managers* do invite *all* the Royal Family, as done at the fetes before given by the club,' and this question was carried by a considerable majority. The discomfited then proposed that 'The ball be postponed.' The advocates for this point were again beaten, and it was carried by three to one that the ball should proceed as before intended. And the next day after my friend wrote, namely, yesterday, the managers were to be chosen, I believe by ballot.

The most important consequence of this convulsion is that the only person on the club fit to manage a fete (Charles Herbert), and who conducted the former ones given by the club (being one of the Prince's family), declines having a part in the management. It is said that the courtiers intend to withdraw their names, but there is a question whether they can do so. The Regent, it is supposed, will not accept of his invitation, and will do his utmost to injure the fete. If his design should extend to the obstructing the royal strangers it will destroy your purpose in attending the fete; but otherwise I should imagine the country gentlemen will be required to do something extraordinary to render the absence of his Royal Highness less regretted.

Boodle's was not the only club to hold masques and masquerades at the Pantheon and Ranelagh. Some were held by rival clubs; while Boodle's was partly involved with the organisation. The Savoir Vivre Club, whose premises Boodle's took over in 1782, hosted a masked ball at the Pantheon on 18 May 1775. The Pantheon's dome, based on the original in Rome, was that night decorated in imitation of 'the vaulted sky and, and gave a tolerably just representation of a star-light evening.' Admission tickets, based on the designs of Giovanni Battista Cipriani and engraved by Francesco Bartolozzi, depicted a winged and bowed putto, its mouth bound, with 'muto, non ciecho' (mute, not blind) in a scroll.

In the following month, on the 23 June 1775, a grand regatta on the Thames (styled after those in Venice) followed by a fete at Ranelagh, was organised by the Savoir Vivre. One of the members, Thomas, Lord Lyttleton, an immoderate gambler and well-known libertine, was named regatta Marshall. The extent of Boodle's involvement is unclear but

at the minimum there was some financial assistance. This is recorded in a ballad recited at the post-regatta celebrations: 'Since the six Clubs have join'd to defray all the charges/ And the Lord Mayor and Alderman lent us their barges'. Boodle's was one of the 'six' as is made clear in the announcement that 'every subscriber must be a member of one of the following six clubs at the west end of the town, viz. Bootle's [sic], White's, Stapleton's, Almack's, Savoir Vivre, Goostree's'. It is of interest to note that this was the first regatta held in England and is possibly the earliest recorded use of the word in the English language.

Magnificent decorations were strung along the Thames, and scaffolding was erected for ease of viewing. Barges and boats were moored along the river bank and, despite the inclement weather, it was estimated that around two hundred thousand people watched the water procession. The river was transformed into a 'floating town'. Richmond House, Montagu House and Pembroke House, the grand London mansions with their gardens running down to the Thames, hosted 'splendid companies'. After watching the boat race that began at Westminster Bridge, the ticketed guests removed to Ranelagh, either by barge or on land by carriage, for dinner.

Among those in attendance were William Henry, 1st Duke of Gloucester and Henry Frederick, Duke of Cumberland, both of whom were barred from the royal residence having angered their brother (the King) by entering into secret marriages (they would eventually reconcile). Others guests included the French, Spanish, Prussian, Russian and Neapolitan Ambassadors; the artist Sir Joshua Reynolds, the architect Sir William Chambers and the actor David Garrick. In total two thousand subscribers were said to have supped.

The balls and masquerades hosted by Boodle's were as much political events as social occasions and inevitably as fashion and taste changed so too would the desire to arrange such events. In 1838 Boodle's was invited to join with White's and Brooks's in hosting a ball in honour of the Coronation of Queen Victoria. Brooks's proposition was intended to divest the celebration 'of anything approaching to political feeling'. In the event the two clubs declined the

REGATTA BALL AT RANELAGH
XXIII JVNE MDCCLXXV

Ticket to the Regatta Ball at Ranelagh on 23 June 1775 organised by the Savoir Vivre Club. A river god stands in a boat shaped like a giant scallop shell attended by mermaids with putti rowing bravely against the tide

invitation, with Boodle's rejecting it with a vote of ninety-one to seventeen. A debate then ensued in which Brooks's determined that it would be 'inexpedient singly to give an entertainment which, under present circumstances, might bear the appearance of a party festival'.

Long before this date however, it seems that the vogue for hosting such events was in decline. Even before the Pantheon was destroyed by fire in 1792, it had been converted into an opera house, and just one year after the Boodle's ball of 1802, Ranelagh was shuttered and its contents sold at auction, the building destroyed. If it were not for the contemporary recording of these 'most brilliant' events, Boodle's superb and highly sought-after celebrations would too have been lost to the ruins of history.

Thomas Malton's engraving of St James's Street in 1792 looking down to St James's Palace with the elegant front of Boodle's on the left facing Brooks's on the right

CHAPTER 5

The Search for Style

MARCUS BINNEY

The gentlemen's clubs of Mayfair and St James's are one of the architectural glories of London, the more so since so many of the capital's great aristocratic mansions – Chesterfield House, Devonshire House, Grosvenor House and Norfolk House to name but a few – were demolished between the wars for speculative development before listed building controls were thought of. London's other great interiors, those of the City Livery companies, so splendidly rebuilt after the Great Fire of 1666, were also devastated during the Blitz. By contrast the West End clubs fared remarkably well, with the notable exception of one of the grandest of them all, the Carlton Club in Pall Mall, designed by Robert and Sydney Smirke. This was struck by a high explosive bomb at 7.48pm on October 14, 1940 which crashed through the roof and exploded in the library. About half the British War Cabinet were dining in the Club one floor below but escaped injury.

Despite this tragic loss – the Carlton's site was developed as a featureless office block in 1959 – the clubs along Pall Mall and St James's Street still make one of the grandest architectural set-pieces in London. They begin with the stucco splendours of the United Services Club (today the Institute of Directors) on the corner of Waterloo Place. Opposite is the more Grecian Athenaeum by the young Decimus Burton who designed the elegant Ionic Screen at Hyde Park Corner. These were followed by the Travellers' and the Reform Clubs, both designed by Sir Charles Barry in a magnificent, restrained Italian Renaissance palazzo style. Next came the Oxford and Cambridge Club, ablaze with richly sculpted classical detail, and then the *Beaux Arts* splendours of the Royal Automobile Club, the work of Mewes & Davies who had made their name with the London Ritz.

Earlier than all the Pall Mall clubs are the trio of clubs towards the top of St James's Street, Boodle's, Brooks's and White's. Boodle's came first in 1775–6, followed quickly by Brooks's in 1776–8, the first major work of the young Henry Holland. White's new clubhouse came a decade later in 1787–8, designed by Robert Adam's great rival James Wyatt, whose portfolio of grand country houses was to include work at Belvoir Castle, Cobham Hall, Croome Court, Dodington Hall, Goodwood and Milton Abbey.

These 18th-century clubs were not just places to eat, drink and gamble. Their principal purpose was explained by the anonymous author of *The Clubs of London* 1828. He explained that 'Since the time of Dr Johnson, the Clubs of Eminence in London have, for the most part, been assemblages of noblemen and gentlemen connected with the Court and with the Houses of Parliament.'[1]

This point is exquisitely made in Thomas Malton's engraving of St James's Street in 1792,[2] looking down to St James's Palace with the elegant front of Boodle's on the left facing Brooks's on the right. Both have the character of private residences more than public buildings, without the grand flights of steps up to the entrance which were a feature of later clubs.

Incessant gambling was a second feature of the St James's Street clubs and the magnificent first floor Saloon at Boodle's was almost certainly intended principally as a Gaming Room, extravagantly decorated to encourage reckless betting. This is the view of Ralph Nevill in 1911 who was as close as anyone to the lore of the West End clubs: 'The saloon on the first-floor has a very fine and stately appearance and opening out of it on each side are two little rooms. One of these, according to tradition, was, in the

The St James's Street front completed in 1775 is dominated by the great fan window of the first floor Saloon. The bay window below was added to the design of J B Papworth in the 1820s. The white stucco contrasts with the warm golden London stock brick which replaced the red brick of the Queen Anne period

Robert Adam's front of the Royal Society of Arts in the Adelphi, completed shortly before Boodle's, was the model for both the fan window and the entrance porch flanked by pilasters

days of high play, occupied by a cashier who issued counters and occupied himself with details connected with the game; the other was reserved for members wishing to indulge in gaming undisturbed by the noise of the crowd which thronged around the faro tables in the saloon. These tables, it is said, are still in the club. Towards the middle of the last century, though gaming had long ceased to take place in the saloon, there was a great deal of high gambling in the card room upstairs. So far as can be ascertained, faro was once again played at that period'.[3]

Boodle's was built for the Savoir Vivre club, whose meteoric brilliance was short lived. On August 1, 1775, Nicholas Kenney, the proprietor of the Savoir Vivre obtained the

lease of three 'old and very low houses' on the east side of the street. These were demolished and the new clubhouse, costing £10,000 and upwards, was erected in their place.[4]

The new clubhouse opened early in 1776. On March 22 Horace Walpole noted that 'a new club is opened in St James's Street, that piques itself on surpassing all its predecessors'. On April 5 James Boswell 'mentioned a new gaming-club, of which Mr. Beauclerk had given me an account, where members played to a desperate extent'. A later proprietor of Boodle's, Mr Richard Miles, wrote 'The house when built was furnished in a style beyond any preceding club: classical pictures, sofas and chairs covered with satin. And when opened I will venture to affirm that no club ever did, or ever will flourish as this club did for some years.'[5]

For many years the design of Boodle's was linked to Robert Adam. Ralph Nevill's well-informed *London Clubs: Their History and Treasures* (London 1911) noted the clubhouse was built 'by John Crunden, from the designs of Adam', continuing that 'from an architectural point of view, Boodle's is an admirable specimen of the work of Robert Adam'.

The attribution to Adam was dismissed by Arthur Bolton, curator of the Soane Museum, in his two impressive folio volumes The Works of R. and J. Adam in 1922. Here he firmly, if a little cruelly, dismissed Boodle's as Adam copyism. The question of authorship was however resolved by Beresford Chancellor in *Memories of St James's Street* citing Thomas Malton's *Picturesque Tour*. This states that Brooks's on the right of his view of St James's was 'designed by Mr Holland, and another called the Savoir Vivre, nearly opposite on the left, designed by Mr Crunden'.[6]

The splendid fan topped window which dominates the façade of Boodle's was undoubtedly taken from Robert Adam's strikingly handsome front of the Royal Society of Arts in the Adelphi completed in 1774 the year before Boodle's was begun. Both have Venetian windows with Ionic columns surmounted by the rippling fan that was one of Adam's favourite motifs. Adam's distinctive porch at the RSA was also clearly the model for the entrance of Boodle's. Both have a pair of columns framing the front door with pilasters framing the side windows. This is a version of the well-known Roman triumphal arch motif. The side windows bring extra light into the hall, always important in London houses where a fanlight was often the only means of doing this.

To make his new club front doubly *à la mode* Crunden also paid homage to London's most fashionable Assembly Rooms, the Pantheon in Oxford Street, which had opened in January 1772 to unprecedented acclaim, attended by 1,700 guests, including all the foreign ambassadors, the Prime Minister, Clive of India, and eight dukes. Horace Walpole pronounced it 'the most beautiful edifice in England'.

The Boodle's front is almost the same width and height as Wyatt's Pantheon which had a central Venetian window

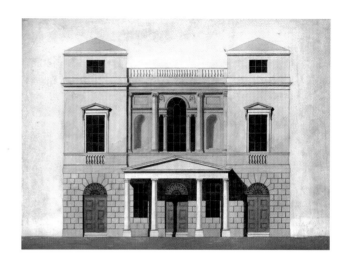

James Wyatt's design for the front of the Pantheon, his famous Assembly Rooms in Oxford Street, which were completed four years before Boodle's. The twin pavilion towers are echoed at Boodle's

flanked by twin Palladian towers rising above the main cornice with low attic windows. The twin towers on both Boodle's and the Pantheon derives from a well-known work of Palladio, the Villa Trissino, and were a favourite motif of the architect Earl of Burlington who designed Tottenham Park in Wiltshire in 1721 for Lord Bruce with twin towers of this kind.

Other handsome features of the Boodle's front are the Apollo heads set in plaques or pateras on the porch and in the spandrels of the Venetian arch. These were ordered from the famous Coade stone manufactory founded in Lambeth in 1769 by the redoubtable Mrs Eleanor Coade. Her speciality was a form of stoneware which produced architectural ornament of unrivalled crispness and durability which survived especially well in the polluted London air. Mrs Coade's catalogues offered no less than 98 different sizes and designs of patera. They were divided into three groups *Pateras for elevations from 30 to 40 feet; Pateras for Elevations from 20 to 30 feet; Pateras for elevations of 10 feet and under*. In other words, the size of the patera should be based on the distance from which it would be viewed. The Boodle's examples remain in first class condition – with Apollo heads set in a sunflower motif.[7] The early members of the Club, all with a classical education, would have been quick to note the attributes of

One of the Coade stone plaques on the porch at Boodle's, inset with the head of Apollo, the sun god who embodied the classical spirit and the arts.

The oval Coade stone plaques beside the fan window are also inset with an Apollo head.
Below: Mrs Coade's catalogue showing the pateras

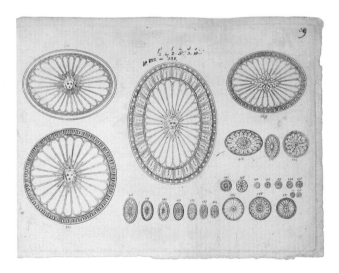

Apollo, proclaiming the clubhouse as a temple of the arts, as well the equally numerous allusions inside the Club to Bacchus, or Dionysus to give him his ancient Greek name. Apollo was also the personification of Reason.

The columns of the porches at Boodle's have distinctive capitals with a collar of palm leaves. Again this is an Adam motif, which appears in Robert Adam's *Works in Architecture* published in 1773 two years before Boodle's was complete.

Adam had observed the motif during his travels in Italy, on the peristyle of the Emperor Diocletian's Palace at Spalatro (modern day Split) on which Adam published a magnificent folio volume in 1764. The same motif is also found on the octagonal Tower of the Winds in Athens, published by two other renowned architectural travellers Stuart and Revett in their *Antiquities of Athens* in 1762.[8]

John Crunden, (*c.*1741–1835), practised as both architect and surveyor and is best known as the author of several popular architectural pattern-books. His *Convenient and Ornamental Architecture, consisting of Original Designs* [from] *the Farm House . . . to the most grand and magnificent Villa* first published in 1767, when he was in his 20s, was the most successful pattern book of town and country houses of the century, in continual demand, and repeatedly reissued, finally in 1815.[9]

Crunden was some four years older than Henry Holland and both were notably young to receive such important commissions – though Holland was by then the partner of Lancelot 'Capability' Brown, the landscape architect, and went on to become a favourite architect of the Prince of Wales. Both learnt their profession with Holland's father, also Henry, a successful Georgian master builder who was Master of the Tylers' and Bricklayers' Company in 1772–3.

Crunden appears to have been a capable draughtsman and was a regular exhibitor at the Society of Artists from 1766 to 1777. In 1809 he received the unusual accolade of having a design for a gothic garden pavilion published in a handsome French volume, J. Ch. Krafft's *Plans des plus beaux jardins pittoresques de France, d'Angleterre et d'Allemagne* (Paris 1809). The first two plates are of a Gothic garden pavilion 'exécuté dans un parc, sur la route de Westminster près de Londres, d'après les dessins du célèbre Jean Grunden [sic]' and is believed to have been situated near Fulham.[10]

In 1774 Crunden was appointed District Surveyor for the parishes of Paddington, St Pancras and St Luke Chelsea, a useful and steady source of income. Crunden's known works are relatively few and his abilities as an architect unclear as most of his town and country houses have been demolished. The losses include Brooklands in Weybridge (1767) which Crunden illustrated in his book, though here he was 'imploy'd to direct' construction by Henry Holland Senior and may have done no more than that.

This was followed by Halton Place, near Hellifield in Yorkshire (1770) for Thomas Yorke (whose descendants still own the property). Here Crunden's authorship is confirmed by the survival of 'The Ground-Plot, Plans, Elevations and Section of Halton-Place in Yorkshire. The seat of Thos. Yorke Esq. Designed by John Crunden Archt 1770'.[11] Portswood House near Southampton (1776) was built for Giles Stibbert, a retired general in the East India Company, and had unparalleled views down the River Itchen and Southampton Water and over the New Forest. Crunden's Audit House in Southampton built shortly before Boodle's in 1771–73, was also demolished.[12]

The Assembly Rooms Crunden designed for the Castle Hotel in Brighton 1777 suffered the same fate, demolished in 1851 but rebuilt nearby. In London, Crunden's houses in Park Street and Hereford Street were demolished in 1865,[13] as was a house he built at No 45 St Paul's Churchyard for Francis Newberry in 1778–9.[14] Only Belfield near Weymouth survives as testament to Crunden's talents, built c.1775–80 for Isaac Buxton.[15] Here there are echoes of Boodle's in the

Left: An urn topped by a globe in the railing. Right: According to Boodle's tradition the brass flowers symbolise a link with the Scarlet Pimpernel. They are always highly polished

large Palladian windows on the piano nobile and panelled pilasters at either end on the façade in the manner of Adam and echoing the Saloon at Boodle's. Highpoints of the Belfield interior are a geometrical stair with stone treads and wrought-iron balusters and an octagon room.[16]

A description of the accommodation Crunden provided at Boodle's is included in a set of auction sales particulars of 1802.[17] Here the club was described as a 'spacious and singularly elegant . . . . Mansion with suitable offices etc . . . desirably situate in the most eligible part of St James's Street with a neat compact house adjoining, suited for the residence of a single man of fashion . . .'

On the first floor there was 'A suit of five splendid apartments', consisting of an ante-room, 18 by 15 feet, a superb drawing room or saloon', 36 by 24 feet, near 20 feet high and 'fitted in a superior style of magnificence', a 'back drawing room' 33 by 21 feet , and an elegant oval room,' 23 by 16 feet. On the second floor there were three 'neat bed chambers and two water closets', and in the attics were five bed chambers and a spacious wash house and laundry.

The entrance porch showing triumphal arch and lantern. The capitals of the columns are ringed with palm leaves. A window head is inset with a tablet of winged griffins, attributes of Apollo. The ornamental Victorian shutter box was installed for sun blinds.

The bow window added by Papworth in the early 1820s follows a shallow Regency curve. It was inspired by the bow added to White's a few years earlier which was notorious for the critical eye members cast on the dress of passers-by.

In 1802, the proprietor of the Club was John Harding, who had been joined by Richard Cuddington in 1796. On Harding's death in 1808 Cuddington had become sole proprietor and ten years later invited the wine merchant John George Fuller to run the club as his partner. Together they embarked on a major set of improvements, including the addition of the famous bow on ground floor. They also took in the separate house on south side integrating its rooms in the Club and making the second porch redundant.

Their architect was John Buonarotti Papworth whose early talent for drawing was spotted by Sir William Chambers, the architect of Somerset House in London.[18] The young Papworth also received instruction in drawing from the sculptor John Deare and learnt perspective from Thomas Malton, the artist of the delightful view looking down St James's Street showing both Boodle's and Brooks's. After a three year apprenticeship with a builder to learn the practical side of his profession, Papworth worked for a year at Sheringham's, a well known firm of decorators in Great Marlborough Street. He also assisted the Polish theatrical artist and architect Michael Novosielski who reconstructed the Opera House in the Haymarket in 1790–1. The choice of Papworth was presumably prompted by Fuller for whom Papworth had designed Leigham Court in Brixton in 1820.

Papworth's fertility as a designer led to many commissions for furniture, silverware and glassware. He was employed as townplanner and landscape gardener and worked on numerous town and country houses for wealthy and aristocratic clients. His versatility was hailed by his contemporaries and when, in 1815, he produced a design for a 'Tropheum' to commemorate the victory at Waterloo, his friends dubbed him a second Michelangelo. This prompted him, a touch grandiosely, to add Buonarotti to his name

Some of Papworth's drawings for Boodle's are preserved in the collection of the Royal Institute of British Architects and copies hang in the annexe to the Coffee Room. The first phase of Papworth's work dates from 1821. The distinctive Regency bay window he introduced on the ground floor was clearly inspired by that added to White's just a few years earlier.

The White's bay window quickly earned notoriety, as members, far from nodding off in arm chairs, used to cast a critical eye on everyone walking along St James's. This was noted by the wit Henry Luttrell in his *Advice to Julia* which took the form of a letter in rhyme, giving advice on London society and fashion:

> Shot from yon Heavenly Bow, at White's,
> No critic-arrow now alights
> On some unconscious passer-by,
> Whose cape's an inch too low or high;
> Whose doctrines are unsound in hat,
> In boots, in trowsers, or cravat.

The book was published by John Murray whose premises were just across Piccadilly in Albemarle Street. A footnote in the 1820 edition adds 'the *bow-window* at White's is now enlarged, and affords a much better view than it did before of all that passes in the street.' [19] Because of this, it was said, many women avoided walking down St James's Street.[20] This establishes that the Boodle's bow window, added by Papworth in 1821 followed that at White's.

Lithograph of a Regency buck in front of Boodle's

Another distinguishing feature of the Boodle's street front are the highly polished brass flowers on the front railings. At Boodle's they are referred to as pimpernel flowers echoing a tradition, never substantiated, that Baroness Orczi's famous hero, the Scarlet Pimpernel, was modelled on a member of the Club. Her novel was published in 1905 and the pimpernel flowers show in early 20th-century photographs.

The porch at Boodle's opens into a modest but well proportioned entrance lobby enlivened by a glowing fire in winter with a dignified porter's cubicle. Today it has a black and white marble floor but the sale particulars of 1802 state that it was 'paved with stone' as the lobby at Brooks's is today. To the left of the entrance is a handsome lyre shaped barometer by Harris and Co of Holborn – Apollo, as God of Music, was often depicted with a lyre. This was a standard

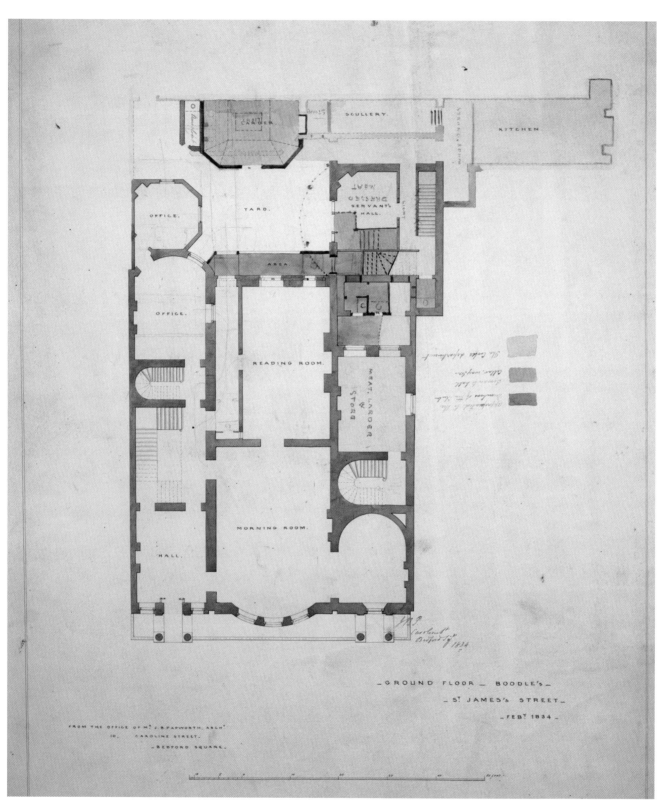

CARDER.

SCULLERY.

KITCHEN.

OFFICE.

YARD.

DRESSED MEAT

SERVANTS HALL.

OFFICE.

AREA.

READING ROOM.

MEAT. LARDER & STORE

MORNING ROOM.

HALL.

_GROUND FLOOR _ BOODLE'S_

S.T JAMES'S STREET

_FEB.T 1834 _

FROM THE OFFICE OF M.R J.B.PAPWORTH, ARCH.T

10, CAROLINE STREET.

BEDFORD SQUARE.

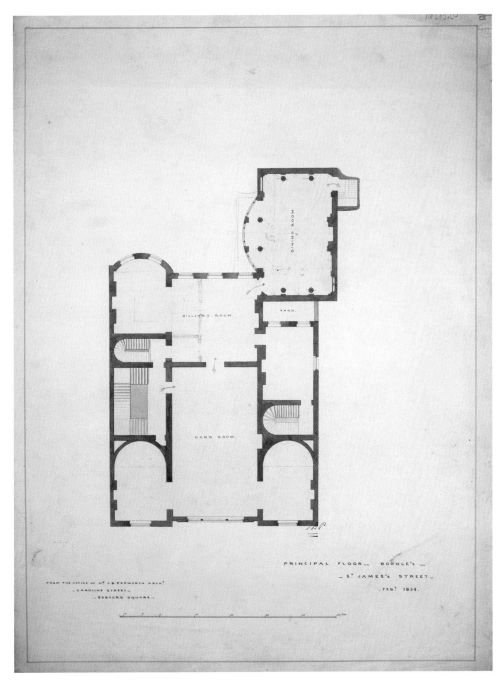

Papworth's plan of the First or Principal Floor. This shows his proposal to form arches from the Saloon, then the Card Room, to the adjoining rooms, the present Undress and Radio Rooms. The present Coffee Room behind, then a Billiard Room, was to be given a bow window. Papworth's Dining Room was beyond with pairs of columns on three walls and a broad shallow Regency window

Opposite: Papworth drawing of 1834 for remodelling the ground floor of the Club. The Morning Room was extended into the entrance hall of the neighbouring house making the second porch redundant. The back part of the Morning Room, then the Reading Room had not yet reached its present broad proportions. On the left, the plan also shows the half rounded back staircase which was later removed

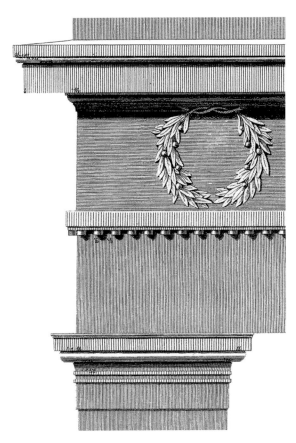

Detail of the Choragic Monument of Thrasyllus as illustrated in Stuart and Revett's highly influential *The Antiquities of Athens* (volume II, 1789). This is the precedent for the cylindrical dentils above the Morning Room doors looking like wine corks

Papworth drawing of 1834 for the door in the Morning Room Opposite: One of Papworth's handsome mahogany doors with a shallow Grecian pediment

feature in Georgian clubs and houses where people tapped the barometer for a weather reading as they check the forecast in the newspaper or television today. Old photographs show the porter's in a polished wooden cabin like those at Brooks's and White's. This was replaced by the present neo-classical design surmounted by three-part Diocletian arch in plans by Heering, Daw and Manners approved in 1969.[21] Over the fireplace – in which a coal fires glows every day in winter – is a gilt mirror evidently by Papworth and close to one of his drawings preserved in the RIBA.

The scale and internal layout of Boodle's, as first completed, was similar to large private houses being built at this time in both Mayfair and St James's. Under the building acts, London houses were codified in four grades – Boodle's being the equivalent of a first rate house. The main staircase is typical of these houses with elegant cantilevered flights rising round an open well and lit from above by an oval dome. Very beautiful examples are to be found north of Piccadilly at 3–6 Grafton Street built in 1768–75, completed at the same time as Boodle's.

The beauty of these 18th-century stone cantilevered stairs lies in the graceful way the stone steps extend from the wall without support from below. The treads are set into the wall by no more than two or three inches and the engineering load is carried down from one step to another until it reaches the bottom. Like a Roman arch they are extremely solid.

as Small doors

Section shewing the side next Entrance.

as Large doors

Section shewing the end.

A Papworth drawing of 1834 showing alternative treatments of the Morning Room. At the top are single doors characteristic of the 1770s when the Club was built. In the centre Papworth proposes taller doors with a central mirror. In pencil Papworth has sketched pediments over the doors and a wider central door into the back of the Morning Room (at the bottom) as exists today

The Boodle's steps are not rectangular blocks of stone but cut away on the underside to increase the feeling of lightness. As they have aged, later generations have sometimes wondered if they are still safe and decided to strengthen them from below. This happened at Boodle's, when in 1966 Clutton's reported to the Crown Commissioners that 'the main staircase is now in dangerous condition' stating there were two options – either to replace the staircase 'entirely in reinforced concrete to the same pattern' or to introduce two steel beams – RSJs – 'supporting the flights from below'. The second they pointed out would destroy the proportion the first would result in 'a loss of detail'.

An official at the Crown Commissioners observed that the recent authoritative *Survey of London* had described the stair as 'somewhat lacking in character'. He continued 'I cannot find anything to recommend it other than its being original'. This was a trifle hard – the Boodle's staircase is handsomely proportioned with a an elegant neoclassical cast iron balustrade. The straight square banisters are adorned with palm flowers. These are 'addorsed' to use the heraldic term which means placed back to back – one facing up, the other down. The Commissioners left the choice to Boodle's and thankfully the stair was retained, albeit with supporting beams that are a little too visible and hopefully may one day be discreetly replaced.[22]

Grand toplit staircases like that at Boodle's usually rose only from ground to first floors with a secondary or back staircase providing the link with upper floors and the basement. This was the case at Boodle's where the semi-circular shape of the second stair is visible at the back of the space members now use as a cloakroom. Arthur Bolton, writing in *Country Life* in 1916[23] observed 'the plainly treated staircase may be assumed to be original, though it is doubtful if it extended above the first floor'. This suggests that the flights leading on to the second floor are later, though before 1916. Certainly the arrival at the top landing is a little cramped.

Beyond the alcove where members hang their coats and leave their cases, the Boodle's Gents is hung with cartoons and equipped in best club style with piles of

Overleaf: The Morning Room with the central doors folded back

Detail of Papworth's double doors carved with a vertical band of pateras

freshly laundered towels, ivory hair brushes, bottles of mineral water and shoe shine stand. Beneath the main stairs for many years stood racks with complete series of telephone directories for the whole of Britain, vanished and forgotten in a world of mobile phones and the internet.

To the right of the hall and staircase hall, doors open into the Club Morning Room, two large rooms linked by double folding doors. No new member of Boodle's can fail to notice a very odd thing – the doors opening into the Morning Room are completely different on the other side – small and single in the hall and larger in the Morning Room.

The explanation is that Papworth completely changed the character of the Morning Room, introducing a more masculine treatment that perfectly illustrates the change in taste after Trafalgar and Waterloo. It was a question of away with 'effiminate' Adam decoration, based on the painted decoration of interiors at Pompeii and *in* with a more 'massy' Grecian look, with a renewed monumentality.

The change can be seen in one of Papworth's drawings in which he shows alternative treatments of small and large doors in the front of the Morning Room. The large doors

are much taller and in pencil Papworth has suggested further flourishes – drawn in a freehand scribble – as if he was discussing the interiors with the proprietor or members of the Club. These changes are the more interesting as they were actually carried out – shallow Grecian pediments over the doors and larger double doors between the front and back halves of the room with a Grecian scroll above.

Subsequently Papworth made a beautiful presentation drawing of the new tall Grecian doors with pediments. This shows double doors in the French manner but made of solid mahogany as was the English fashion. The door however backs onto a single door into the hall. The top of the new door as constructed is also false – though given hinges at the top to complete the illusion that it is a full height door.

The raising of the doors accorded with the Regency taste for higher ceilings, party a reflection of the new grandeur that victory brought but also of the need for more air and ventilation as a result of the introduction of gas lighting. Obviously Papworth could not raise the ceiling so he resorted to an optical device of pushing the cornice up, so that it spreads across the ceiling but takes up only a few inches of the top of the wall. Papworth's decorative motifs are all Grecian rather than Roman – palm buds, flowers and leaves.

His prime motif was the introduction of unusually broad or 'massy' pilasters faced in the most beautiful golden Sienna scagliola veined with red. This is of superb quality obviously executed by the best craftsmen, possibly Francesco Bernasconi, one of the leading Regency stuccoists. Instead of the familiar Ionic or Corinthian capitals these have a necking band inset with what look at a glance like scallop shells. On closer scrutiny these are palm flowers alternating with palms buds.

Above them is the very minimal cornice consist of little

18th-century chimneypiece in the Morning Room introduced between the Wars

Above: Detail of Papworth's unusually monumental skirting
Opposite: Pilasters faced in the most beautiful golden Sienna scagliola veined with red

more than a traditional 'egg and dart' moulding. Darts of course are an attribute of Cupid, and the egg is more properly described as a cupid shield. The more unusual motif is the ornamental band around the ceiling with a repeating motif a little like a spear head. This is more probably a version of a palm leaf. It is also close to the cresting on one of the most admired of Greek monuments the circular, pillar box like Choragic monument of Lysicrates, illustrated in Stuart and Revett's *Antiquities of Athens*.

Papworth again subtly increases the sense of height by dispensing with the traditional horizontal band of the chair rail and introducing in its place an unusually massive double height skirting. Though the decorative detail is somewhat chokes by layers of paint it is adorned with pairs

of addorsed palm flowers alternating with the spearhead or palm leaf motif found on the ceiling.

Papworth's new mahogany doors have both raised panels and narrower sunken panels (a little like letter boxes) in the French manner. The mahogany is of superb quality. Another intriguing detail are the unusual dentils. These are not the small squared blocks familiar in a Roman or Palladian cornice but little cylinders exactly the size and shape of wine corks. This motif is taken from the Choragic Monument of Thrasyllus in Athens.

Between the two mahogany doors is a large mirror which

The Morning Room looking towards Papworth's bay window
Overleaf: Papworth introduced a shallow Regency arch to open
the Morning Room into the front hall of the neighbouring house.
Note the ventilation grilles over the arch essential in an age of
candles and gas lighting

corresponds to a Papworth drawing. The matching mirror, which must have hung over the fireplace opposite, is now in the entrance hall. Facing mirrors were very much a feature of French classical interiors and in England the architect Sir John Soane was a genius in his placing of mirrors to creating reflections and vistas and bring light into dark corners. Humphry Repton noted the fashion: 'No more the Cedar Parlour's formal gloom with dullness chills, 'tis now the Living-Room; where guests, to whim, or taste, or fancy true. Scattered in groups, their different plans pursue.'[24] Another intriguing feature of the Morning Room are the numerous ornamental ventilation grills set in the upper walls, presumably cast iron. Though the detail is clogged by paint they have a five-pointed acanthus motif – surrounded by a pearl string. These ensured that Papworth's rooms were both well lit and amply aired – all to the very latest standards.

Door furniture was an important feature of Georgian interiors and some of the mahogany doors have round black handles with a metallic ring. The best preserved pair is on the door by the window which has a silvery collar which was probably originally gilt lacquered – another subtle element of gilding adding to the brilliance on the room. The

Above: the unusual two-sided clock suspended from the arch in a scrolled and gilded frame. The air vents above are in the form of a six-pointed flower

Below: Papworth's drawing for the clock

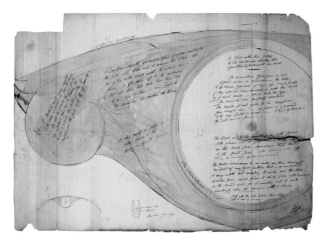

black handles were probably intended to suggest darkened antique Greek bronze rather than ebony. Another superb detail is central vertical band of button-like medallions, actually carved libation pateras. An antique patera was a shallow dish for libations, here each one is studded with a pearl.

The pairs of central folding doors are painted and inset with larger medallions – a feature French architects used to vary the geometry of the door panelling.

Papworth's drawings show he intended the back half of the Morning Room as a library with smart built-in bookcases set behind screens of Greek Ionic columns on either side. This may not have been executed as the back half of the Morning Room has the same golden Sienna scagliola pilasters as the front.

Between the two world wars Papworth's chimneypieces

The half moon alcove in the Morning Room now hung with Georgian cartoons

were replaced by late 18th-century marble fireplaces considered more appropriate to the 1776 date of the building. For this the Club received a gentle rebuke from Christopher Hussey in his 1932 *Country Life* article. 'Recent introductions, in the shape of chimneypieces, mirrors, etc, while excellent in themselves, may be regarded as misplaced by amateurs of Regency *décor*, which is so admirably suited to a club.' Papworth's chimneypieces had presumably been considered too severe. In design they must have been similar to those which survive in the Undress and Radio Rooms on the first floor.

The scrolled motif crowning the double doorway between the front and back of the room is repeated on both sides. This is one of the most striking and appealing decorative motifs in the vocabulary of the Regency with a luscious honeysuckle flower in the centre and set within the scrolls. It is a motif used by Sir John Soane on the magnificent screen wall that enclosing the Bank of England, on the corner of Threadneedle Street and Prince's Street. In Antiquity, the motif appears most impressively in the Ara Pacis, the monumental altar commissioned by the Roman Senate in 13BC to celebrate the Pax Augusta established by Augustus's victories in Hispania and Gaul, though this was not fully excavated until the 20th century. It would be nice to see the Boodle's scrolls as symbols of the Pax Britannica established by Waterloo but the point is not yet proven.

Above: Papworth's ornate Grecian scroll over the central doors in the Morning Room is carved with honeysuckle flowers

Below: A plaster model of a Grecian scroll ornament for the Bank of England in the Monument Court at Sir John Soane's Museum

This combination of scrolls and carved honeysuckle decoration was very popular in both England and France around 1800 and used by designers such as Percier and Fontaine, Charles Heathcote Tatham and Thomas Hope as well as Papworth and Soane. It was adopted from Roman funerary chests, carved in stone which often have a lid with a scroll top – what is known as a cippus altar. Examples were to be seen in the Park Street house of the great classical collector Charles Townley, whose marbles were acquired by the British Museum.

This motif also appears on top of the Papworth mirrors in the hall and opposite the fireplace in the front of the Morning Room where the central motif is not a honeysuckle but a *thyrsus*, the pinecone top of a staff borne by Dionysus and his votaries – another allusion to Bacchus early members would have enjoyed.

One principal source for this scroll motif was a handsome folio volume by Tatham, *Etchings . . . of Ancient Ornamental Architecture drawn from the Originals in Rome and other Parts of Italy* (London 1799–1800). The subscribers to Papworth's book included many of the leading architects and patrons in London.

Papworth illustrates examples of the double scroll on antique Roman thrones and tombs. These include a *rosso antico* seat in St John Lateran and an 'Antique seat of parian marble in a Chapel near Rome' and 'An Antique Seat of rosso antico marble used anciently as a Bath, now in the Collection of the Museum of the Vatican'.

Papworth's most unusual feature is the hanging clock he placed in the alcove arch to the south of the Morning Room. His design is preserved in the RIBA Collection and the clock unusually is Janus-like with two identical faces. On his drawing Papworth provides interesting details: 'A clock with two faces to be suspended between the two apartments and beneath an arch. The enamelled clock face is to be 15 inches in diameter and well legible. If [the hours] will not shew decidedly in gold they might be of dark brown – black looks too poor. The minute arm properly marked. The hands if not gilt, to be bronzed as gun barrels are – in fact it is required to be very legible and neat – glazed of course with curved glasses. The clock is to be complete on both faces. Both glasses are to open – and to wind up on the back face . . . all the sides will be hid by carving'. The rich gilding of the acanthus frame of the clock adds another glowing touch to the room, playing up the golden Sienna scagliola.

The name of the maker is inscribed on the face, Johnson of the Strand. Clocks in almost every room were a feature of all the clubs in St James's and Pall Mall. Members liked to be able to check their watches against a well-regulated timepiece as they arrived and left. Equally if they were with other members or guests it was easier to check a clock rather than look at one's watch which could seem precipitate or rude.

Today the Morning Room is one of the most comfortable and relaxing of London club rooms. Its subtle transformation from a very traditional club interior dominated by leather upholstered furniture has been effected by Stuart Richmond-Watson, who has long had a hand in looking after the Club's building, working with Stefa Hart over more than fifteen years. Stefa Hart's business grew out of Hambledon Hall in Rutland, one of the most attractively

A hanging lamp in the form of a shallow glass bowl or tazza wreathed in Bacchic vines with a central sunburst in the glass

decorated and furnished country house hotels in England, using colour and beautiful fabrics to bring out the character of a room. The aim at Boodle's has been to create a lighter, more relaxing interior, without the slightest hint of an institution, rather a home from home for the members. The Morning Room has been arranged for members to sit relax and talk with side tables for drinks. The walls have been painted a strong yellow to match Papworth's scagliola pilasters, beautifully cleaned some twenty years ago while Simon Leatham was chairman on the club.

A new carpet has been commissioned from the French house of Braquenié. It is woven to ressemble three large rugs – for the front and back rooms and the alcove, with

99

outfil to the walls. The colours are a stagey green and russet red. Stefa Hart went to the company's factory north of Lille and looked through their archives. 'I found a Persian design, an arabesque which could be varied in size till we achieved the right proportion. They had a bolder modern version but I wanted more muted colours so they wove me a special sample.'

The picture lighting has been reworked following advice from Stephen Cannon-Brookes who was closely involved in the lighting scheme for Waddesdon Manor, and subsequently set up his own lighting consultancy advising museums, including the Hermitage, and London clubs such as the Garrick and the Oxford and Cambridge. His approach is to find a way of lighting paintings in historic interiors that looks 'aesthetically coherent'. Hidden holes in ceilings and masked light sources are not his style. His aim is to provide solutions which will discreetly provide good value over a

Detail of a Grecian mirror designed by Papworth and now hanging in the Entrance Hall

long period. One problem today, is that for all the concern for energy saving, people unconsciously expect warm, welcoming lighting in interiors by day and in the evening. 'Imagine a shop with the lights off' he says. At Boodle's chandeliers are left off during the day.

The large Regency banquettes upholstered in red buttoned leather are evidently to Papworth designs. Their deep seats make them particularly comfortable to sit in – one is a settee with scrolled ends. There is a Papworth drawing for a large upholstered armchair with deep buttoned leather dated May 1828 and inscribed 'Messrs Cuddington & Fuller'. The chair with Greek 'sabre' legs does not survive. Instead of the usual loose cylindrical squab cushion it had a triangular shape – with a distinctly Egyptian sloping front. Other armchairs

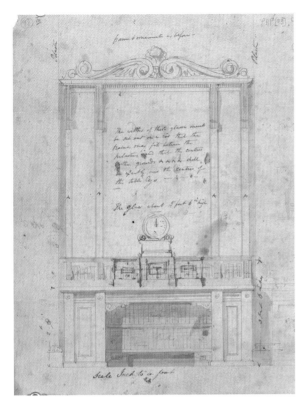

Papworth's design for the mirror now in the Entrance Hall

The Entrance Hall in the 1950s

The main staircase: like all grand townhouses of the 1770s in Mayfair and St James's Boodle's has a cantilevered stone stair with wrought iron balustrade and mahogany handrail lit by a dome at the top.

Sketch of 'An Adam Saloon in a famous London Club' by Hanslip Fletcher published in *The Sunday Times* February 4, 1934. This shows the archways introduced by Papworth and his scrolly brass clock on the mantelpiece

Opposite: The Saloon laid for an evening dinner looking towards Crunden's large and elegant Venetian window

have been upholstered in beige corduroy to provide a softer lighter touch. A deep half moon sofa has been made for the alcove room covered in a pale green cut velvet. Handsome new reeded curtain poles with gilded finials have been supplied by Edward Harpeley and Co and hung with red and gold silk and linen damask curtains specially woven in France.

The large and splendid bird painting in the back of the room is by Pieter Casteels, born in Antwerp in 1684. He accompanied his brother-in-law, the sporting painter Pieter Tillemans, to London. Here he painted numerous still lives of flowers, birds and animals dying in Richmond in 1749.

Old plans show that the Bar at the back of the Morning room was previously a Card Room. One early photograph shows an impressive but severe black stone chimneypiece, presumably by Papworth. This has now migrated to the Billiard Room on the second floor. With the ban on smoking indoors, a new smoking terrace has been create outside the bar, given privacy by an elegant screen of Doric columns. This has been designed by Peregrine Bryant, the Club's architect. His is also the new door opening onto the terrace, barely noticeable as the top of the door is glazed to match the adjacent sash windows. The trellis was designed by Stefa Hart.

The bar, which previously had a 1950s buttoned leather

An early 20th-century photograph of the Saloon showing Crunden's trios of columns and pilasters

Matching photograph of the chimneypiece on the opposite wall showing the room before the ornamental ceiling was introduced

front has now been faced in plain leather, and the television recently concealed within a mirror. On the walls hang two paintings by Susan Crawford, painted for Arthur Budgett, a Boodle's member and racehorse trainer, and one of only two people to have bred, owned and trained two Derby winners. These were Blakeney who won in 1969 and Morston in 1973, both named after neighbouring villages in Norfolk. The nearby Card Room has a Robert Kime wallpaper, a version of a smoky green cut velvet fabric. The carpet has been supplied by Avena in Halifax. The curtains are a French cotton with a bullion fringe supplied by George Spencer.

On the first floor is the grandest room in the club, the 1775 Saloon. Christopher Hussey writing in *Country Life* thought it 'one of finest rooms in London – its lofty proportions

exceeding everything except the ball rooms of great houses'.

The bravura treatment of the room comes with the clusters of pilasters – three on either side of the fireplace, echoed, on the wall opposite, by pairs of square and rounded columns providing an answering salute. The architectural treatment takes over the whole room, intentionally leaving no space for hanging pictures. Interestingly, the paneling is not in plaster as is usual with Adam interiors but in wood. This may have been because of the heavy entertaining in the room – plaster is easily chipped if people are squeezing past and knocking against it.

The walls are inset with delicately painted murals. Two of these are in colour, those over the fireplace and above the

The Saloon as repainted following paint research in the 1990s. The ceiling added in the 1920s, cleverly designed in best Adam style, matches Crunden's elaborate wall treatment of the 1770s

The sliding doors Papworth introduced were inset with a 'wicket' door for discreet service

mirror opposite. The first is said to portray the Aldobrandini Marriage but appears more likely to be Bacchus taking leaving of Ariadne, the daughter of King Minos of Crete who helped Theseus to escape from the labyrinth. Theseus left her on the island of Naxos where Bacchus found her, consoled her, and married her, only to take leave of her. Opposite is a line of Greek maidens in flowing dresses. The other panels are a set of *grisailles* with reclining figures representing the arts and sciences. These include Architecture with her dividers, Urania, the muse of Astronomy and Euterpe, the muse of lyric poetry.

The pilasters have recessed panels in the manner made popular by Adam. One close parallel is with the exquisite Glass Drawing Room Adam created at Northumberland House in London in the early 1770s which was completed just as Boodle's was begun. A portion of this was reassembled at the V&A Museum following demolition of the house in 1874.

The capitals in the Boodle's Saloon are especially rich with a collar of palm leaves. The sections of frieze above the pilasters are further enriched with urns celebrating the plentiful libations which must have flowed when the room was in use.

Another close parallel is with the dining room or back parlour at Home House 20 Portman Square, one of Robert Adam's finest works, and today a flourishing proprietary club. Interestingly it was completed in 1776, the same year as Boodle's, built for the rakish Countess of Home. According to William Beckford, who attended her parties, she was 'Known by all the riff raff of the Metropolis as the Queen of Hell'. This has similar panelled pilasters and relief panels over the doors.

The use of pilasters presents architects with the challenge of how to treat the corners of the room – Crunden solves it by placing mere slithers of pilasters in the angles with a fragment of capital and base – unnoticeable by most people but a neat if expensive solution. By contrast to the rich treatment of the pilasters and columns the pedestals on which they stand are completely plain – perhaps because they would have been concealed by furniture much of the time.

The ornamental plaster ceiling, though in the same style as the walls, is a clever addition of the 1920s to the designs of the Club's architect at the time Professor Beresford Pite of the Royal College of Art. Pre-1st World War photographs show a plain ceiling. [25]

The very rich white statuary marble chimneypiece must be original and is inset with a splendid steel grate introduced by Papworth with flanking brass torches. The gilt girandole mirrors, which must have hung in the room since it was completed, have the same medallions as the cornice. Two survive – there may have been more. They are comparable to a set at Osterley Park attributable to Robert Adam. [26]

Papworth's first floor plan shows that, when he linked the club to the house next door, he created a pair of archways opening into the matching anti rooms on either side of the Saloon overlooking St James's Street. These archways have

The elegant capitals of Crunden's columns and pilasters carry a frieze of Apollonian wine urns with griffin-headed handles and libation pateras

Below: a carved relief panels of twin sphinxes and twin griffins confronting sacred urns

One of the carved ram's head beside the central double doors with a wine ewer above. Papworth's drawing below suggests he designed a new door to match Crunden's original

now been suppressed but are visible in the delightful sketch of the saloon by Hanslip Fletcher, an etcher and illustrator who worked for *The Sunday Times* and the *Daily Telegraph*, sketching architectural scenes and interiors in London. The arches were fitted with pairs of paneled sliding doors – the arches and the door paneling are still visible in the side rooms, apparently neatly preserved as a 'reversible' alteration should the Club ever wish to put them back into operation. A photograph of May 1941, taken by Hubert Felton of the National Monuments Record (presumably as a record in case of bombing), shows a 'wicket' door set into one of the sliding doors so staff could enter discreetly from the side rooms without causing a disturbance by opening and closing the sliding doors. Fletcher's view also shows the Papworth clock now in the Committee Room on the mantelpiece.

The double doors through to the Coffee Room are adorned with splendid carved rams' heads. Though very much in the Adam style they appear in one of Papworth's drawings at the RIBA suggesting they may be one of his alterations. Rams' heads are a symbol of Bacchus, the god of wine, and therefore again appropriate to a temple of the grape. Other attributes celebrate Apollo, whose head adorns the Coade stone medallions on the façade, for example the griffin. Early members would have understood these pointers to their duty to promote the nation's arts and sciences.

The Papworth plan of 1834 marks the Saloon as the 'Card Room'. Brigadier-General C G Higgins, writing in *The Field* on July 22, 1939 recalled the heavy betting at the Savoir Vivre: 'To find the additional members to enjoy and pay for this magnificence, about 200 members were combed out of White's and Almack's. The betting now in these new premises was very heavy. Colonel Crawford of the Guards (Equerry to the Queen) won 100,000 guineas in a season. A Kentish baronet, Sir Edward Dering, lost in a night 11,000 guineas, and brought the money to the house the next day. On the night of this same day he lost 19,500 guineas, the house giving credit to the winners for their respective shares. This sum was all repaid in a fortnight. This mad rage for gambling in these St James's Street clubs had now being going on for years.' Lord Lyttleton of Hagley wrote a few years earlier 'I tremble to think that the rattle of a dice box at White's may one day or other (if my son be a member of that noble academy) shake down all our fine oaks. It is dreadful to see, not only there, but almost every house in town, what devastations are made by that destructive fury, the spirit of play.' [27]

Old photographs and illustrations suggest that in the early decades of the 20th century at least the Saloon was intermittently used. Fletcher's sketch shows the Saloon sparsely furnished with little furniture apart from a circular table at which a member sits writing while two other take coffee at an occasional table behind. *The Sunday Times* noted on May 22, 1938 that 'it was in this room that, in the 19th century, the annual general meeting of the Royal Yacht Squadron, English's premier yacht club, was held'.

Research by Ian Bristow, a pioneer of historically accurate paint schemes, concluded that the original colours of the room were pale green white and pink. [28] Early in the 20th century this was changed to a Wedgwood blue and white. In 1932 Christopher Hussey described 'its faint lilac, green, and white colouring', which survived until the 1960s. Though no colour photograph has yet been traced this was certainly an unusually lovely paint scheme. [29] In 1968 the room was redecorated by the architect Claude Lord Phillimore (1911–1994) at the suggestion of the 11th Duke of Grafton. Under his direction the walls were painted cinnamon brown picked out in primrose yellow and off white. Bristow found that the pilasters had been stripped of their original layers of paint between the wars but architectural logic suggested they were painted pink and white as the frieze had been shown to be.

At the same time the mirror frames were repaired and regilded by David Horden. New green damask curtains, woven by Gainsborough Silk, were hung by A E Chapman and Sons who adapted a Chippendale design for the window head, retaining the shape of the arch but obscuring the window.

The rooms on either side of the Saloon are known as the Undress Room (to the south) and the Radio Room (to the north) and remain as Papworth designed them. Inspired by

Detail of one of the Crunden doorcases given added emphasis by flanking half-pilasters

Detail of a golden brass Regency column with honeysuckle ornament and flaming torch framing the fire grate

One of a pair of gilt girandoles. The oval medallions match those in the main frieze of the room

Above: A procession of maidens with garlands of flowers in the Saloon dancing to the sound of a tambourine. The artist is unknown but the style recalls Biagio Rebecca

Above right: Grisaille panel of the figure of Architecture using dividers to measure the plinth of a column

Left: Painted panel over the Saloon chimneypiece said to be the Aldobrandini marriage. The air of resignation suggests it may be Bacchus taking his leave of Ariadne, who he married in Paxos where she had been left by Theseus after she had liberated him from the Labyrinth at Knossos

Detail of Papworth's marble chimneypiece and mirror in the Undress Room with the glass lustres he designed and a reflection of the chandelier

the work of Sir John Soane at his house in Lincoln's Inn Fields, Papworth created the illusion of shallow saucer-domed ceilings, supported by triangular spandrels smoothing the transition from square to circle. At one end he introduced an arch over a sideboard. Here, in contrast to the rooms below, Papworth's austerely elegantly Grecian chimneypieces survive in purest white statuary marble, far less ornamental than the Adamesque chimneypiece in the Saloon. On them stand pairs of beautiful lustres with tops like lotus flowers and superbly sharp drops ensuring they reflected candle light to best effect. They can be attributed with some confidence to John Blades, Cut Glass Manufac-

turer to George III and known as 'the Great Glass man of Ludgate Hill'. Blades regularly employed Papworth as a designer of his glass.[30] The feet are not the more usual lions' paws but Apollonian griffin's paws.

Country Life in 1932 noted the Undress Room 'contains a well-worn table, the top of which has a groove and central socket for a revolving wine trolley'. This deficiency was happily made good by Mr Simon Leatham during his tenure as chairman of the Club. The Club tradition is that the Undress Room derives from the time when members riding up from the country wanted to eat without the need to change into evening dress.

The double doors at the east end of the Saloon today open in to the Coffee Room. Papworth's plans and drawings

The Coffee Room as illustrated in *The Field* in 1939 showing the original richer 1920s wall treatment

show that his dining room was in a wing at the back which today serves as a first floor kitchen. The elegant shallow bay window remains, visible from the courtyard at the back of the club with three sash windows. A coloured drawing by Papworth survives, dated 1834, showing the wall treatment with Ionic columns on three sides and matching pilasters on the inner wall. It includes mahogany sideboards similar to those now in the Coffee Room.[31]

The present members' dining room has long been known as the Coffee Room, the custom in other London clubs such as White's, the Travellers' and the Garrick. The name is supposed to derive from the origins of the early West End clubs as coffee houses. At Boodle's the Coffee Room is a double height space matching the Saloon, with the attractive feature of two tiers of windows, with tall sashes below and square ones above. The central part already had a 21-feet high ceiling in 1802, according to the sale particulars,

but the removal of the floor between the first and second storeys is apparent above the bow window opposite the main door. The room as configured today is a creation of the 1920s. Christopher Hussey, writing in 1932[32] says the room 'which runs the whole width of the site at the back, was remodeled a decade since from designs by Messrs Hoare and Wheeler. The architects aimed, not unsuccessfully, at catching the spirit of Regency design, but – perhaps unfortunately – seem to have taken a cue from the ponderous style of Robert Smirke rather than the lighter variants of Nash, Papworth and Soane.'

The room's finest feature is the very architectural neoclassical ceiling with dome, shallow coffered vault and half dome – an unusual touch of asymmetry. By contrast the cornice is non-existent, playing up the geometry of the square ceiling panels along the sides. The room has subsequently been altered, rather to its detriment, but it is

The Coffee Room as redecorated in the 1990s showing the elegant 1920s domed and coffered ceiling

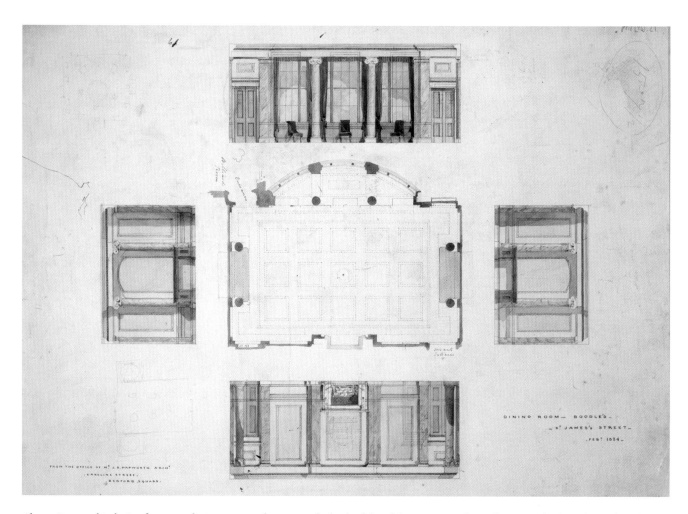

Above: Papworth's design for a new dining room in the wing at the back of the Club. Opposite: The Coffee Room looking through to the saloon both laid for an evening event

illustrated as it was in the 1939 article in *The Field*. This shows that the plain panels on the walls originally had banded borders typical of the stripped-down classicism of the interwar years, and looked less bare. The tabernacle motif framing the hunting picture on the north wall added a note of richness as did the decorative brackets to the door through to the Saloon.[33] Without the bands the panels looked bare, and they were further enlarged and bulked out in 1997 by the architects Purcell Miller Tritton, to make them more suitable for the hanging pictures.[34] A copy of their proposals hangs in the dining room annex signed KH 27th January 1997.

Hoare and Wheeler were architects of some talent.

Edward Hoare, educated at Harrow and Magdalen College Oxford, went into practice with Montague Wheeler in 1898 and they designed some good houses on the Howard de Walden estate in and around Harley Street. They also rebuilt Lees Court, Kent after a fire in 1913 and designed colonial buildings in Karachi.

The fireplace in the Coffee Room is modern, supplied by Chesney's. On it stands a distinctly architectural clock similar to one shown in a Papworth drawing for the Morning Room where it stands in front of a mirror. Unusually it has both Latin and Arabic numerals and stands on a Grecian scroll capital like a miniature altar. Beside it, built into the wall, are two splendid mahogany sidetables of Papworth

date, and presumably removed from the dining room Papworth installed beyond the present Coffee Room. The mahogany is of the very best quality, finely figured with a silky texture. Other more recent introductions are the polished service stations concealing the radiators.

In 2012 a new carpet arrived, specially commissioned for the Club by Stefa Hart. This is a modern version of an 1810 Savonnerie carpet woven in new colours – designed so that it can be taken up and turned round every few years so it is less vulnerable to wear near the entrances to the room.

The large stag hunt hanging on the end wall is by Abraham Hondius (1625–91) a Dutch painter known for his animal pictures who settled in London in his later years. Another large Stag Hunt of his is in Norwich Castle. To the right is a John Ferneley loaned to the Club and on the left a Lynwood Palmer bought from the estate of Marshall Field III.

On the second floor above the Coffee Room is a committee room which also serves today for meetings and receptions. This has an unusual 'egg box' ceiling with nine square compartments each with a pyramid vault or a roof light. It must have been created at the same time as the Coffee Room and the unusual ceiling appears in a drawing of 1933 in the Crown Commissioners' records.[35] The marble fireplace is recent, supplied by Chesney's. The unusual ceiling

Opposite: The back of Boodle's showing the bay window of Papworth's former first-floor dining room

The elegant Doric screen introduced by Peregrine Bryant, the Club architect, discreetly encloses an outdoor smoking area, the only place where members may smoke

created an uncomfortable echo at committee meetings and the walls have been hung with fabric to absorb sound – an Italian moiré cotton with braided edging. To make the room more elegant four pretty side tables in satinwood were commissioned from Richard Phillips and a series of engravings of Rome have been bought to hang on the walls framed by Serena Vivian Neal.

Beyond, steps lead down to the billiard-room, in a rear wing above Papworth's former dining room. Originally a smoking room as well, it was added in 1862–63 by Messrs Mayhew and Knight with what *The Survey of London* dismisses

a little cruelly as 'crude Corinthian pilasters and entablatures'. Old photographs show that the large black stone fireplace originally stood in the present bar. The arched fireback is evidently a Papworth design, enriched with bold acanthus scrollwork. Recently book cases have been installed at the end, and a start made to rebuilt the club library with books relating to Boodle's history, architecture and possessions. For the walls Stefa Hart has chosen an American damask green paper while the carpet has been woven to a Turkish design by Avena.

Early in the 20th century the Crown Commissioners (from whom Boodle's still leases its premises) devised a grandiose scheme for converting St James's Street into an imperially proportioned highway like Kingsway and Regent Street (the latter as rebuilt after Nash's original buildings were demolished). Suddenly Boodle's found itself sandwiched between much higher Edwardian neighbours in monumental Imperial baroque style. There was a flurry of rumours that Boodle's itself was in danger. Ralph Nevill, the respected author of the then recent *London Clubs: Their History and Treasures* wrote to *The Times* on July 28, 1914 expressing concern that 'in addition to a new storey being added to the club-house the front shall be refaced or rebuilt. The object in view is apparently to assimilate the façade of the rest of the modern buildings – monstrosities for the most part – which now disfigure an historic London thoroughfare'. The Crown Commissioners files in the National Archives show officials angrily dismissing such rumours. A letter from A R Powys, the distinguished secretary of the Society for Protection of

Ancient Buildings requesting a denial of the plans, is annotated 'this is a silly letter which might well be left unanswered'. It fell to Colonel F C Romer, the honorary secretary of the Club, to reassure readers that Boodle's was not under threat. Nevill, now under attack from the Commissioners, replied that he had written 'as I did on the suggestion of a well-known architect'.[36] This may well have been Arthur Bolton curator of the Soane Museum who wrote up Boodle's in *Country Life* two years later.

Boodle's nonetheless had ambitious plans for remodelling the Club in hand, drawn up by the Club's architect Professor Beresford Pite of the Royal College of Art. The plans, originally costed at £7,000, were delayed by the war. A new scheme, costed at £21,000, was put forward in 1919 and an extended lease granted in 1922 in recognition of the investment the club was making. On completion the sum had risen to £26,905 1s 5d with 'a large sum in addition for

The entrance to Boodle's Chambers and the Ladies' Side is set behind a deep arcade

Looking from The Economist Plaza towards Brooks's Club. The
flank of Boodle's is on the right with the bay window added by
the Smithsons

Below: Plan of the proposed plaza published in *The Economist* in 1981

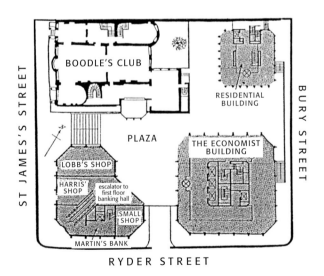

decorations'.[37] Beresford Pite's plans dated March 1916 survive
in the National Archives.[38] They show the Morning Room
in two almost equal parts as today with a library in the
position of the present bar. At the bottom of the main stair
there a telephone for members' use and two more just
beyond, with lavatories and a dressing room further back.
Pite's plans show the Coffee Room or Club Dining Room
enlarged to its present proportions though there is no indication of the present domed and vaulted ceiling. This was
evidently part of the additional expense of the post war
scheme completed in 1922. This scheme rendered Papworth's
dining room beyond redundant and it was converted into
a serving kitchen.

No sooner were the great works completed than the Club found that several of the main timbers above the saloon were 'defective through age'. Faced with these new costs the Club was under financial pressure. On January 15, 1934 there is a note that an 'appreciable saving was effected by employing manservants in place of women, the wages being somewhat lower' and 'the requirements of manservants' less.'[39] Boodle's therefore sought a rebate on rent. Cluttons advised the Commissioners that if Boodle's were to depart 'difficulty would be experienced in reletting either as a club or for other purposes at the present time'. A rent rebate of £500 was granted.

The post-war years saw many clubs struggling to survive. Boodle's sold books and silver but in the early 1960s the Club was able to do a remarkable deal with the owners of *The Economist* magazine who were seeking to build a prestige new tower as their headquarters. They chose as their architects the leading modernist practice Alison and Peter Smithson. Seeking to respect the street and building line of St James's Street, the Smithsons composed the accommodation in three separate buildings set around a raised, paved plaza. This had long been one of the most admired pieces of modernism in London and was listed Grade II* in 1988.

The project was explained in detail in *The Economist* – in an article, as always unsigned, 'A new home for *The Economist*' published in July 1961.[40] The development included the property then occupied by the magazine as well as three buildings on St James's Street and one on Ryder Street 'all of nineteenth-century construction', and three eighteenth-century brick houses in Bury Street. The plans, said *The Economist*, had from the start been governed by two considerations. 'First, the greatest care should be taken to ensure that any new building fits in with its neighbours, and, in particular, that the general aspect of St James's Street is not damaged. This is almost entirely a matter of proportions. The individual buildings of the street include few that are really good, and some that are downright hideous . . . If the street as a whole is one of the most satisfactory in London, that is a function of the ratio between its width and the general height of the buildings that line it. But the

The Print Room in the Ladies' Side serves as a private room for parties

proportions having been preserved, the second principle was that there should be no fake antiquarianism'.

The article continues 'It was also desired, other things being equal, to give an opportunity to a British architect whose work had not yet had the chance to become widely known. This was not conceived of simply as a piece of artistic patronage. The complications of modern construction produce the double result that the work of successful practitioners rapidly degenerates into salaried team-work, and that it is very difficult for fresh ideas to break in. We thought we stood a better chance of getting a building thought out afresh from first principles by going to an architect who represented himself and not a large office. After the most careful inquiry, the husband-and-wife team of Alison and Peter Smithson were appointed. Mr Maurice Bebb, who has been involved as our architectural adviser right from the start, has been appointed as associate architect.'

The ruling planning policy at that time was a permitted plot ratio of 5 to 1. 'In theory, the whole site could be covered with a building five storeys high . . . Or the same amount of floor area can be provided by going up high on one part of

The Ladies' Dining Room as redecorated by Stefa Hart

the site, leaving the rest free, in which case the possibilities are further restricted by the angles of light to neighbouring buildings and by an overall height limit'.

The virtue of the Smithson scheme said *The Economist* was that it lifted 'a good proportion of the accommodation provided to where it will enjoy unrestricted light, but it also makes it possible to open up a large part of the site for use as a small *piazza*, open to the public.' The penalty, 'if indeed it be a penalty', was quite a high tower. *The Economist* view was that 'it will not be long before the double advantage of space at ground level, and of light up above, produce a complete revolution in the accepted canons of British Urban architecture.' The magazine also pointed out that the tower would only be seen from a stretch of about 60 yards along St James's Street.

In retrospect the Economist Tower is more successful than the other major tower of this period – the 19-storey New Zealand House tower at the bottom of Haymarket, completed in 1963 to the designs of Robert Matthew, Johnson-Marshall & Partners which brutally interrupts the established cornice line of the street. Indeed the Smithsons saw themselves as rescuing the gracefully proportioned façade of Boodle's from its much higher Edwardian neighbours. The roofline of the front block matches that of Boodle's and the main cornice of the handsome stone faced building across Ryder Street. The Smithsons also matched the cut off corner across Ryder Street, repeating this on all the new buildings as a kind of leitmotif. They also introduced a piano nobile matching the height of the Boodle's Saloon. This provided a 'fine first-floor banking hall' for Martin's Bank (taken over by Barclays in 1969) which was approached by an escalator set in a corner entrance – a novel feature for London.

The success of the *piazza* remains debatable. Its glory moment came in the cult 1966 film *Blow-Up* directed by Michelangelo Antonioni, about a photographer played by David Hemmings who believes he has unwittingly taken photographs of a murder. In the opening scene an open top jeep sweeps up the ramp crowded with whooping youths in fancy dress, face paint and flowing robes, much the most exciting thing that has ever happened here. Today it is used for changing displays of sculpture, which often look self-consciously out of place. A change of policy might revolutionise the popularity of the place. Yet for Boodle's the quietness and seclusion of the plaza is a bonus – no voices echo up from the pavement disturbing members in the bedrooms or the card room and dining room above.

One problem in creating the plaza was that it exposed the party wall of Boodle's which was never intended to be seen. The Smithsons gave the wall a facing of fine new London stock brick very carefully pointed and much brighter and cleaner than the 200-year-old stock brick on the front façade.

Compared with many office blocks of the nineties and the noughties of the new century, which are on a deep plan, the Smithsons designed their 16-storey tower (14 storeys from plaza level), so than 'no part of the building', excluding lifts and lavatories, was more than 18 feet from a window . 'There will be no inside rooms and no dark corners whatever'.

The construction is of reinforced concrete not steel but the visible portions especially the prominent vertical ribs are of Portland stone 'Roach bed'. This has the textured, slightly pitted quality of Roman Travertine stone. The Smithson's son, Simon, himself a distinguished architect working with the Richard Rogers practice, points out that the corner block on St James's Street is cut back behind so sharply that it is almost triangular in plan. 'Only my parents would provide that kind of generosity, sacrificing prime office space within to enlarge the open space outside'.

The best views of the Economist Plaza are those where the new buildings frame the old buildings around, notably Henry Holland's handsome front of Brooks's. This openness is heighted by the octagonal form of all the Smithson buildings – square in plan with chamfered corners. The entrance floor of both the tower and the block containing Boodle's chambers are set back behind arcades 'increasing the seclusion' says Simon Smithson. The chamber block was conceived as a little brother to the main tower – all its major horizontal dimensions are exactly half those of the main tower. The basement provides a Ladies' Side for Club and the first three floors contain bedrooms for the members. The upper floors were designed as flats, to meet the demand of the planners for a residential component.

Today a smart name stone on St James's Street, painted pillar box red, announces The Economist Plaza. It is an interesting point as to when *The Economist* adopted the American Plaza in place of the 'piazza' used by the Smithsons. This was added in 1990 when the leading American architectural practice, SOM, remodelled the podium stairs to Bury Street and refurbished the Economist Tower.

Contriving an elegant ladies' annexe in a basement was inevitably a challenge, met initially with bright fabrics and shafts of daylight through a large roof light. In 1992 Stefa Hart was charged with creating a more traditional look, with rooms which would look warm and welcoming even without natural light. The rooflight was removed 'it made the place feel like a swimming pool' was one comment. The dining room was painted a warm apricot and the walls enlivened with stenciled porcelain from the V&A painted by Dione Verulam whose company, started with her mother, has done work at Cliveden and Hambledon Hall. The room was furnished with modern versions of Hepplewhite chairs which add a light and graceful touch with banquette sofas along the wall covered in corded sage green velvet. As the Club had no spare paintings to fill the walls, simulated books were supplied by Philip Bradford to provide texture and touch of colour. These are complemented by the very pretty print room created in the private dining room beyond which can be closed off by sliding doors. Arches were introduced around the bar to create more intimate seating areas. The

One of the tall arches introduced by Papworth in the 1830s

The Billiard Room

Below: Papworth's writing desk in the Morning Room

Below: The rounded end of the former back staircase

Boodle's Ladies' Side now has a life of its own, at lunch and dinner and late in the evening on the Club's regular theatre nights.

After hard times in the years before and after the Second World War, Boodle's is now in first class health, enjoying its fine architecture and interiors as never before. The search for style in everything the Club does, dating back to the masquerades of the late 1760s and 1770s, and taken up by Crunden and Papworth, continues to this day. A summer break now never passes without a team of workmen ensuring the Club is in smart order when the members return.

Exquisite carved detail on the white statuary marble chimneypiece in the Saloon dating from 1776. The carved tablet portrays the Continence of Scipio who declines the beautiful virgin presented to him as a spoil of war and returns her to Allucius, her fiancé, waving aside the presents offered by her parents to secure her release

Opposite: One of Papworth's glass lustres in the Undress Room

The furnishing of Boodles

Above: One of a set of 1780s candlebra with a Roman Bacchic priestess holding a wine urn issuing candle branches. The figure is on a white statuary marble altar plinth with rams' heads and ormolu mounts

Top right: A hall chair with Grecian tablet back bearing the marks of two centuries of use

Below right: A Papworth door handle with gilt brass surround

Regency writing
desk in the Morning
Room

A decidedly
masculine
looking sofa
table in the
staircase hall

Regency sideboard in the Undress Room

One of a pair of sideboards in beautifully figured mahogany now in the Coffee Room and attributable to Papworth

Opposite: A writing desk in the Morning Room with palm-flowered legs on Grecian scroll bases

Late 18th-century longcase clock in mahogany case

A Grecian clock set on an Ionic-scrolled altar pedestal attributable to Papworth in the Coffee Room. The face has both Roman and Arabic numerals

Golden brass mantel-clock richly embossed in the French fashion with a Venus shell emerging from waved scrolls guarded by mermaids. It alludes to the sun-deity Apollo's control of the Elements. Attributable to Papworth

This handsome arched fireback in the Coffee Room has acanthus scrollwork attributable to Papworth

Gout stool in the Morning Room

Plain black stone chimney and grate in the Billiard Room attributable to Papworth

131

Rowlandson's satirical view of the newly introduced gas lights in Pall Mall dates from 1809

CHAPTER 6

St James's Street from Piccadilly to the Palace

DANIELLA BEN-ARIE

On 29 May 1835 Frederick von Raumer, a professor of history in Berlin, and visitor to London, strolled from Kensington towards St James's Palace, taking in Hyde Park, Green Park and St James's Park. Arriving at the Palace mid-afternoon he was just in time to observe the festivities that had been organised to celebrate the official birthday of King William IV. A long line of horses and their carriages – von Raumer estimated he saw nine hundred waiting to enter the palace – ran down St James's Street, each one 'brilliant' in their presentation.

Moreover, he observed, the passengers in the carriages were so magnificently attired that the slow-moving procession enabled him to scrutinise each of the ladies by taking the 'liberty of moving on in a parallel line, and of keeping by the side of certain carriages which contained the greatest beauties'. He gloated that he had no better 'opportunity, no company in the world in which one may stare ladies in the face with so much ease – I might almost say impudence – for so long a time'.

Von Raumer was able to get so close that he enjoyed the diversion of trying 'to figure to myself all their circumstances, and to read the thoughts of each in her eyes'. After the carriages had dispersed he headed towards his own club (not to one of the many that lined St James's Street but a more recent addition to the scene, the Athenaeum on Pall Mall). As von Raumer ventured out again later that night he returned to St James's Street where he described the illumination of the buildings as being some of the best he had seen, both 'splendid and beautiful by coloured lamps and moving gas lights.'

Nineteenth-century London was widely considered the greatest city in Europe, and visitors such as von Raumer regularly described the city in superlative terms, or as one writer put it, 'the glory of the island, the admiration of every stranger – and the first city of the world!'. Thomas Pennant, the well-regarded writer and traveller observed in *The Complete Guide to the British Capital* (in an edition revised posthumously) that London was 'one of the largest and most opulent cities in the world' being a city that 'contains 200 inns, 400 taverns, 500 coffee-houses; 1,500 hackney coaches, 7,000 streets, lanes, courts and alleys, and 130,000 dwelling houses.'

Of the West End of town it was noted that 'for the conveniences of fashionable life, is certainly preferable to any other; and if lodgings and other charges are proportionally higher, they are often repaid by connexions which may be formed, better air, &c. Hence many of the most opulent merchants in the city have other dwelling houses in this quarter.' At the centre of this 'first city' was St James's Street, considered one of the 'most elegant and noble', which ran between St James's Palace at its southern end and abutted Piccadilly at its northern end.

Towards the beginning of the nineteenth century many changes to London's infrastructure were under way. The cobbled pavements slowly began to be torn up and replaced with asphalt, sewers were being laid, and gas lighting began to replace oil. Indeed one of the first experiments to introduce gas lamps for public benefit was along the entire length of Pall Mall, ending at the Palace, in around 1807.

A satirical print made by Thomas Rowlandson entitled *A Peep at the Gas Lights in Pall Mall* shows these lamps on the pavement in front of Carlton House. These lights had been installed by F A Winsor, a self-styled 'inventor and patentee' of the Intended Light and Heat Company, who was trying to sell off the remainder of the shares in his new company, boasting of the gas lamp's 'superiority, safety, and salubrity'. In an advertisement in *The Observer* from 1808 Winsor describes his intention to light 'Boodle's Subscription House' to give 'additional public conviction' to his endeavour. If indeed this was carried out then Boodle's would have been among the first to adopt gas lamps in London.

Unlike many of the surrounding streets, such as the western end of Piccadilly near Park Lane or along Arlington Street which ran parallel, the 'houses' in St James's Street were mostly not private residences intended for an individual's use.

Instead the buildings were occupied by the private subscription clubs with which the street has long been associated, as well as with various hotels, chocolate houses and taverns that lined its east and west sides. The clubs included Boodle's (from 1782), Brooks's (from 1778), White's (from 1755), Cocoa Tree Club (closed 1932) Thatched House Tavern (both the Literary Club and Society of Dilettanti met here), Miles's Club (dissolved 1809), Arthur's (ended in 1940), the Carlton Club, the Conservative Club, the Union Club, and Crockford's (from 1828).

Among the shops was James Lock & Co, Hatter's, at number 6, where the bowler hat originated in the middle of the nineteenth century (and in which premises the business remains). Peter Wirgman, goldsmith and jeweller, worked in a building on the corner of St James's Place and the well-known bibliopole Robert Triphook had premises for several years at number 37 before relocating to Old Bond Street. The counters of his bookshops were professed to be 'for more than forty years the rendezvous of the aristocracy and gentry'.

Some private individuals did live on the street, although their residence was often short-lived. The poet George Gordon Noel Byron, 6th Baron Byron resided at number 8 in 1811. Byron belonged to several clubs on the street, and as a guest was so sought after that Elizabeth, Duchess of Devonshire, the second wife of the 5th Duke, and herself the subject of much salacious gossip, depicted him as 'really the only topic almost of every conversation – the men jealous of him, the women of each other'. He was also said to have been a frequent visitor to Triphook's shop.

On the other hand George Salting lived above the Thatched House Club at number 86 for many years in an extremely modest manner, particularly when compared to his means. While living here he would go on to build an

Tallis's views of London form a record of every building along a street. White's is second from the left

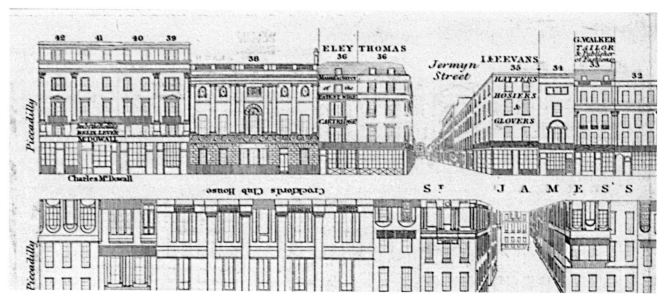

extensive collection of decorative art and paintings that were eventually left to the Victoria & Albert Museum, the National Gallery and the British Museum.

The establishment of St James's Street (and shortly afterwards Pall Mall) as the centre of club life, with its close proximity to the Houses of Parliament and the Royal Palaces, meant the street, and the clubs, lay at the nexus of political power and social influence. An account of London in *The Builder* in 1844 describes the clubs as 'aristocratic larders in which anything can be obtained for money – repositories of peers, politicians, poets, continental perambulators, and wealthy plebians; of statesmen in place and statesmen wanting place; of churchmen, embryo-warriors, and matured veterans; representing *en masse* the wealth and power of the country.' John Britton, the well-known antiquarian and historian of London life, observed that the Club's location was 'highly useful to eminent political and fashionable Characters'.

Many of the clubs along St James's developed a reputation for excessive gambling, raucous drinking, and lavish entertainments, the stories from which could satiate even the most gossip-loving member. Indeed it was not unusual for a newspaper story to appear after a particularly raucous night's gambling, such as in *Lady's Weekly Miscellany* in 1807: 'a few nights ago, a young sprig of fashion, not eighteen years of age, lost five hundred guineas, his gold watch, and his phaeton and horses, to the *merry caster*, at one of the gaming houses in St James's street'. Visitors to London were directed by the growing number of guidebooks (published by both locals and foreigners alike) to stroll down St James's Street and take in the scene, even though the club's themselves would have been off limits to non-members.

An account in *Boyle's Fashionable Court Guide, or town visiting Directory* in 1793, lists all the subscription houses, with Boodle's then designated 32 St James's, under the proprietorship of Benjamin Harding. The street was described in detail, sometimes in purely architectural and historical terms; occasionally in a more judgmental tone, particularly if the writer was a churchgoing man like the Unitarian minister Joseph Nightingale who wrote in 1815:

It is proper that I should not mislead the reader by leaving unexplained the true nature and character of the hotels, as they are called, with which this fashionable street abounds. A stranger naturally associates with the idea of an hotel, that of a public licensed house, for the

Boodle's is easily recognised by its large fan-headed window

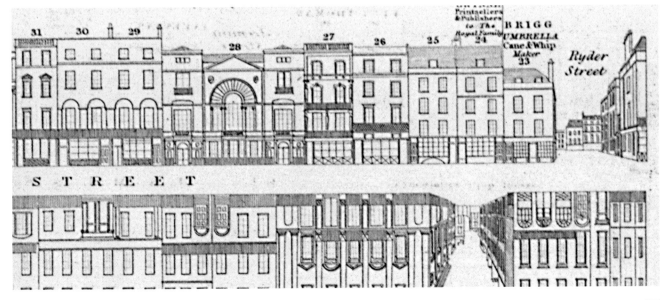

reception of individuals and families, for temporary refreshment and accommodation. Hence he would, (as many are) be induced in his walks through St James's Street, to call, as at any other respectable house of the same name and ostensible destination in the metropolis; but what would be his surprise to find himself abruptly stopt at the door by two or three waiters and door-keepers, earnestly enquiring his business, and when they found that rest and refreshment were his only objects, absolutely refuse him entrance?

The fact is, that, with one or two exceptions, these hotels are those sinks of vice and dissipation – the bane of human happiness, and domestic peace, – *Gaming Houses*! I need not add one word more to caution the prudent not to be misled by these spacious houses, with a foreign name. It is not necessary to distinguish the respectable hotels from these haunts of cupidity and dishonesty, not fashionably called *Subscription Houses*.

The magnificent illuminations and crowded streets that von Raumer described during his visit in 1835 was not in fact a one-off. St James's Street and its Palace lay at the centre of the annual celebrations marking the monarch's official birthday.

The external elevation of St James's Palace was often disparaged (as in *A Companion to all the Principal Places of Entertainment in and About London and Westminster* of 1795): 'an irregular building, of a mean appearance'. Thomas Pennant noted in his guidebook that the palace was used primarily for social occasions, such as birthday celebrations, and was otherwise being 'nearly deserted, excepting some apartments occupied by the Duke of Cumberland [presumably the unpopular 5th son of George III, later Ernest Augustus, King of Hanover] and the persons belonging to the royal household'.

Shortly after Boodle's moved to St James's Street in 1782, a variety of newspapers carried detailed accounts of the crowds that would gather on special occasions to honour the monarch. A report in *The Times* (20 January 1787) described the street as 'crowded with carriages of the first distinction, to witness the procession of the equipages

to St James's on the Queen's Birth-Day; some of the most celebrated women of fashion were among the spectators'.

By 1800 'his Majesty, not-withstanding incessant rain, never appeared in better spirits, seeming much gratified by the sentiments of loyalty and affection evinced by so considerable a portion of his subjects.' The crowds on these occasions were always large despite 'umbrellas [being] the order of the day'.

Tremendous care was taken every year to illuminate the clubs, taverns, shops and hotels that lined the street. In 1810 the 'houses in St James's-street were particularly crouded yesterday' and as Louis Simond observed, 'the King's birthday has been celebrated with more than usual pomp. The crowd was immense, – the town illuminated, – the people full of joy and loyalty, – and quite on a cordial footing with the horse-guards on duty among them.' Celebrating the Queen's birthday in 1821 the newspapers recorded 'we cannot help mentioning some of the club-houses in St James's-street' where Boodle's 'seemed to vie with Brooks's, on the opposite side of the street, in profuse light and tasteful decoration.'

A typical illumination contained the initials of the ruling monarch alongside a crown, with some minor variation year to year, such as the addition of laurel leaves. On occasion one of the club's would try, and succeed, to outdo the others. In 1828 Crockford's at 50–53 St James's Street put on a most 'brilliant exhibition. No expence had been spared, and, in fact, a flood of light reflected from the front of this magnificent building, and threw the minor effects of the neighbouring Club Houses into the shade'. The entire street was also 'brilliantly illuminated'.

On other occasions St James's Street appeared from end to end as 'one blaze of light, and the brilliancy of the scene attracted vast crowds of people during the night'. Boodle's would be decorated with the monarch's initials, such as a 'G.R.' with an 'IV' between, and on each side was a diamond of gold-coloured lamps festooned, surmounted with a leaf of laurel, above which was a very beautiful Imperial Coronet.'

It was not just the clubs that emphasised their loyalty to the Crown by bearing these illuminated displays, however. Along St James's, the Royal Hotel, the 'linen-drapers' W and

T Nicholls, the 'sword-cutler' Palmer, the Royal Music Repository of Willis, Sam's' Royal Library, and Willis's the tailors, were surmounted by and decorated with various devices showing George IV's initials, crowns, and laurel leaves. By the time of Queen Victoria's reign the royal initials were accompanied on Boodle's' façade by 'a splendid Brunswick star'.

The illuminations would have been the focus of the celebrations as the evening approached but the festive atmosphere would have started many hours earlier. Preparations had been under way since dawn, and 'the west end of town presented a very animated appearance' and the 'bustle and crowd in the neighbourhood of St James's exceeded any thing we ever before witnessed on a similar occasion.' St James's must have been among the most densely crowded of the streets as it was the main thoroughfare for guests invited to the Palace.

The waiting spectators who were lined up alongside were entertained by detachments of guards stationed in the vicinity of the Palace and who took turns playing popular tunes. One group was stationed right at the bottom of St James's Street. Police were dispersed throughout the crowd to maintain order, and as one observer drolly noted, there were no accidents or incidents 'except the transfer of divers handkerchiefs, purses, and watches from the pockets of the owners to those of the light-fingered gentry.'

Among the most anticipated events must have been discussing and dissecting the outfits and jewels worn by the guests, sitting in their carriages, waiting to be let through the palace gates. Their progress inside was hindered by their large numbers as well as by the crowds in the street. (One wonders if this must have been the source of some frustration considering many guests lived within close walking distance, or even within sight of the Palace itself.) During the celebrations for the King's birthday in 1828 there was already by midday a crowd of ladies lined up 'anxious to see those who were going to the Drawing room'.

The carriages, in two rows, reached most of the way up St James's and were soon backed up into Bond Street, giving ample opportunity to examine the 'beauty, the rank, the talent, the genius, the wealth and the enterprise of the British Empire'. It was duly noted that 'on no former occasion was there so great a display of elegant dresses, more particularly as regards the magnificence of the ornaments, of diamonds and other jewels, worn by the ladies.'

Among the most magnificent jewels were those worn by Harriot Beauclerk, Duchess of St Albans, wife of the 9th Duke, who lived around the corner at 80 Piccadilly. Her head was adorned with a diamond tiara, and her chest with a stomacher of diamonds. Princess Mary, Duchess of Gloucester and sister of George IV, wore a white satin dress and robe 'intermixed with rich and brilliant gold tissue.' The front of her dress was 'entirely covered with superb medallions of costly brilliants, forming a stomacher' and her headpiece was 'a magnificent plume of ostrich feathers, with a profusion of diamonds.'

Charlotte, Duchess of Northumberland, the amiable wife of the 3rd Duke; the extremely well-connected Dorothea Khristoforovna, Princess Lieven, wife to the Russian Ambassador; and the preeminent hostess, Elizabeth, Marchioness of Stafford (later the Duchess of Sutherland), whose husband had just acquired the neighbouring Stafford House, were among the many exceedingly elegant guests wearing 'splendid displays of diamonds' and other precious stones, and headdresses of feather and diamonds. These women must have had to endure some discomfort, and extreme patience, as they sat waiting for their carriages to make its way down St James's.

It was not just the women who garnered the attention on these occasions. In June 1800 at a 'Drawing-Room' in the Palace to celebrate the birthday of George III one of the 'most conspicuous' guests, among the foreign ambassadors and cabinet ministers, was Mirza Abu Taleb Khan who had been an official at the Courts in Oudh Province (Uttar Pradesh) and in Bengal. Travelling under the patronage of Charles, 1st Marquess of Cornwallis, then governor-general of India, the 'Indian Prince' as he was contemporaneously described, was aware of the Club's role in English life. 'Hospitality is one of the most esteemed virtues of the English', he wrote, and that of all the institutions he saw, 'none of them pleased me more than their clubs'.

While St James's street was clearly the focus of many

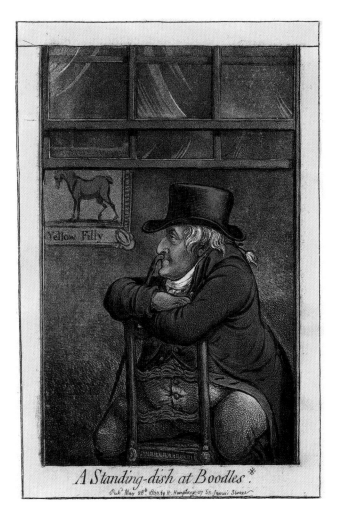

This Gillray cartoon portrays Sir Frank Standish, a well-known member of Boodle's, who Gillray, as a resident of St James's Street, had plenty of opportunity to observe

official celebrations there are many wonderful prints that depict the hive of activity that made up everyday life in the street. Among the best known as relates to Boodle's is the etching by James Gillray depicting *A Standing Dish at Boodles*. The 'Dish' is Sir Frank Standish, 2nd Bt (c1746–1812) sitting near the Club's window. Sir Frank had been elected a member of Boodle's in 1767 when the Club's premises were in Pall Mall, and had subsequently been voted on to the Management Committee on four separate occasions (1791, 1798, 1805 and 1809).

Gillray was in an unusually good position to observe life

on the street as he lived next door to the Club, above the shop of his publisher, the printseller Hannah Humphrey situated at number 27, the shop being the subject of his popular print *Very Slippy Weather* in 1808. Having moved here from Old Bond Street in 1798 there could have been no better-located address for an artist who made his living satirising his contemporaries – and within an arm's reach of where many of his subjects spent their days, whether George, Prince of Wales at Carlton House, the politician Charles James Fox at Brooks's across the street, or the members of Boodle's itself.

If the clubs and taverns of the street could not prove enough of a draw then Gillray's latest print was certain to entice. A visitor to London in 1802 observed that 'they are fighting here to be first in Ackermann's shop and see Gillray's latest caricatures. The enthusiasm is indescribable when the next drawing appears; it is a veritable madness. You have to make your way in through the crowd with your fists'. One could also inadvertently find oneself in the middle of a rowdy crowd as with William Pitt the younger, when he was attacked in his carriage by supporters of Fox on 28 February 1784.

By the mid-nineteenth century the association between the clubs and St James's Street was so entrenched that Frederick Locker wrote a poem on the subject:

> St James's Street, of classic fame,
> For Fashion still is seen there:
> St James's Street? I know the name,
> I almost think I've been there!
> Why, that's where *Sacharissa* sigh'd
> When Waller read his ditty;
> Where Byron lived, and Gibbon died,
> And Alvanely was witty.
>
> The dear old Street of clubs and *cribs*,
> As north and south is stretches,
> Still seems to smack of Rolliad squibs,
> And Gillray's fiercer sketches;
> The quaint old dress, the grand old style,
> The *mots*, the racy stories;

James Gillray's *Promis'd Horrors of the French Invasion, or Forcible reasons for negotiating a regicide peace*

The wine, the dice, the wit, the bile –
The hate of Whigs and Tories.

One of the 'fiercer sketches' mentioned by Locker may have been Gillray's *Promis'd Horrors of the French Invasion, or Forcible reasons for negotiating a regicide peace*, from 1796, in which the French troops are shown marching up St James's Street. Two of the clubs, White's and Brooks's, are clearly visible. Gillray lived out the remainder of his life at number 27 and eventually succumbing to his reoccurring bouts of depression 'he was seen for the last time, naked and unshaven at midday standing in the shop where his caricatures were sold'.

St James's Street as a centre of London society is reinforced

in a letter written in 1822 by the Frenchman, a Monsieur Le Vicomte de L——, whose full name was not published. He laments being in London and finding the city, and St James's Street in particular, empty and deserted. His visit in that year coincided with Boodle's being 'full of paint and bricklayers', presumably referring to the alterations undertaken by the architect and designer John Buonarotti Papworth, about which relatively little is known.

He compares a 'somber' and 'lifeless' St James's Street to Pompeii and Herculaneum, where no one is seen, 'not a dandy at W[hite]s; not a radical at B[roo]k's. All this is stark contrast to how it is during the Season – 'the very air breathed of gaiety, bustle and pleasure'. In essence he goes on to complain about what is missing from London, 'at least *habitable* London' as he sees it, and consequently summing up exactly what the strong appeal of the Club is to its members:

[It used to be] from three to six o'clock what an emporium of dissipation and fashion! What strings of equipages! What crowds of horsemen! What phalanxes and files of loungers! What an animating buzz on the pavement (a thousand times finer than Delille's buzz of the insects in the sunny fields at noon) – what rencontres of friends – what nodding of lovely face from carriage windows, – not a vacant chair or an unoccupied *Morning Post* at a club-house: B——m conning over a flaming speech in the back-room at Brooks's, and H——s beating up voters for the House among the country gentlemen (*gentilshommes de province*) at Boodle's.

The Rue Vivienne is a mere *magazin de bas et de souliers* compared to St James's-street; and the Boulevards, delightful as they are, are too large, too rambling, and too much thronged with *canaille*, ever to offer this delightful concentration of fashion rank, taste, finery, caricatures, and club-houses. A-propos, *Vous ne savez pas ce qu'ils sont que ces Clubs. Je m'en vais vous dire.* A club is a grand hotel, in a fashionable street, with a handsome *vestible – un Suisse à la porte –* a lofty saloon *qui donne* on the street with a bow-window, from which loungers exercise their spy-glasses on passers with great comfort and ease.

The walls hung with maps on rollers rarely unrolled, an immense table covered with journals, newspapers, blue *Edenbourg* Reviews, court-guides, peerages, inkstands, and wax-tapers. Noblemen and members of parliament, with boots and horsewhips, are lolling over the chaos of periodical literature; and young dandies, who have just escaped the black-ball, are yawning in the window – making bets on the numerical amount of the Ministers' majority, or the favourite horse at Newmarket – and scanning with languid *nonchalance* the passengers, who look up at this castle of indolence,

without being privileged to enter its sacred precincts....

Besides these, there's B[ood]le's, the rendezvous of foxhunters and country gentlemen (where the Duke of B[edford] was un-ceremoniously blackballed (*rejeté*) the other day) ... In short, no man can now show his face in London society unless he belongs to some one or more of these juntas, which have well nigh ruined, by their competition, all the *cafés* and *restaurateurs* of London, and which present so powerful counter-attraction to the joys of home and a domestic fire-side.

Even before Boodle's and Brooks's relocated from Pall Mall, there was little doubt that St James's Street would hold an important role in London's social history, in particular because of its proximity to political power. The establishment of so many clubs there, and their enduring presence, has ensured that this *would* be the case. It became a *de facto* second (London) home for the political, economic, social and artistic elite, those who were the trendsetters, the most sartorial, and the moneymakers.

Perhaps the last word on how the people who frequented St James's Street, the clubs that were established on it, and the events that took place alongside it have become integral to its popular perception can be left to T S Eliot:

Bustopher Jones is *not skin and bones* –
In fact, he's remarkably fat.
He doesn't haunt pubs – he has eight or nine clubs,
For he's the St James's Street Cat!
He's the Cat we all greet and he walks down the street
In his coat of fastidious black:
No Commonplace mousers have such well-cut trousers
Or such an impeccable back.
In the whole of St James's the smartest of names is
The name of this Brummell of Cats;
And we're all of us proud to be nodded or bowed to
By Bustopher Jones in White spats!

Opposite: A Regency iron and glass lantern hanging over the porch

140

The Quorn at full gallop. An 1835 aquatint by F C Lewis

CHAPTER 7

When Foxhunting was run from Boodle's

MICHAEL CLAYTON

There are, I am sure, very few foxhunters, and certainly no foxhunters of the Victorian era, to whom Boodle's is not a household name. For many generations it was the great club of foxhunters, and there are very few famous Masters of past times who were not members of Boodle's

Brigadier-General C G Higgins *The Field* July 22, 1939

Who is Boodle? This is the plaintive question expressed by puzzled Leicestershire farmers after the Club had assumed a key role in foxhunting in 1854. Boodle's foxhunting committee, The Masters of Foxhounds (MFH), was recognised as the body which laid down or interpreted the 'rules' of foxhunting. The MCC had a similar task in ruling cricket, but its role was somewhat easier to maintain than that of the Masters of Foxhounds of Boodle's.

When it came to arbitrating on Hunt boundaries they were confronted by local feuds, with ancient arguments in far-flung areas of rural society unwilling to accept arbitration from any outsider, least of all of a group of gentlemen in London acting under the mysterious title, Boodle's.

Not all Hunts had written rules and constitutions; this element of 'progress' was still being sought by the foxhunting world as a universal requirement of Hunts late in the twentieth century. 'Who is Boodle?' was the appropriate title of the chapter in Colin Ellis's excellent history, *Leicestershire and the Quorn Hunt* 1951, describing the Great Inter-Hunt Row which divided the foxhunting world.

Ellis remarks that 'prolonged, passionate and public controversy was an indispensable element in Victorian life,' and the Quorn row fitted that description exactly. When landowning, territorial jealousy and sporting rivalry are involved in the mix, such a dispute boils up into an especially bitter stew.

The Quorn's problem was to reveal the need for just such a body as Boodle's Foxhunting Committee, but it would also disclose its weakness – a lack of teeth in making its decisions final in circumstances where like-minded groups of country gentlemen were not always inclined to accept compromise. Additional cooperation was necessary from farmers, owners or tenants, far outside the world of gentlemen's clubs in St James's Street.

The Quorn row came to a head in 1878, when the Hunt sought to recover its southern country near Market Harborough which had been loaned on imprecise terms to a private pack owned and hunted by Mr William Ward Tailby from 1856. Leading landowners and farmers in that country refused to allow the Quorn to resume hunting their land after Tailby retired in '78, and rural warfare commenced. Duels with whips in the hunting field, and attempts to 'cut down' opponents taking fences were part of the conflict. Some hunting people tore off their hunt buttons, and wore safety pins instead, as a form of protest against the rival faction.

The Great Row was a major factor, although not the official cause, of the winding-up of Boodle's Foxhunting Committee, and the founding of the Masters of Foxhounds Association (MFHA) in 1881.

Boodle's can rightly claim that it had until then played a valuable role in assisting foxhunting to evolve in the nineteenth century as a great national sport which cemented rural communities, and increasingly earned support from urban based sportsmen who flocked to the countryside to enjoy the Chase. Many of them purchased estates and country houses, putting their new wealth into Masterships. Surtees satirised the input of London businessmen through his creation of John Jorrocks, the grocer from Great Coram Street, who was the Cockney Master of the Handley Cross

The drawings in this chapter are Boodle's Golfing Society vignettes

Hunt. British Army officers were encouraged, in many cases expected, to take up foxhunting not only as a healthy risky sport, but as a means of improving their horsemanship, and acquiring a 'bump of locality' in a natural terrain. These were considered valuable assets in 19th-century battlefields.

Throughout the century there were many men much higher up the scale of commerce and the law in the City and West End who were to support packs of hounds. An increasing number of the old squirearchy were pleased to accept funding from 'trade' in running their local Hunt; many of the new industrialists were keen to establish their rural credentials through the hunting field. The trend continued into the twentieth century postwar years; as well as entrepreneurs in property the new estate owners could be stars of the pop and entertainment world. Many new landowners have learned to enjoy the balm of the hunting field as an antidote to city life.

When Boodle's was founded in 1762 the Quorn was already a decade into its history which would revolutionise foxhunting. Hugo Meynell, a Derbyshire squire and not a Leicestershire landowner, rented property at Quorn, north of Leicester, to hunt the great swathe of grassland from Nottingham down to Market Harborough. He took the Quorn Mastership in 1753, and during the next half century bred faster hounds capable of hunting the fox at speed in the open.

The enclosure of land made possible the hectic sport of

leaping fences in pursuit of hounds, and the Quorn led the way in the nineteenth century's love affair with the speed and dash of a newly glamorised hunting field. Foxhunting was a shared passion among Boodle's' membership of the rural squirearchy. Young bloods increasingly spent much of their winters in Leicestershire, lured by a thrilling risk sport, before the days of fast cars. They spent the winter in lodges at Melton Mowbray and other country towns, riding to hounds with desperate valour, despite warnings that they would break their necks, or lose their horses, their money or their wives – in any order. Many others were loyal and devoted followers of their local Hunts throughout the British countryside.

Accounts of foxhunting's fortunes in the Shires and less fashionable areas were published in London's growing array sporting magazines, and read assiduously in Victorian clubland. The Quorn's renowned huntsman Tom Firr had the status of a modern soccer star, but with far more dignity; he was said to ride like a jockey, but looked like a bishop.

The advent of new Hunts to meet the news of new foxhunters throughout the nineteenth century made the problem of boundaries more acute. Landowners in the seventeenth and eighteenth centuries made mutual agreements with neighbours as to the boundaries between their hunting territories. These could remain flexible and mainly amicable until foxhunting's mounted fields began to swell with 'carpet baggers' from the cities. The practice of taking fixed subscriptions from mounted followers grew in the latter nineteenth century. In the shires many foxhunters rode to the meets on a hack, changed to a hunter at the meet, and a second horse followed, ridden by a groom, to be handed over to the foxhunter in early afternoon. All the 'second horsemen' rode in a large group on roads and tracks, usually under the command of a groom employed by the Master. The unwritten law of foxhunting was that if a fox found in your own country ran across the border into your neighbour's it could be pursued all the way until it was either caught or irretrievably lost.

It was essential the pack then returned within their own boundary to find another fox. The phalanx of second

horsemen were always stopped at the hunt boundary in such circumstances, to await the return of the mounted field. Transgressions of these 'laws' became more frequent as pressure increased to provide maximum sport for expensively mounted followers who began to make substantial contributions to the cost of the Hunt.

All too often the excuse for ignoring boundaries and access to draw coverts could be that they had mysteriously moved to the 'other side' of a stream or road, or some ancient correspondence was quoted as doubtful evidence of a past agreement between former Masterships. When landowners and farmers were drawn into boundary and covert disputes the outcome became far more critical for the chairman, committee and Masters of the Hunts concerned.

The creation of an arbitrator on boundaries and coverts became all the more necessary by the mid-nineteenth century when there were at least three hundred formal packs of Foxhounds, and more than a few *ad hoc* packs brought together by local sportsmen on the day of the hunt; they were known as 'trencher fed' packs. The inclination of some Harrier packs to hunt foxes as well as hares, although the latter was their true quarry, could be a problem for Masters of Foxhounds. Deer hunting with hounds had lapsed, except for the West Country packs on Exmoor and the Quantocks, and the New Forest Buckhounds, although the nineteenth century saw increasing popularity for carted deer hunting, notably by the Royal Buckhounds based at Windsor.

All these factors ensured that Boodle's Foxhunting Committee fulfilled an essential role. Its advent was timely: in

1856 the Masters of Foxhounds who had previously met informally to discuss such matters, agreed to become members of the new committee, with John Mitford, 1st Earl of Redesdale elected as the first chairman. According to the minutes, still in Boodle's' archives, at a meeting on 12 July 1856, it was deemed that membership of the Foxhunting Committee comprised every member of the club on that day 'who shall be, or who shall have been, at that time a Master of Foxhounds'; each member paid an annual subscription of £1. This was an unwieldy body to act as an arbitrator, and for this role it was decided to appoint five Stewards, one going out of office on 1 July each year, and not eligible for re-election for one year. His successor would be announced at an annual dinner in the preceding month of June.

The first Stewards were representative of the upper strata of foxhunting: the Duke of Beaufort, Lord Southampton, Lord Redesdale, Sir Bellingham Graham and Mr Greene. The 8th Duke of Beaufort was hereditary Master of his own famous pack at Badminton from 1853–56; the 3rd Lord Southampton was MFH of the Grafton (1842–61); Lord Redesdale MFH, the Heythrop (1835–37 and 1842–53); Sir Bellingham Graham was in turn MFH of seven packs: Badsworth, Atherstone, Pytchley, Hambledon, Quorn, N. Shropshire and Enville & Albrighton (covering 1815–25); Mr E. Walter Greene was Master of the Suffolk (1871–75; 188?–83, and the Croome 1883–89).

The Committee was to continue to exercise a beneficial influence, as well as fulfilling useful arbitration, for the next

twenty-four years. To some extent the new body attempted leverage on Masters of Foxhounds in arbitrating by stipulating that 'every member of the (Foxhunting) committee shall submit to the decisions of the committee, under pain of expulsion.' Rule Eleven said that in a case of dispute between two Hunts 'as to the rights of any coverts', the Masters of or members of one Hunt declining to refer the case to the Committee, then the Committee could inquire into and decide such a case 'according to the Laws of Foxhunting, if the owner or owners of such coverts shall request them to undertake such an inquiry, whether those concerned with the Hunts shall appear before the Committee or not'. This laborious rule exposed the major

problems of arbitrating on matters concerning private property. The so-called 'Laws of Foxhunting' were later to be exposed in the courts as being subordinate to common law on property ownership and trespass.

The Committee could not therefore guarantee absolutely binding self-regulation for hunting, but Boodle's was highly influential in helping to suppress practices which brought the sport into ill-repute, and it succeeded in solving various boundary and covert disputes, although some remained intractable. The minutes reveal an immense amount of painstaking work in researching and deciding cases. The Stewards and other members of the Foxhunting Committee must have engaged in a considerable amount of expense

146

and effort in engaging in local inquiries, as well as pains-taking consideration of great sheafs of written 'evidence' submitted in boundary and covert disputes. All had to be rendered into long hand-written reports, culminating in decisions which were often lengthy and complicated. Often the dispute covered many decades of inter-Hunt correspondence and discussion.

An example of this was a long running dispute in Yorkshire between the 4th Earl Fitzwilliam and the Sandbeck and Badsworth Hunts. It started with a letter from the 6th Duke of Leeds to Earl Fitzwilliam in 1800, and the matter rumbled on for nearly seventy years until Boodle's painstakingly, if not painfully, unravelled it and produced an 'award'.

The Duke of Leeds sought to draw certain coverts for the Sandbeck Hunt, later part of the Grove Hunt country, which had become 'available' due to a Mr Savile relinquishing the country he had hunted. It seemed that Lord Fitzwilliam only hunted this area during the cubhunting season. It was agreed the Sandbeck should hunt the country fully throughout the season. By 1860 the 6th Lord Galway was Master of the Grove, and the next Lord Fitwilliam wished to hunt some of country by the River Don more extensively, describing the earlier arrangement as merely 'of a neighbourly and friendly character'. This appeared to have been agreed, but later in the century the Badsworth Hunt became drawn into various complicated claims over coverts which all three Hunts wished to draw.

Boodle's decided eventually that the 6th Earl Fitzwilliam had established a right to continue to cubhunt the country in question with his own Wentworth pack, but the Badsworth should hunt for the rest of the season. They held that the Sandbeck had abandoned the country. The 6th Earl Fitzwilliam had in 1857 inherited the family seat of Wentworth Woodhouse, near Rotherham, and from 1860 established his own private pack there. It was known as the Fitzwilliam (Wentworth) and hunted the Yorkshire country which had previously only been cubhunted by the Fitzwilliam family's other pack, kennelled on the family's estate at Milton, Peterborough, paying a visit every autumn. The earl's hounds went out in Yorkshire three days a week during

The 8th Duke of Beaufort

his twenty year's Mastership; meanwhile his brother, the Hon George Fitzwilliam hunted the family pack at Milton.

The latter nineteenth century saw a growing variation between private packs, often owned by aristocratic landowners, and newer packs which took subscriptions. Finding a way between varied claims from such disparate parties to hunt large stretches of the English countryside was indeed a delicate exercise, and Boodle's MFH Committee was always careful to couch its decisions in the politest of terms. Often countries were hunted on the basis of handwritten notes, or verbal agreement, passed between neighbours in the late eighteenth and early nineteenth centuries.

Most significant in the Fitzwilliam finding was the Stewards' declaration, full of commonsense, drawing the attention of 'the members of all Hunts to this award, and to impress on them the importance of having the boundaries of their countries well defined, and of securing sufficient and continued records of the conditions under which any portions of them are hunted by other packs. Roads and waters afford in general the best boundaries, as with the commonest care and knowledge of the country, they cannot be crossed without being noticed.'

Some of the cases decided by Boodle's MFH Committee ensured the survival of Hunts which have survived until the present day. In May 1872 the Stewards ruled in favour of Mr Selby Lowndes in a dispute with the neighbouring Bicester and Warden Hill over land in Buckinghamshire which the latter claimed. The Stewards declared that on the evidence presented they were of the opinion 'that Mr Selby Lowndes having hunted the country in dispute so far back as 1842, and no claim having been made by the Bicester and Warden Hill Hunt until November 1871, nor as any documentary evidence on the subject having been produced to prove that he did so by permission of that Hunt, has established his right to the country.'

Selby Lowndes was Master of the country north of Aylesbury which became the Whaddon Chase Hunt whose best known Master in the twentieth century was the TV commentator Dorian Williams. The growth of the new town of Milton Keynes drastically reduced this country in postwar years, and from 1986 the Whaddon Chase has been amalgamated with the neighbour with whom it had originally been in dispute, the Bicester and Warden Hill.

In 1870 there was an interesting boundary dispute between the North Shropshire and South Shropshire Hunts which called for a veritable 'judgement of Soloman' in making best use of the hunting country available. The Stewards, who may have felt some exasperation, ruled: 'None of the districts have been held by either Hunt separately for a term of twenty years, which might be held to constitute a legal claim, but that the two countries have been hunted at many different times, in different ways and from different kennels. Under these circumstances they are unable to come to any other conclusion than that they must revert to the latest time when the country was divided between

a North and South Shropshire Hunt, namely from 1834 to 1839, and their award therefore is that the boundary between them for the future shall be the River Severn to Shrewsbury, and the road from Shrewsbury to Escall Mill.

It appears however to the Stewards that it may be desirable for the interests of foxhunting in Shropshire that some further concession should be made by the North, if the country thus awarded to the South is insufficient for two days a week: but this must be left to the good feeling of the members of the respective Hunts who may be disposed to agree to the appointment of referees to set out some other boundary between the two countries.

It can be seen that the Stewards did not rely simply on narrow legalistic solutions, but tried hard to establish concord in the best interests of hunting in general; a peculiarly British way of endeavouring to achieve compromise on issues of territory which historically have led mankind not merely to dispute, but to outright war. Since the land in question actually belonged to, or was rented by, numerous people who were not party to the dispute it was all the more challenging to find a solution.

The contentious nature of some disputes is shown in the case of the Cheshire and North Staffordshire Hunts regarding the Doddington coverts. The evidence showed that gaining and maintaining the goodwill of landowners is a prime responsibility of Masters of Hounds.

Boodle's MFH Committee Stewards reported in 1870 that in 1813 the Doddington Coverts belonged to the Cheshire Hunt:

In that year, in consequence of some dispute with the owner, Sir John Broughton, they were warned off by him, and the coverts were drawn by the North Stafford. Sir John allowed the Cheshire to return to them in 1842. Owing to another dispute they were again warned off in 1846. Sir John died in 1847, but there not any evidence produced to show that either then, or when his successor died in 1852, the Cheshire attempted to regain or claim the Coverts which have been continuously hunted by the North Stafford since 1847.

It is considered by the Cheshire that this was by permission from them to Mr Davenport, the Master of the North Stafford, out of personal regard for him; but when he retired from the Mastership in 1865, and the country was hunted by subscription, the Cheshire did not even then make a claim.

It is clear therefore that the North Stafford have enjoyed more than twenty years' continued occupation without dispute up to the present time, although the manner in which they became possessed of the country was contrary to Foxhunting Law.

Under these circumstances, the coverts in question must be held to belong to the North Stafford unless they are disposed to surrender them, or part of them, to the Cheshire on account of the badness of their original title. If the Cheshire had claimed in 1865, the award must have been in their favour.

As far as transgressions against good sporting practice by a minority of Masters and huntsmen in the nineteenth century, the influence of Boodle's was equally beneficial. Surtees who wrote of foxhunting in the first half of the nineteenth century had vilified in his novels and magazine articles the practice of 'dropping a bagman' (a fox kept captive in a bag, until released for hounds to hunt). It was unsporting; it produced an artificial chase; worst of all it was inclined to ruin a good pack of hounds, the creator of Jorrocks warned. When a bagged fox was 'nicked', its feet being punctured to leave droplets of blood which improved scent, true foxhunters were even more outraged. Foxhunting society in general vehemently condemned the use of bagged foxes put into holes, or ejected into coverts, just before hounds arrived. On the other hand, a new, socially insecure landowner was equally in dread of his coverts being drawn blank by hounds immediately after he had entertained the neighbourhood with a meet at his country house. A 'helpful' gamekeeper could drop a fox from a bag without telling his employer, but experienced foxhunters were well aware of such a faux pas, whereas a newcomer to the countryside might be fooled. Shooting foxes was another rural mis-

demeanour likely to make a landowner a social outcast in staunch hunting countries until well after the Second World War, although that does not mean it did not occur.

The main tenet of the Masters of Foxhounds Association when it arrived in 1881, was simple: 'Foxhunting as a sport is the hunting of the fox in his wild and natural state. No pack of hounds, of which the Master or representative is a Member of this Association, shall be allowed to hunt a fox in any way that is inconsistent with this precept.' Boodle's, as the Club most popular with hunting gentlemen, was an effective setting for encouraging this basic rule of good practice before the arrival of the MFHA, and thereafter. It was the most likely venue in London for stories of such practices to be exchanged in confidence. Although records of the Foxhunting Committee's findings were generally couched in conciliatory terms, its members would have been aware of news or gossip of sporting wrongs being committed in certain hunting countries. There were ample opportunities within the portals of Boodle's for senior Masters discreetly to take to task those who were conducting their foxhunting incorrectly. Shaming the guilty party was a significant element of self-regulation long before the rules of foxhunting were written officially.

In more than few cases of boundary and covert disputes heard by Boodle's, the parties concerned often put their case to the Foxhunting Committee, and thereafter resolved the matter amicably among themselves, once they had

A joint Dinner held in March 2012 with the Tarporley Hunt Club of Tarporley, Cheshire which also celebrated its 250th Anniversary in 2012

appreciated the full extent of both sides of the argument. The Quorn case, referred to above, proved not to be susceptible to such compromise, and gained far more notoriety than most disputes coming before Boodle's. The Stewards of Boodle's committee after long deliberation, made a decision in 1879 over the Quorn's appeal to have returned to it, the country it had loaned to Mr Tailby. Boodle's was of the opinion that the Harborough country was still part of the Quorn and Mr Coupland, the Quorn Master, had every right to hunt it.

The minutes of Boodle's Masters of Foxhounds Committee, dated 13 February 1879, state: 'The stewards of the MFH Committee having carefully considered the evidence on both sides in the case submitted to them by Mr Coupland and Sir B. Cunard are unanimously of opinion that the country which was hunted by Mr Tailby in the season of 1878–79 is still part of the Quorn country, and that the offer

of Lord Stamford in 1859 to hunt the Billesdon side, as well as the protest made by Lord Wilton in 1871 on behalf of the Quorn Hunt Committee, which was received and recorded by the Stewards of the MFH Committee in 1872, entirely invalidate the claim on the part of Mr Tailby to undisturbed possession for 22 years. The Stewards therefore decide that Mr Coupland has the right to hunt the Billesdon side of the Quorn country, if he thinks it desirable to do so.' The sting was in the last eight words of the decision, indicating the Committee knew full well that in matters of hunt boundaries and coverts you could take a horse to water but you could not make it drink.

The disputed country was already being hunted by another: from 1869 Sir Bache Cunard had gained the full support of landowners and farmers in the disputed country, and hunted the country to their satisfaction, causing much smaller mounted fields to cross their land than would have been the case with the highly popular Quorn which attracted so many seasonal visitors to Leicestershire. The landowners in the disputed country protested at the prospect of Sir Bache being turned out of new kennels he had built, and they threatened prosecutions in the courts for trespass against Mr Coupland if he attempted to hunt their country. Legal trespass proved more potent that 'Foxhunting Law'.

The powerful John Poynz Spencer, 5th Earl, known as the 'Red Earl', Master and ruler of the Pytchley country, at last achieved an arbitration accepted by the local landowning fraternity. The Quorn accepted the Earl's proposal that they had established a 'right' to hunt the country, but Sir Bache should continue to hunt it, although it should revert to the Quorn on his retirement. This never happened because when Sir Bache retired in 1888 he was succeeded on a similar basis by the great Mastership of Mr Charles Fernie who reigned until his death in 1919. The embers of the old dispute died down, and the Quorn relinquished all claims in 1920, the separated country flourishing as the Fernie Hunt until this day.

The Quorn case has been claimed to be the catalyst for the formation of the Masters of Foxhounds Association outside Boodle's from 1881, but certainly the proliferation of new Hunts full of newcomers to the Chase, made the task of arbitration even more pressing in the late nineteenth century. In Boodle's archives there is a letter signed by Earl Spencer, and other leading Masters in 1880 asking for the Club's manager, Mr Gainer, to deliver over to Earl Spencer, the senior Steward, 'all the awards, letters and other things belonging to the Committee, and to remove from the printed rules of the Club all those relation to the MFHA Committee'.

Reports of a disagreement between members of the Committee and the management of the Club are hinted at in the joint letter which states that the 'undersigned members of the Masters of Foxhounds Committee, formed at Boodle's in 1853, being satisfied that the work of the Committee can be no longer carried on at the Club as the same is now constituted'. It has been said the seeds of disagreement simply concerned the price of drinks in the Club, but whatever the circumstances, the transfer of the government of foxhunting to the MFHA was timely. The 8th Duke of Beaufort chaired the first meeting of the MFHA, held at Tattersalls, offices of the popular London horse sales at Knightsbridge. The original MFHA subscription was ten shillings per head, which was recorded as being 'more than enough to cover all expenses.' Packs were now to be registered officially with the MFHA, which acquired extra teeth in enforcing its decisions. Originally compiled in 1800, the maintenance of the Foxhound Kennel Stud Book by the MFHA from 1886 became an essential element in running a successful Hunt.

The MFHA could punish errant Masters by withdrawing their right to enter their hounds in the stud book. This would not be tolerated by Hunt Committees who would have not choice but to eject Masters debarred by the Association. The expulsion or suspension of Masters became a significant deterrent, and later the MFHA. acquired the power to award or withdraw from Hunts the right to hold an official point-to-point, which would be unpopular with followers and would involve a loss of income to the Hunt.

The MFHA's early development into an effective sporting body would hardly have been possible without the considerable experience gained within Boodle's.

The Club played a key role in ensuring the survival of one of our greatest national field sports throughout the twentieth century into the twenty-first – when even the attempt by New Labour to ban the Chase through the Hunting Act of 2005 has yet to succeed in extinguishing the golden thread of foxhunting from our countryside.

MAY has xxxi DAYS.			Received.			Paid.		
21ſt Week.]	Account of Caſh.		L.	s.	d.	L.	s.	d.
20								
	For Poors rates paving and lighting —					5	17	0
	Door keeper of the House of C					1	1	0
	Dinner &c at Boodles					1	10	—
	To Tody for House —					5	5	0
	Won at Whiſt —		4	4	0			
	Unaccounted articles in 4 weeks					6	12	0
	Total.		78	7	0	56	5	0
	Balance		22	2	0			

A page from the pocket book of Edward Gibbon, renowned author of the *Decline and Fall of the Roman Empire*, recording the cost of a dinner at Boodle's in 1776

CHAPTER 8

Boodle's Food

DAVID MANN

> 'A man seldom thinks with more earnestness of
> anything than he does of his dinner'
> SAMUEL JOHNSON

In May and June of 1776 Edward Gibbon, celebrated historian, writer and, most importantly for this purpose, Boodle's member, recorded in his pocketbook that he dined at the Club. Here he enjoyed a game of cards, and celebrated his gain of £4. 4s: *'Won at Whist'*. Despite having a London home, and possibly even a cook in residence (his wife having retired to Bath), Gibbon spent considerable time at the Club living in his 'usual manner' as he described it. Many of his letters were written from the premises. It is recorded that 'Dinner & c. at Boodle's' cost him £1. 10s and £1. 6s respectively. He was not the only member spending his evenings at Boodle's, the Club then still in its Pall Mall premises, using it as a home away from home.

Boodle's Dining Etiquette

From the time of its establishment in 50 Pall Mall the Club's dining etiquette was set out in a series of rules made known to its members. Rule nineteen required that the 'Dinner to be always upon the Table at a quarter past four o'clock. The Bill to be always called for at half an Hour after six. Supper a Quarter before Eleven. Bill half an Hour past Twelve, any persons in the Room after Dinner or Supper is upon the table or before the time pay his share of the Bill. The Dinner to be at Eight Shillings, the Supper at Six Shillings a Head. Fire not to be paid for. Port Wine at half a Crown a Bottle, Claret at Five Shillings and Sixpence a Bottle'.

Rule twenty-three dealt with hospitality and stipulated that 'it is resolved that from the 1st of May to the 1st of November The members of the Club may each of them bring one stranger (& one only) to either Dinner or Supper, The Stranger paying for himself.' Among the other rules decided by the Committee (in 1867) was number twenty-nine which stated that 'House Dinner be on table in the months of January, February, March, April and September at 8 o'clock instead of half past 7 o'clock.' (Was this rule connected to the hours during which Parliament sat, and of which Boodle's members made up a good contingent?)

Dining was clearly already an important aspect of Club life from its earliest years, but there are no extant records describing the meals that were served to Gibbon and his fellow members. A hint to the type of foods that could have been served is suggested in the satirical poem *Heroic Epistle to Sir William Chambers* that was written by William Mason in 1772:

> So, when some John his dull invention racks,
> To rival Boodle's dinners or Almack's,
> Three uncouth legs of mutton shock your eyes,
> Three roasted geese, three butter'd apple-pies.

Regardless of what was actually eaten one other thing was specified: 'no Healths' and 'no toasts' were allowed to be drunk.

Seasonal Food

In 1815, long after Boodle's had moved into the St James's Street premises, a fascinating book called the *Epicures Almanack* gives some indication into what foods would have been available to the Club's cooks. The book was 'designed to direct any man with a delicate stomach and a full purse, or any man with a keen strong stomach and a

Fox's Cotillon in St James's Market.

This 1784 satirical print, showing supporters of Charles James Fox (the great opponent of Pitt the Younger) who gambled recklessly at Brooks's) is set in the meat market in St James's. In March 1784 the King dissolved Parliament; Pitt was returned with a substantial majority

lean purse, where he may dine well, and to the best advantage in London.' The authors go on to mention the Club, possibly on account of the quality of food coming out of the kitchen, explaining that 'on the east side of St James's Street, is that splendid mansion known by the name of Boodle's Subscription House'. Brooks's and The Cocoa Tree were also mentioned.

Boodle's was well situated to take advantage of the best-stocked markets in London. Not only was Covent Garden market relatively close by, where 'every esculent vegetable in or out of season, indigenous or exotic, natural or forced' was sold, but also in close vicinity to St James's Market, situated between St James's Square and the Haymarket. This

market was held 'in high repute for good meats, and can boast within its precincts several first rate fishmongers, poulterers, fruiterers, and green-grocers'. If indeed Boodle's acquired their produce here then they were in prestigious company as 'from hence the households of most of the branches of the Royal Family are supplied.'

While some twentieth-century recipes from the Boodle's kitchen have survived (and are reproduced herein), a more comprehensive sense of the foods available to Club members in the earlier years can be gleaned from the list of seasonal foods published in the *Almanack* in 1815.

January, which might traditionally be associated with a rather lean month for new food, is conversely described as being 'one of the most distinguished in the calendar for good cheer'. The markets were brimming with an abundance of seasonal produce: 'The bracing air of winter promotes exercise and quickens appetite . . . its long nights and short days, create a relish for social and domestic enjoyments; of which dinner, being the most substantial, is most generally interesting.'

The cooks from Boodle's would have been able to choose between turkey from Norfolk, mutton (Welsh and Highland bred preferred), wild duck from Lincolnshire and Cambridgeshire, as well as pheasants, hares, geese, partridges, beef, veal, pork, lamb, ham, guinea fowl, to say nothing of the seafood. The game and meat dishes would have been accompanied by potatoes, savoy cabbage, sprouts, kale, turnip, onions, carrot; hearty winter fare. Desserts included tarts and pies, apple and mince, as well as custards and jellies, 'and other fruit indigenous or exotic, crude or candied'.

By March turbot was in great supply, and Londoners apparently paid 'vast sums' for this fish which showed their 'good taste and spirit in whatever concerns the glory of the table'. John Dory was also in season, along with a greater variety of fresh vegetables, now available as the colder weather receded. Young cheeses were brought to the table, of the 'Bath' and 'York' variety, accompanied by early-season radishes.

By the following month, as Spring unfolded, the demand for grass-fed lamb was at its height and rich pork meat 'disappears from all polite tables' to be replaced by roasting pigs. In 1815 the fashion for sturgeon, the 'royal fish', whose flavour could be enhanced by a newly created sauce 'which places him almost on par with turtles in richness of flavour'. Halibut, mackerel and sole were also available to eat.

If dining in the Club in May, members could expect to find asparagus, 'expected in abundance', on the menu, typically as a side-dish to 'dovecote' pigeons or salmon. The latter was of the river variety, which was in greater demand than that from the sea. The Thames was one of the main sources of supply. As this was also the high-season for sea-food, carp and perch were also served. Fresh butter was 'particularly fragrant and balsamic, being perceptibly

Boodle's celebrated the birthday of George IV in April 1828 by holding a grand banquet.

impregnated with the juices of fresh herbage and flowery pasture.'

The parliamentary season ran from February to August and Boodle's remained open for most of the summer months. In August the club would close and London was 'so thin that it looks like the ghost of its former self'. It had always been so; even Gibbon described Boodle's in August as 'now no more'.

In October, cod reappeared on the table and seasonal fruits such as apples, pears and plums, much like what is found in today's markets, were at their best.

By the year's end 'the refinements of foreign invention are for once superseded by the simpler products of old English cooking: roast beef and plum-pudding, turkies and chines, ham and fowls, capons and sausages' along with custards and pies such as mincemeat.

The Ball at St James's Palace held on the King's Birthday 4 June 1782, the year Boodle's moved from Pall Mall to St James's Street

The Attorney General's Dinner

While nothing has survived regarding the day to day food preparations of Boodle's, hidden in the back of an extant club book is a menu created for 'The Attorney General's dinner April 23rd 1828 for the Kings Counsel.' The occasion being celebrated is not indicated but presumably was related to George IV's birthday. Wednesday, 23 April had been declared a holiday and festivities kicked off with the 'ringing of bells' as Pall Mall and St James's Street filled with the 'bustle and [the] crowd exceeded any thing we ever before witnessed on a similar occasion'.

Contemporary accounts describe the decorations, the music, but most importantly the people making their way

towards St James's Palace, which was the centre of the celebration, to pay their respects: 'bout twelve o'clock there were two rows of carriages in St James's Street, filled with ladies anxious to see those who were going to the drawing room, the chain of carriages, with company, having even then reached some way up St James's Street; by a quarter before one o'clock the chain had extended nearly to the top of Bond Street'.

Much of the crowd's attention was focused on these guests and it was concluded that 'on no occasion was there a greater display of elegant dresses; & the ornaments which were worn by the Ladies, and which were composed of diamonds and other precious jewels, were of the most magnificent and brilliant description'. Among the large number of

George Cruikshank's 1814 satirical cartoon portrays Lady Hertford holding out a tureen of turtle soup to the Prince Regent

invited guests was the aforementioned Attorney General, Sir Charles Wetherell, who had been appointed to the position for a second time that same year, and who was among those received by His Majesty in the Palace's Throne Room.

The King retired by half past four but the celebrations continued well into the night. St James's Street was so transformed by the brilliant illuminations of the clubhouses and hotels that 'the whole reflected a galaxy of light almost too bright for the human eye to gaze upon'. Boodle's was decorated with 'a bulging Crown and G.R. IV'.

The night's festivities were spread across the West End, from sumptuous dinners hosted by the Duke of Wellington at Apsley House to the Duke of Gloucester at his rooms in the Admiralty, and also by various Cabinet Ministers and Officers of State. Sir Robert Peel, 2nd Bt, the Home Secretary in Wellington's cabinet entertained the Attorney General along with the rest of the Law Court: 'the Judges of the Court of King's Bench, Common Pleas, and Exchequer, the Judge of the High Court of the Admiralty, the Judge of the Arches' Court, the King's Advocate-General, the Solicitor-General, the Lord Mayor, the Sheriffs of London and Middlesex, the Recorder of London, and the Undersecretaries of State for the Home Department'.

It is probable that the dinner mentioned in the Boodle's club book is connected to the one that Peel hosted that night, even though he himself was not yet a member of the Club (he would be elected in 1836). The menu enumerates the spring delicacies prepared in Boodle's kitchen: asparagus and peas, sole, turbot, salmon and mackerel, pigeon and lamb, as well as 'mock turtle' soup, a nod to the expensive, epicurean delicacy of West-Indian turtle soup.

20th-Century Club Menus

Victor Ceserani, MBE, who would eventually become head chef at Boodle's in 1948, wrote a detailed account of food that he prepared when first cooking at the Orleans Club on King Street – the menu here probably much the same as the one he would eventually create for Boodle's:

'All food was of the finest quality – fresh salmon was sent by the Tay Salmon Company from Scotland by overnight express and we used only free-range chickens from Surrey, plump tender birds of good weight, with full breasts and the faint blueish tinge to the skin which is a mark of quality. Fresh fruit and vegetables came in daily from Covent Garden (a stone's

The front of Boodle's festively dressed for Edward VII's Coronation in 1902 with balconies for members to watch the Royal procession. Note the Royal Standard on the flagpole

Boodle's awaits the Royal Wedding of Princess Elizabeth and Prince Philip in November 1947. Post-war austerity is evident in the plainer balconies

throw away). Meat, poultry and game came from Smithfield, and fish from Billingsgate.

Club members liked good, correctly cooked, well-served food with a varied selection of traditional British dishes and interesting international favourites. A typical menu might feature a roast bird or joint mutton – chicken, goose or duck. Other favourites included jugged hare; braised ox tongue with Madeira sauce; salmis of game; devilled kidneys; curried beef, lamb or chicken; fricassee of chicken or veal; hot veal and ham pie; boiled mutton with caper sauce; wild duck with orange sauce; plover with port wine sauce; partridge braised with cabbage, bacon, sausage, onion, carrot and herbs (delicious!); roast pheasant; grouse; woodcock and snipe. These last two long-necked, long-beaked birds were trussed with their own beaks after cleaning.

Most members had a sweet tooth, especially at lunch

time, when we would offer a tempting range of traditional British puddings, the repertoire for which is so vast that there was never any problem finding variety. There was a different milk pudding every day of the week, suet puddings (blackberry and apple, rhubarb and gooseberry), fruit tarts and pies (raspberry and redcurrant, with a feather-like pastry crust – a favourite), spotted dick, treacle sponge, fruit fools and trifle.

In the evenings, whilst we served a few sweets, hot savouries on toast were popular: oysters or chicken livers wrapped in bacon, haddock and bacon (strips of finnan haddock the size of a forefinger cleaned of all bone and skin were wrapped in paper-thin rashers of streaky bacon, grilled and dusted with cayenne pepper), curried prawns or shrimps, soft roes and mushrooms, creamed haddock sprinkled with grated cheese, chopped ham in cream or curry sauce with a grilled mushroom on top, Scotch woodcock, devilled kidneys, sardines (skinned and boned) and the club specials – Welsh rarebit and beef marrow bone. For the Welsh rarebit we grated or finely sliced Cheddar cheese and gently melted it in a little white sauce until smooth. An egg yolk was added and a good measure of ale, which was reduced in a separate pan to a teaspoonful. Two to

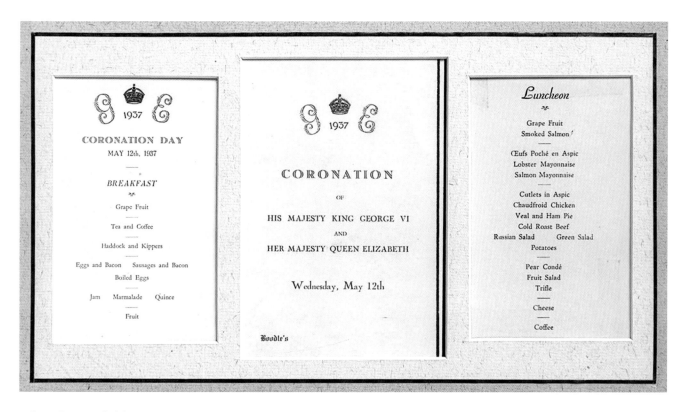

A framed group of Club Coronation menus

three drops of Worcestershire sauce, a dash of English mustard and a snuff of cayenne pepper completed the seasoning.

The mixture was then poured into the inner part of a small, rectangular double silver dish, the outer part of which contained a heated metal block. The ornate silver lid was put on the dish and sent to the dining room where, in the adjoining pantry, fresh toast was made, buttered, crusts removed and served on a hot plate. The club member then proceeded to help himself to the rarebit. I wondered at first why Marie usually swiftly volunteered to prepare Welsh rarebits until I realised that of the bottle of ale drawn from the bar for every order, only a fraction went into the pan. The remainder was considered chef's perks. For the beef marrow we used whole beef shin bones, sawn into halves and placed in a large covered pan with a little stock and steamed. One of these would be served wrapped in a white serviette on a silver dish

and the member, using a special long-handled narrow spoon, would spoon the marrow on to a slice of fresh buttered toast, season it with salt and pepper, and consume it with relish.

Cheeses of the finest quality were purchased from Paxton and Whitfield of Jermyn Street (about 200 yards away), and we always were required to have a large Stilton in prime condition which, as the justly named "King of Cheeses", had a trolley all to itself. Members served themselves with a special Stilton spoon (a practice frowned upon by some today), and once an inch of the cheese had been chiselled away a bottle of good port was gradually poured into the cheese (another practice also now frowned upon). Once the Stilton was within an inch of the bottom it was sent to the kitchen and replaced. When the old cheese arrived in the kitchen (which wasn't very often as a large Stilton contains a great mass of cheese) we would cut it into four and scrape away a considerable amount of very ripe, strongly port flavoured cheese which swiftly disappeared between the staff.'

Food Rationing at Boodle's

Fully stocked larders would be in contrast to the period of severe food rationing that would affect Boodle's during the First and Second World Wars. The rationing was introduced at different stages for various commodities on both national and local levels. During the First World War the peak was mid-1918 to summer 1919. In a letter written by Sir Alan Frederick Lascelles to his father on 6 March 1918 he describes how to make the best of the imposed restrictions:

As to food in London, you will find you can get along quite comfortably, if you make up your mind from the start not to expect much meat, and to be thankful when you get it. On the whole, I have fed extremely well these last ten days and never felt better in my life. Daisy got me a food-card, as she, or Blanche, will no doubt get you one; this is the thing like a sheet of miniature postage stamps, which one can easily carry in a treasury-note case, or pocket-book; four of these postage stamps represent your meat-ration for a week. If you want a meat-meal at Boodle's, or a restaurant, you hand the card to the waiter, who cuts off one, or half (according to the amount of meat you want) of these postage-stamps, and keeps it. It is really quite simple. But at all clubs and restaurants you can always and at any time get an excellent meat-less meal – soup, fish, eggs, stuffed onions, etc. The meat-less food at the Traveller's I consider quite excellent, and I am sure it is equally good at Boodle's. On meatless days, I don't think you can get meat anywhere, except in private houses, whose owners have bought their ration overnight.

If you are going to stay a few days in London before you go in, I should strongly advise you to make a definite arrangement to lunch each day at Boodle's; hand in your meat-card to the head waiter, and he will then see that you get your full meat-ration during the week. For dinner, you would then have to do the best you can

with poultry, oysters, fish, etc.; in private houses they give you pheasant as if it were still January. If you want sugar or butter, you will have to get a separate card; but I have got along very well without either, so I should recommend you not to worry about a second card.

Charles Ritchie, who was Second Secretary in the High Commission of Canada in London (and would later be made Canadian Ambassador to Washington) describes dining at the Club on 1 September 1939, 'in the candlelit gloom' of the dining room where 'all but two waiters had been called up. It was the first time in history that members were permitted to dine in the dining room in day clothes'. Ritchie emerged after dinner 'into coal-black St James's Street'. During the War the Orleans Club was accommodated by Boodle's to whom it eventually sold its cellar of port (it would eventually be merged with Wyndham's and the Marlborough Club).

The clubs were also subjected to rationing as Boodle's Club's General Committee Minutes indicates. On 18 November 1943 it was resolved to 'ration vintage or tawny Port to one small glass at or after lunch and one small glass at or after dinner' and in April 1944 rationing was extended to include whisky 'to two large or four small glasses per day. A Member who lunches in the Club to be allowed one large or two small . . . in addition to the above. Similarly for gin and cocktails.'

According to one story a certain member, in order to feel sufficiently satiated, would lunch firstly at Boodle's and then move on to the St James' Club to have a second lunch. The high prices of the unrationed foods were felt by the Club and taken under discussion.

The rationing would long outlast the war, only coming to an end on 4 July 1954. Ceserani himself describes the extent to which the chefs at Boodle's had to go in order to provide enough food even though, as he tells it, club members were luckier than most:

Food remained on ration for several years after the war and catering establishments were only allowed to spend a certain amount of money on meat – in our case, four pounds ten shillings a week – which in 1946 would buy one whole lamb and a wing rib of beef. The Club was open seven days a week for lunch and dinner, and the staff also had to be fed. The meat allowance barely covered two days, but occasionally it would be supplemented with a few sausages or some offal. For the purchase of groceries, eggs, fats and tinned foods, an allocation of points was made which was very tight, so that we had to organise and plan with great care and economy.

Inevitably, a flourishing black market existed, and if you were prepared to pay the price, almost any quantity of any commodity could be purchased. Respectable clubs and establishments frowned on this practice and we were never allowed to buy food other than the legal entitlement.

The Club was more fortunate than most establishments, as members who farmed, hunted or fished would send in surplus requirements. British Rail vans were regular callers, bringing large hampers of assorted game from Scotland and salmon in a wide variety of sizes in long, woven rush containers. Salmon would vary in weight from 7 to 50 lb. All 14-pounders were sent to a salmon-smoking company in the East End of London who, after smoking them, would keep the sides in store until required.

Whole carcasses or sides of venison wrapped in sacking would be dumped unceremoniously on the floor of the larder. These would be butchered, keeping the haunches marinaded in red wine, vegetables and herbs for forty-eight hours, before being roasted and served with a sharp, peppery sauce. The tender fillets were kept for steaks to be fried or grilled and served with a variety of well-flavoured sauces and garnishes.

The remaining meat was trimmed, diced and left under running cold water for forty-eight hours, which made the meat much lighter in appearance. After blanching and refreshing, it was then used for a variety of stews, pies and curries, or minced for cottage pie, pasties, steaks and casseroles. The bones would be chopped and browned, along with any other game carcasses, and made into rich well-flavoured stock with the addition of herbs and vegetables. This stock would then be made into an ever popular game soup, to be finished at the table with the addition of a glass of port, madeira or brandy.

One club member reared pedigree turkeys in Norfolk and, in addition to the excellent birds he supplied for roasting, we were also able to purchase turkey eggs, one of which in size roughly equals two hens eggs. Another member had a large estate of prize-winning fruit trees, specialising in English apples. At the beginning of the season, a large wooden box containing 56 lb of Beauty of Bath, together with a typed card giving all relevant information, would arrive.

Some time later would follow the Worcester Pearmains, and so on, right through numerous varieties of

Silver sauce boats and (right) asparagus tongs inscribed with the Club name

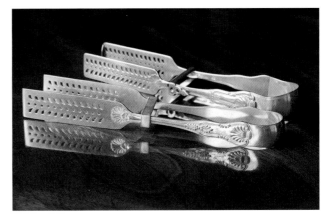

The Boodle's Christmas pudding being made, overseen by Chef Carter

the very best of dessert and cooking apples, ending with Cox's Orange Pippins. All the apples were packed with loving care, and on opening each box, it was like looking at the gold medal winner at the autumn Royal Horticultural Society show at Vincent Square, Westminster. His Charles Ross were magnificent, often weighing a pound each, a splendid cooking apple that can be eaten or cooked. If I was a painter, it is one I would clearly love to put on canvas.

When Christmas puddings were prepared, a week before mixing we would put all the dried fruit – raisins, currants, mixed peel, sugar, mixed spice ginger, chopped almonds, prunes, dates and apples – into a large wooden barrel. Next was added twelve bottles of ale, six bottles of stout, and one bottle each of sherry, rum and brandy. The barrel was securely covered and

left for seven days, and stirred occasionally so that the fruit became thoroughly impregnated with the liquid. Flour, breadcrumbs, butter and eggs were added and the mixture was then put into basins and steamed in the traditional way. We would make thirty-five 2 lb and twenty-two 3 lb puddings annually, and usually served them with brandy butter or brandy sauce.'

Ceserani goes on to describe one particular event which stuck with him after his usual walk through Soho calling on 'some of the suppliers whose shops were *en route*. Slater, Cooke, Bisney and Jones, butchers in Brewer Street, were the last stop where I called daily in the hope that there might be a little something not on rations.'

A surprise awaited me one morning, when the manager

replied to my usual question, 'Anything going this morning?'

'Yes, I've got something for you.' With that he opened the door of his large cold room and removed a tray on which lay a skinned animal resembling a short fat rabbit.

'What's that?'

'It's a beaver.'

'A beaver? What am I supposed to do with that?'

'Don't ask me,' he replied. 'I'm only the butcher, you're the chef.' On close examination, the animal looked clean and plump. There was a fine grain to the meat and it looked good quality.

'All right, I'll have it,' I said. 'Send it in.'

When the butcher's delivery boy arrived an hour or so later, Cecil and I had a discussion about how it should be prepared and cooked. We made a tasty herb and onion-flavoured stuffing for the inside, covered it with thin slices of fat beacon and pot-roasted it slowly on a bed of vegetables and herbs.

Around eleven-thirty as usual, Mr Sharp, the club steward, came down for the day's menu. When I said roast and stuffed beaver he thought I was pulling his leg, whereupon I took him out to the kitchen. Cecil opened the oven door, slid out the tray, removed the lid and basted the animal. 'We can't put roast and stuffed beaver on the menu, the members won't eat it!' he said. I replied, 'I can't call it anything else, that is what it is and that is how we shall have to put it on the menu.' Somewhat reluctantly Mr Sharp finally agreed.

The club had one or two members who lived in grace and favour residences in St James's Palace, from which at twenty-five past twelve daily one elderly knight would totter up St James's Street in order to be first in for lunch. After seating himself in his customary chair, he perused the menu, called for the head waiter, and said in a loud peppery voice, 'What the b— hell is this?'

'Exactly what it says, sir', replied the head waiter.

'What the blazes is the club coming to? They'll be serving cats and dogs next! I'll have the escalope, I like

Selection of cheeses: Vacharin, Double Gloucester, Yorkshire Blue, Golden Cross Goats' Cheese, Keen's Cheddar, Lancashire

a bit of veal.' Little did he know that the escalope (which was not called veal on the menu) was prepared from the cut of meat from one side of the saddle of an imported frozen rabbit.

Two members ordered the beaver and ate it without complaint. I had some for my lunch and found it acceptable, but the remainder went through the mincer and ended up in the staff rissoles for supper.

Occasionally, we were able to obtain a case containing twelve frozen rabbits, which made a useful variation as they could be prepared in a variety of white or brown stews, curries, pies and pasties. The saddles were always used by boning out the two cuts of meat

Boodle's Partridge and Game Chips

163

Boodle's Hare Royale

and soaking them well in cold water in order to whiten the flesh. Then, by cutting length-wise three-quarters of the way across, opening out, and carefully beating using a little water, they could be made into thin slices about the size of a dessert plate. Covered with flour, egg and crumbs shallow-fried and served with a wedge of lemon or a variety of garnishes, they were very popular, and on more than one occasion brought forth the comment, 'Nice piece of veal!'

Fine Food

More than any other English gentlemen's club, Boodle's is known for its food. A large number of recipes in cooking books are identified with the Club as well as with those chefs who won competitions and went on to build careers in restaurants. It is not known when and how this tradition started. Richard Edmonds, former Boodle's Secretary (1966–98), has his own clear recollections of how the menu looked when he first arrived at the club in 1966, on a 'roneoed foolscap piece of paper with a huge selection besides the ten daily dishes. You could see that it had been made by a committee incorporating all the items the members had requested. I expect this was a natural successor to the austerity menu during and just after the war'. He goes on to recollect:

In my early travels I visited the Nouveau Circle in their original clubhouse on the Isle San Louis. They were most charming and so concerned I should be made welcome they even found some English speakers to sit at the Club table with me. My host was a General, he explained that the club was like a private home and there was a three-course menu and the only choice was at the main course, a grilled steak. With such a simple menu only one chef was required. This gave me much to think over; the idea of no choice would not be accepted by everyone but there would be a huge saving in staff and wastage. A few years later I went to America for the first time and visited the Pacific Union Club in San Francisco who have a very small menu.

The Club finances as always were not good and if I could reduce wastage and staff it would help a great deal. I set out to reduce the menu, to get the Committee to agree. I suggested we would abolish the bread and butter charge; it was agreed immediately.

I first of all reduced the number of permanent dishes on the menu (the à la carte) to the minimum I thought I could get away with although I knew some members would be disappointed; some regularly came and ate the same thing every day. I think those dishes I chose are still the same today.

I took over the menu writing and was still doing it when Keith Podmore as Chef arrived some ten years later. I also did all the menus for the private parties and the Ladies' Side. I decided that the Club menu should cater for all the members' requirements. One fresh soup made on Monday and again on Wednesday (on the old menu there were four, all from packets). A mousse or pate and two other dishes that could be eaten as main courses. There would then be a fresh fish course which could be eaten as main or starter if a member was entertaining someone special.

There would moreover be three main courses unless it was the game season when there would be four. I was aiming to please all the members, the member lunching/dining alone, with his brother (reasonable and filling) or entertaining someone special. By control-

164

ling all the menus I was able to bring them all together, and many evening and private parties had the same combination of dishes – a great saving in labour and ingredients. About ten years later we brought in the pudding menu, before there had been one pudding and a huge cheese selection.

I had two chefs. Cecil Pierre Bill was very stuck in the past having joined the kitchen just after the war with ration books and members bringing in their game. When I arrived it was a traditional menu. I had not long been out of the Savoy, and it was practically the same. I arrived at Boodle's the same time as the Roux brothers opened the first Gavroche restaurant in London in 1967 and things started to change. I could give you a list of all the great chefs who arrived. I couldn't get Bill to change, so on pretext of increasing profits I took over the buying and, more important, all the menus.

By Thursday night all private parties, the Ladies' Side and the backbone, the Coffee Room menu, were done. Everyone knew the most important place was the Coffee Room, and I never had complaints in thirty-two years. The menus were put together to support each other. It was then I created the small menu that you have now.

With the young sous-chefs we started to put on new dishes. I bought them all the best cookery books and even sent them out to shop in China Town for spices and different vegetables. It was a great time. Gerry Boriosi who had completed his apprenticeship was in the Ladies' Side and several chefs were in the Coffee Room. Boriosi later went on to win the most prestigious competition of the time, the Mouton Cadet competition supported by Baron Rothschild.

In January 1983 Keith Podmore became Head Chef of Boodle's, a position he retained until 2006. After his retirement he was invested with the honorary doctorate for services to Culinary Education by Thames Valley University. What follows are Podmore's recollections of his twenty-three years at the Club:

Cold Veal, Ham and Egg Pie

During my interview with Richard Edmonds I realised that here was a man I could work with, even though the kitchens were somewhat dated and in need of upgrading to modern standards. I soon recognised that the members were very knowledgeable and composed of many gourmets and gourmands! They were also very appreciative, and I enjoyed the many occasions that they would come to pass the time of day or just talk about food in my office. I learnt a lot from them!

Soon after I started at Boodle's I began introducing changes by first tackling the basics, such as improving the stocks and sauces, and the butchery and fish mongering to get control of consistency and profitability. The style of food would be fresh; classically British and French following the Seasons and the underlying fashion as it evolved. All the food was prepared in house including all our pates and terrines. We did try to make our own bread but because of all the different varieties needed and the specialist flours and equipment required we purchased it from very good producers.

The format of the inherited menu was good. I reduced the number of dishes cooked to order at luncheon (serving a daily roast and a braised dish, pie or pudding) so improving the speed and reliability of service, much appreciated by members and my soon to be very good friend, the Coffee Room manager,

Boodle's Crème Brulée

Luciano. At dinner I increased the number of dishes cooked to order because of the more sedate dinner service and the fewer members dining. This also gave me better control of the quality, and the cost. The banqueting menus and Coffee Room menus were also dovetailed.

'Bloody odd being treated to a slap up lunch by a sexy little bank manageress with excellent legs – hope you won't be expecting me to put you up for Boodle's next …'

I wrote the menus weekly with the input of each sous-chef in charge of the Coffee Room and the Ladies' Side, with the sous-chef in charge of the larder contributing cold dishes. The Ladies' Side was a problem because everyone wanted to eat at the same time and service was fast and too furious – we had approximately forty seconds to prepare each dish. Proper booking times were needed but this took longer than expected to introduce and proved hard work, but we eventually succeeded. We were able to produce good food and retained some very talented cooks (including Laurent Tourandel who now has many restaurants in New York).

There was a training programme in place when I arrived, and I set to work to improve this. It was to prove a great investment of time and effort for all. We were serving good food with the philosophy of "simple elegance and perfection" which of course was impossible to consistently achieve, but it was a good goal. My own maxim was "always better". The apprentices (who mainly lived in) were, and are, the mainstay of the kitchen. I always had the support of Richard Edmonds and my sous-chefs in the training scheme.

We did, of course, follow the seasons; the British seasons where possible. Game was the main season much anticipated by members and staff alike. Woodcock, Teal, Snipe, Hare Wild Duck, Widgeon, British Grey Leg Partridge (alas now so badly under pressure) Pheasant, Hare, Venison, Blackcock, Plover (not many) and of course the Grouse. One might describe it as the Boodle's Bird; the most served in two months (we closed for annual holiday in August) was 2,000 birds.

With help from the Academy of Culinary Arts (I was Chairman of the Education Committee) we consolidated an apprenticeship scheme using Thames Valley University, as well as Bournemouth and Poole College. We entered the apprentices in many competitions and had much success. Andrew Fairlie won the first Roux Brothers Scholarship and he now has his own two star Michelin Restaurant in Gleneagles Hotel. Our apprentices were in demand and able to find good jobs to

further their career. We encouraged them to build on their training and many went on to gain experience and work in many fine hotels and restaurants.

I felt we were having success in the kitchen achieving reliable profitability. In 1991 we built a state of the art kitchen for the Coffee Room and eventually some ten or so years later a state of the art pastry and larder – the engine room of the kitchens. The Ladies' Side kitchen was also upgraded during this period. Our reputation for quality food and training was spreading and recruitment was becoming easier and we were able to attract staff even from France. This also had the effect of helping "Clubland" to become an attractive place to work, with some high profile Chefs coming to work in the Gentlemen's clubs.

Banqueting was also an important area for members as we catered for weddings and other private and family functions. Fine wine dinners were also attractive to members, and at them a Château from France would come and show their wine. We would create a menu to suit that particular wine and the challenge was always welcome. Among those served were Chateau Gruaud-Larose, Château Palmer, Château Mouton-Rothschild, and famously Château Pétrus. The châteaux would present various vintages starting with the youngest and finishing with the oldest they wished to show. We always tried to understate the menu because the wine had to take pride of place. Simple elegance and perfection were key.

In 2005 I felt that I needed to think about retirement as I found it increasingly difficult to maintain the standard. I had an excellent brigade, probably the best I had ever had, but I still needed to be involved in everything, and was beginning to lack the drive. I retired on 6 April 2006. It was time for someone of Stephen Carter's ilk to bring refreshment and maintain the standards and traditions, which he certainly has.

Silver and Stilton displayed on one of the splendid Regency mahogany sideboards in the Coffee Room

CHAPTER 9

Boodle's and Wine from 1762

DUNCAN McEUEN

'There are regular clubs which are held in coffee houses and taverns at fixed days and hours. Wine, beer, tea, pipes and tobacco help to amuse them at these meetings . . . everything necessary for convivial jocundity. Each member drank what he liked, in quantity which he thought proper. The master of the house had nothing more to do than to produce a fresh supply of licquors as soon as they were emptied.'

Jean Pierre Grossley on London Clubs, 1765

It is a sad but inescapable fact that no records whatsoever of what Boodle's members were drinking in the Club between 1762 and recent times have been preserved. It is fair to say also that we can only guess at what they were eating in those early days, but perhaps that is more predictable and therefore, with due deference to our current superb cuisine, of less interest today. 250 years ago lamb was lamb and beef was beef and other than recipes, not much will have changed. Wine, however, has changed out of all recognition. While we have no records of our own, it is fortunate that Michael Broadbent, then head of Christie's Wine Department, produced *Christie's Wine Review* annually between 1972 and 1980. While predominantly a record of auction wine prices, each edition contained wine related articles, among which each year was a piece by Edmund Penning-Rowsell, then wine correspondent for *The Financial Times* and *Country Life* as well as Chairman of the Wine Society, on the history of wine sales at Christie's. The eponymous James held his first auction in 1766 in Pall Mall and wine featured regularly from that date. So while we cannot know precisely, the wines that went under his hammer are likely to have mirrored those in Boodle's coffee room.

In 1762 the wine trade as we know it was only just emerging. While the cork was found efficacious as a bottle stopper about one hundred years earlier, it was only just before Boodle's was founded that the cylindrical bottle was developed. This made all the difference. Wine could be laid down and matured and the word vintage achieved some importance. However the fly in the ointment was the almost perpetual state of war which existed with France and by the Methuen Treaty with Portugal in 1703, French wines were subjected to a punitive duty of £55 per tun, while Portuguese paid £7. Port and Iberian table wines were to become the most popular wines in England and accepted as an alternative by a population that had become soaked in gin. Indeed it is incredible that there was any trade in claret here at all, when duty in 1766 was 14s 6d a case and a dozen of 'fine claret' under the hammer went for 24s. The result of this discrimination was that the table wine which would have appeared at Boodle's in those early days was likely to be called Colares, Tent, Calcavella, Algarve, Setubal and Lisbon, all from Portugal. Also Spanish Red Alicante, Sack, Mountain and La Mancha. Other Mediterranean wines would have been seen, 'Cyprus' for one, together with wines from Hungary, Germany and the great Constantia from the Cape.

There is evidence that much of the wine consumed in the mid-eighteenth century was imported in cask by the purchasers in England. Private buyers would have the wine bottled at home by the butler and so it seems likely that Boodle's cellarmen would have had a busy time bottling our own wines. Bottles were reused and even with the advent of the cylindrical bottle, wines would have been consumed very early in their lives. For over 150 years first-growths have been bottled two years after the vintage, often drunk fifty and more years after bottling; 250 years ago in the English market they were mostly kept five or six years in cask, bottled and drunk immediately. Vintage years and estate names were deemed unimportant until the turn of the nineteenth century and it is amusing now that in 1772 you could purchase parcels of 1748 Hock and Hungary (quite separately of course) and to imagine how they had resisted oxidisation after twenty-four years under rather less than the sophisticated corks we are used to. Also in 1772, the year of our founder's decease, a trade parcel of seventeen pipes (probably as now about six hundred and sixty bottles each) of 1769 port (no shipper named) fetched £35 apiece. Perhaps it was so irresistibly priced, at just over a shilling a bottle, that Mr Boodle bought a pipe and one might just imagine hastened his demise by rolling it along Pall Mall the few yards from Christie's to his Clubhouse at 49, 50 and 51. A few years later, in May 1777, Boodle's bought, from the cellar of Mr Francis Latour, gone abroad, 3 ½ dozens 'Genuine old Hock, of the First Quality' 1719 at 31s 6d per dozen. Shipped from Mayntz (*sic*) in 1775, the incredible age of this wine laid before our members must have been due to the barrel being refreshed over the years in the way that 'solera' Madeira, seen today, might too have a starting date in the eighteenth century.

By the 1780s and 1790s Burgundy was beginning to feature at our tables. Descriptions were often vague. 'Chablet', Vin de St Georges, Romanie and Mont Rachet; however Chambertin, Volnay, Pommard and Beaune would have been served, but with no indication of vineyard, grower or vintage. Labels were virtually unknown, bins of cellared wines identified by lead or porcelain bin-labels and bottles by silver or enamel 'bottle-tickets'. The most fashionable wine in this era was undoubtedly Madeira. The word 'fine' in the description was reserved for those wines which had undertaken a long sea voyage or had been kept in the tropics. It was early recognised, and indeed part of its production, that great heat produced great Madeira and a 'Pipe of Madeira 5 years in the West Indies' would have been much prized. As would thirty-nine pipes 'of most excellent London Particular Madeira which had been to the Brazils'. Perhaps Benjamin Harding (the Club's proprietor after Boodle's death in 1772)

sent his cellarman along to get one of those as well. Champagne would have figured, often called Sillery, either sparkling or still. And one wonders where the 148 dozen champagne, sold in 1788 by the retiring French Ambassador from his cellar at Hyde Park Corner, ended up. This included Hautbillet Roset, probably pink from Hautvillers Abbey, the location of Dom Perignon's earlier activities.

At this time, in spite of the discrimination against French wines, claret, the most accessible in terms of distance, remained a prestige product. Champagne and Burgundy too, were sought after and one could speculate that tables in St James's groaned under the weight of smuggled products. Or would our patriotic members have eschewed claret and camembert? It is also comforting to note that when the French were convulsed with their Revolution, the benevolent English government reduced duty to 4s 6d per dozen. However in 1796 it once more bared its teeth at Napoleon and raised the tax to 10s 2d. As a result a plethora of strange names would have graced our tables at the end of the century, a few faintly recognisable now: Essence of Oldenburgh, Bacharet, Vidonia, Nice, Bristol Water, Riveselte, Vin de Size, White Lunel and Vin de Sichey.

As a postscript to the eighteenth century a fascinating insight into what was being consumed on top tables in the year of our creation is illustrated by the 'Wine Consumed at the Lord Mayor's Installation Banquet in 1762':

Port	438 bottles
Lisbon	220 bottles
Claret	168 bottles
Champagne	143 bottles
Burgundy	116 bottles
Madeira	90 bottles
Hock	66 bottles
Malmsey or Sack	4 bottles
Brandy	4 bottles
Total	1,249 bottles

Intriguing to wonder about how many attended and about the iron nature of their constitutions when only four bottles of *digestif* were required to settle that vast quantity of port and probably rather more than a cheese sandwich.

At the dawn of the nineteenth century one of the benefits the members of Boodle's would have enjoyed was the proliferation of wine merchants in the immediate area. Pall Mall was the favoured address, but nearly all the old names have now vanished and just Berry Bros. & Rudd remain. The main advance in the first half of the century was the development of the modern bottle, permitting laying down for maturation. In earlier days, age was considered more important than a single vintage, particularly for port, madeira, claret and strangely enough for hock. And then, when vintages began to be noticed and appreciated, claret, the prestige wine in spite of all economic and political barriers, was drunk anonymously or under the name of the merchant who bottled it. Private bottling now disappeared, the ability for long term maturation demanding professional care, (more) sterile conditions and far better corks. As time went by château names began to appear, but massively led by the first-growths, although the actual 'classification' did not take place until 1855. So much so that many must have been 'stretched', as indeed was the custom at the time.

The punitive tax rate for French wines was coming to an end. In 1812, when Napoleon invaded Russia, it had soared to £2 per case, (£50 plus today), but in 1831 anti-French preference was abandoned and all foreign wines paid 10s, to be reduced to 2s in 1860. Wine prices through most of the century were amazingly stable. As the years went by château names would have begun to appear more frequently on our tables. Leoville, La Rose (probably Gruaud) and Rauzan, but contemporary wine writers complained about the lack of interest in wine and that connoisseurship was rare and adulteration, falsification and sophistication all too common. Perhaps the paucity of any historic wine records at Boodle's reflects the fact that prices through a long period were flat, investment was not an issue and wine was just a beverage. Perish the thought!

Two rather bizarre auction events did take place in Club-land, which may reflect the above: in June 1815 there was a sale of wines from Brooks's, 'Sold in consequence of a dissolution of Partnership'. Eleven thousand bottles port; three thousand bottles East India and West India Madeira

and one thousand bottles Sherry – bottled 1809. Even more odd, in July 1836 the Travellers sold five thousand bottles Costello's Sherry – bottled 1831 because 'the Committee is desirous of making room in their Cellar for East India Sherry'. It is a fact that madeira was a popular cargo as it provided ballast for the return voyage from the Indies, when ships carried bulky, but very light cargoes such as tea and spices. How something as delicate as sherry survived can only be a matter of wonderment.

The second half of the nineteenth century proved to be a roller-coaster ride for wine drinkers in St James's. Early in the piece the fungoid disease *oidium tuckeri* swept through the vineyards of France, particularly Bordeaux and it seems fortunate that Mr Tucker, the gardener who first detected it in a Margate greenhouse, was not hauled off in a tumbrel. After extensive treatment with sulphur the 'Comet' vintage 1858 was extremely expensive, a great shock when prices had been broadly unchanged for the previous century. As if in sympathy, in 1860, William Gladstone, Chancellor of the Exchequer reduced table wine duty from one shilling to tuppence a bottle. Overall the 1860s and 1870s were decades of great prosperity for both the English and French middle classes and the combination of demand, speculation and disease caused wine prices to spiral upwards. This trend was assisted by a succession of really great claret vintages: 1858, 1861, 1864, 1865, 1869, 1870, 1875 and 1878. A truly purple patch, the zenith of the ungrafted vine, followed by a desert until the great twins of 1899 and 1900.

As is its wont, nemesis had been lurking around the corner and with the 1880s arrived the phylloxera louse which decimated European vineyards. Only American rootstock appeared to be impervious and so each and every European vine had to be grafted on to an American-grown root. Allied to this came the outbreak of mildew and the widespread economic slump in France and Britain which lasted until 1914. Champagne largely escaped these diseases until the early twentieth century and so with growing technical skills became increasingly popular with the affluent classes. Corks would have been popping in Boodle's.

If it seems reasonable to draw conclusions from auction records to identify what was being imbibed at Boodle's at this time, then one could speculate that our members were far too busy trying to work through the colossal cellars they had at home. Or perhaps they had expired in the attempt to do so. For example John Pender MP, selling his house near Manchester disposed of 1,100 dozen, including 240 dozen sherry and 600 dozen port. Mr Hoare from his house in St James's Square offered 600 dozen and in 1881 Sir Richard Musgrave Bt MP succumbed before he was able to tackle the twenty-four dozen Lafite 1864, forty dozen Leoville-Barton 1868, twenty-two dozen Rauzan 1874 and eight dozen Fine Liqueur Brandy 1811 binned away in his cellar. In the same year the late Duke of Portland's cellar of eight-hundred dozen included 150 dozen 1864 pale sherry. Finally, in 1897, to illustrate the popularity of champagne before phylloxera struck, among the eight-hundred dozen laid down by the late A G Guthrie of Duart Castle, Isle of Mull were 340 dozens of various champagnes. Transport alone must have been a major headache.

There is not much evidence of what actually was in the cellars of London Clubs in the nineteenth century. Odd snippets do surface from auction records but more questions are raised than answers supplied. For example what was the story behind the vast stock sold from Crockford's Club in St James's in 1852: five hundred dozen sherry, four hundred dozen port, three hundred dozen claret and ninety dozen champagne offered as 'the very extensive and justly celebrated stock of wines in consequence of Mrs Crockford's determination to relinquish the Business entirely'. And why was the Carlton Club selling, in June 1878, as 'surplus', twelve dozen Lafite 1865 and three dozen magnums Latour 1861? Each at around £4 a case, incredible for two of the greatest pre-phylloxera wines ever made. Even more bizarre, the sale included ninety-two dozen Sandeman 1868, a lovely vintage at just 42s a case. But perhaps that is unfair. Wine in those days had little investment value and 'surplus' meant just that.

The Edwardian era is often regarded as a kind of British *belle epoque*, with large and prosperous gentlemen strolling into St James's Clubs in top hat and tails, puffing fat cigars and quaffing draughts of champagne. In fact since the 1880s and lasting until the First War, there had been a long period of economic depression and accompanying it, deflation. So while wine was commonly regarded as a rich man's drink and exclusive, it was remarkably cheap and it is somewhat surprising that there were such large and frequent dispersals of liquor from both Club and private cellars. The fact is that until after the First War little was consumed and indeed auction prices look dismal in this period. There was certainly no investment value in wine. For example five thousand dozen sherry accumulated in the cellars of the Royal palaces since the death of Prince Albert in 1863, none younger than 1890, and sold in 1901 fetched an average of £3 a dozen. This proved such a blow to the fashion conscious that sherry went into decline for thirty years and the age of the cocktail was born. That champagne and brandy became such stalwarts of Club drinking was due to complete lack of interest in burgundy and hock and the run of dreadful claret vintages between 1880 and 1919. Apart from the fabulous 1899 and 1900, only 1893 and 1896 were of any note. Luckily the stocks of great pre-phylloxera vintages still available would have satisfied the rather few connoisseurs around. Indeed magnums of 1870 Lafite, from a cold Scottish cellar (Glamis), were deemed 'now perfect for drinking' a century later.

The twenties tried hard to make up for the failures of the previous forty years, but the five really good vintages, culminating in another pair of greats, 1928 and 1929 could barely compensate for the dire thirties. The only decent claret vintage was 1934 and it seemed as if the gloom of the Depression had settled everywhere. But a few bright lights shone out in Burgundy and the lovely 1934s and 35s and perhaps, just, the 37s before war broke out, were shipped to Britain. At that time much would have been shipped in barrel, bottled by a myriad UK Merchants and supplied to London Clubs

The war years must have placed quite a strain on the Club's stocks. That we survived the stick of incendiaries that fell along King Street, a few yards away, must have been a relief to those returning on leave and to the older members still regularly using the Club. When post-war austerity was over in the early fifties, wine buying for the Club would have

Opposite: Traditional wine bins in the basement cellar

Decanter and tumbler made for members

settled into the pattern that remained largely unaltered until the big step forward when we started buying *en primeur* claret in 1998. The tradition for thirty years after the war (and indeed, before) was for wine merchants to buy their stocks following the vintage and then hold them for assessment until they could confidently advise their customers. Up until 1975 importation in bulk, either in cask or tank, was quite usual, even for classed-growth clarets. After all, our merchants were pretty good at it, bottling all year round in their bonded warehouses. However the 1975 port vintage and likewise claret, was universally bottled at source. And so it has remained.

With no recorded knowledge of what was in Boodle's cellars in our first two hundred years, first in Pall Mall, a little later on in St James's Street, it has only been possible to speculate. There is evidence that the volume of individual wines far outweighed their variety and fortified far outweighed table wines. It seems that wine, much of which was high strength, was considered a beverage to accom-

pany food and neither the name nor the vintage seemed to matter much. The alcoholic effect of all that port, madeira and sherry would have been mitigated by the prodigious amount of food that was consumed. A great cellar was an asset not an investment. Through discrimination tax was a far more potent part of the price than it is today, and in any case a very limited percentage of the population would ever have tasted wine.

How different it all is today. With the splendid 1982 claret vintage, the influential American Robert Parker, rhapsodising on its soft and forward tannins, helped to promote the attractions of early consumption and the surge of *en primeur* buying. Boodle's cellars now contain more than 180 different clarets with an average of fifteen dozen of each, excluding the club claret. A mere fifteen hundred bottles of fortified wines are consumed annually, just 6.5 per cent of the total. Champagne, rhone, red and white burgundy are consistently (in context) in demand and for whatever reason, the catholic range of 'other' wines is consistently ignored.

If one accepts that the consistency of Boodle's members' drinking habits motivates the actions of the Wine Committee, then it follows that it has not been too difficult to take advantage of the three driving forces that have prevailed over the past fifteen years. They are intertwined and serendipitous. First, the ability of modern wine-makers to make good-to-excellent wine every year. Twenty years since the dreadful 1991. Second, the sheer quality of 'lesser' Bordeaux growths. Coffee Room lists a generation ago would have been bursting with Palmer, Ducru, the Leovilles, Pichon Lalande, Cos d'Estournel and even several vintages of several first-growths. Now we see Potensac, Poyferre, Patache d'Aux, Poumey and Poujeaux, just to mention one alliterative group. Third, price. Wine is finite. Demand is not. The result has been inevitable and prices have soared, recently to new heights for very specific wines. Fortunately some of the bottles under our feet had a certain oriental appeal and Carruades de Lafite, made from the Château's younger vines and Château Duhart-Milon, owned by Lafite have achieved cult status in the Far East on the back of their passion for the *grand vin* label. Selling at prices far above their intrinsic (to us) value, forty cases

of Carruades paid for our entire 350 case purchase of the great 2009 claret vintage and a similar sum from the sale of seventy-five cases of Duhart-Milon has paid for 320 cases of the even greater 2010.

Boodle's is blessed with thirsty and very hospitable members and the need to replace the three hundred cases of fine claret they consume each year is relentless. As mentioned above, this is now easier to achieve than it used to be and our current list contains every year of the last decade, bar 2007, but the oldest wine is 1996.

Looking back to 1984 there was a greater spread of older vintages in the cellar. Plenty of 61s (Latour cost £2.27 per bottle), 66s (Latour now £6.20), 70s (Latour cheaper at £5.76) and no less than thirty wines of the great 1982 (Lafite, £24.80 per bottle). From this bedrock of great wines of great vintages, carefully set aside over the years, came the prize list for a great Boodle's innovation in Clubland, the triennial Wine Lottery, first held in 1983. The happy coincidence of Boodle's members' appetite for a flutter, a superb dinner, great wines to drink and general conviviality guaranteed the success of the 1983 event and the nine subsequent reprises. May it continue, as the funds generated help fill the cellar and the continuing maintenance of our splendid eighteenth-century mansion.

Hilaire Belloc in 'Heretics All' had some apt words as closure:

> Catholic men that live upon wine
> Are deep in the water, and frank and fine
> Wherever I travel I find it so
> Benedicamus Domino

The Committee Room in Almack's Assembly Rooms showing the seven patronesses discussing membership applications

CHAPTER 10

A Ladies' Boodle's in the Eighteenth Century

DANIELLA BEN-ARIE

On 12 May 1770 Elizabeth Harris, writing from the family house in Salisbury, composed a letter to her son, James, the future Earl of Malmesbury, then a young diplomat based at the Spanish court. Filling him in on the news from home she went on to describe a 'new assembly' that had been 'set up at Boodle's'. The Club's *raison d'être*, she wrote, was to 'meet every morning, either to play cards, chat, or do whatever else they please.'

Mrs Harris opined that this was 'a most ingenious thought, for no one yet ever hit on a scheme that should occupy the fine people all the day, without inflicting on them the torment of being, some part of their time, in their own houses. The first meeting was Thursday, and probably you will have a more accurate account from some of your correspondents who are in town, but if that should not be the case, I did not think it proper you should remain in ignorance of so fashionable a thing.'

The exact location of this newly established club had in fact been variously assigned. While Mrs Harris specifically mentioned that members met at Boodle's, then in Pall Mall, Horace Walpole told his friend George Montagu that this 'new Institution that begins to make, and if it proceeds, will make a considerable noise. It is a club of *both* sexes to be erected at Almack's, on the model of that of the men of White's'.

In addition, Frances Evelyn Boscawen, known as Fanny (1719–1805), and the great niece of the diarist John Evelyn, wrote to Mary Delany that 'The *female club* I told you of is removed from their quarters, Lady Pembroke objecting to a tavern; it meets, therefore, for the present at certain rooms of Almack's, who for another year is to provide a private house. It is much the subject of conversation'.

This confusion may have been related to the close relationships that the clubs then had. Boodle's had been operating from its Pall Mall premises for approximately eight years, by the time that this 'new assembly' was formed in 1770. As has been discussed elsewhere regarding the early history of Boodle's, William Almack opened a tavern at 49 Pall Mall in 1759. By 1762 he acquired the lease for number 50 right next door and straight away established a club or 'society' which by 1764 had split itself into two distinct entities: Boodle's, and Almack's (the latter club would become Brooks's). Boodle's club, under the management of Edward Boodle, remained at 50 Pall Mall and Almack's took over the Tavern's premises at number 49.

To further complicate matters, in 1765 William Almack founded Almack's Assembly Rooms in King Street, just around the corner from the Pall Mall clubs. These Rooms, it was decided, would be run by seven ladies each of whom had their own 'Subscription Book . . . to contain the Names of 60 Subscribers'. This became known as the 'Ladies Club'. It was into this mix of Boodle's at 50 Pall Mall, Almack's at the former tavern at number 49 and Almack's Assembly Rooms on King Street that the 'new assembly' was launched. Despite being widely referred to as a 'female club' it would be open to both sexes.

Whether at 49 or 50 Pall Mall, this new club was apparently also referred to as Lloyd's Coffee-Room after the 'sole-inventor' Rachel Lloyd (1722–1803), who was then a Housekeeper at Kensington Palace. Lloyd had spent considerable time travelling in the company of Elizabeth Herbert, Countess of Pembroke and Montgomery (1737–1831), and her irascible husband, Henry Herbert, the 10th Earl.

In Paris, Lloyd was 'not admitted into all the Company

where Ly Pembroke went' as she was considered a common 'Consierge' or, as her friend Mary Coke put it, 'an Office so low in France that She cou'd not be received at the Palais Royal, nor in any of the houses of the Princes of the Blood'. Used to being treated with greater deference, this was clearly of 'great mortification to her'. In any event, it appears as though she was not so constrained back in London. Her mastery of cards, particularly the game of Loo (which she played in her apartment at the Palace) was well-known. Other founding members included Lloyd's good friend Elizabeth Herbert, who was described by Walpole as having the 'face of a Madonna'. Many years later, during George III's period of madness, it was to her whom he thought he was married.

They were assisted in the endeavour by Anne Warren, later Lady Southampton (then known as Mrs Fitzroy) about whom it was rumoured that George III had fathered one of her sons; Mrs Meynell, probably the Anne Boothby Skrymsher who married the politician Hugo Meynell; and Lady Molyneux, probably the Isabella Stanhope who married Charles William Molyneux, 1st Earl of Sefton in 1768. Walpole, who as a member of this club, observed that 'I am ashamed to say I am of so young and fashionable a society; but as they are people I live with, I choose to be idle rather than morose. I can go to a young supper, without forgetting how much sand is run out of the hour-glass'.

Miss Lloyd's new club was indisputably the subject of much fascination and discussion. One contributor to a contemporary magazine decided to 'confine my observations to those adventurous and spirited females, who seem resolved to break through the whalebone and buckram fences of modesty and decorum, and would no more endure starch in their manners than in a pair of laced ruffles. A certain masculine air now distinguished the ladies; and if you see a female enter a public place with a bold *knock-me-down* freedom, set her down for a person of quality.' As the author explained, these ladies 'have arrogated the old Salic laws of libertinism, and openly set up a tavern in protest rivalry of Boodle's, Arthur's, and Almack's.'

Satirical prints of the 'Female Coterie' also made the rounds, illustrating the 'fashionable club, instituted at a polite part of town, for the reception of ladies as well as gentlemen'. Members are shown drinking and playing cards; one arrives carrying his mortgage (for surety presumably). On these occasions, as one commentator sardonically suggested, 'a lady may soon perhaps intrigue, and game, and swear, and drink, and smoak tobacco, more openly then her husband does at present'.

Taking the gentlemen's clubs (whether it be Boodle's, Almack's or White's) as their model, the founding members set out a series rules that established how the Club would be run. These 'Authentic Rules of the Female Coterie' were published in *The Gentleman's Magazine* in September 1770, and included:

Rule II. That the ladies shall ballot for men, and the men for ladies.

Rule XI. That dinner be upon the table at half after 4 o'clock exactly, and that every member present pay 8 shillings, exclusive of the wine, which the men are to pay.

Rule XIII. That supper be upon the table at 11 o'clock exactly, and that every member present shall pay ___ shillings, exclusive of the wine, which the men are to pay.

Rule XIV. The name of each candidate proposed, shall be placed and remain over the chimney in the eating room, at least a week before he or she is balloted for.

Rule XXI. No play in the eating room, on penalty of paying the whole bill.

Rule XXIV. That no supper be allowed in the card room.

Those individuals who were omitted from joining the club generated as much gossip as those who were admitted. Mrs Harris wrote that 'my intelligence is that the Duchess of Bedford and Lord March have been black-balled; this I cannot account for.' Lady Gertrude Leveson-Gower, Duchess of Bedford (c.1718–94), who was the formidable and politically active second wife of John Russell, 4th Duke of Bedford was (unsurprisingly) ultimately asked to join.

The exclusion of Lord March, bon-vivant extraordinaire (and whose title was normally preceded by 'the notorious') remained firm. March is better known as William Douglas, 4th Duke of Queensberry (1725–1810) and was considered

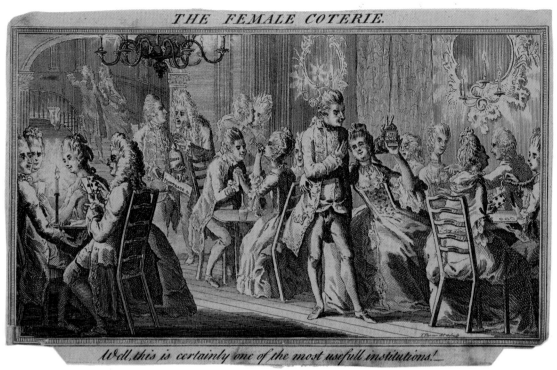

THE FEMALE COTERIE.

Well, this is certainly one of the most usefull institutions!—

This print of 1770 by Thomas Bonner portrays an evening scene of ladies playing cards. Miss Lloyd's club, modelled on Boodle's, had just such a card room

'the most fashionable, most dissipated young man in London, the leading character at Newmarket, the support of the gaming table, the supreme dictator of the Opera-house, the pattern whose dress and equipage were to be copied by all who aimed at distinction and . . . the person most universally admired by the ladies'. According to Fanny Boscawen 'Lord March, Mr Boothby, and one or two more who think themselves pretty gentlemen *du premier ordre*, but it is plain the ladies are not of their opinion.'

Rejected too was the noted beauty Lady Harrington, presumably Lady Caroline Fitzroy (1722–84), married to William Stanhope, 2nd Earl of Harrington (1719–79). Others, such as the Duchess of Beaufort, presumably Elizabeth, wife of the 5th Duke, and also daughter of the aforementioned Frances Boscawen, declined membership 'as her health never permits her to sup abroad'.

By September 1770 membership was around one hundred and thirty people. Rule eight stipulated that 'upon any lady's becoming a member of this club, her husband shall become a member of course' and so membership included

five dukes and four duchesses: the Richmonds, Marlboroughs, Buccleuchs, Bedfords, and William Cavendish, 5th Duke of Devonshire who was not yet married to Lady Georgiana Spencer. Rule twelve stated that foreign members were accepted but not 'allowed to pay an annual subscription'. A group of French members included Messieurs and Mesdames de Masseran, du Chatalet and Messieurs de Meniliet, de Lauvagne, Francois and Madame de Villegagnon.

Perhaps, unsurprisingly, much of what was published contemporaneously about this club had a gossipy, jeering, and mostly mocking tone. Having started in a tavern, then moved into the premises of a men's-only club, Lloyd's finally settled in a house in Arlington Street where its original founders – Miss Lloyd, Mrs Fitzroy and Lady Pembroke – remained on the managing committee. Unlike the gentlemen's clubs of Boodle's, Almack's and White's this 'so fashionable a thing' did not stand the test of time. In 1777, the year after James, the future Earl of Malmesbury had completed his diplomatic service and returned home, this coterie was no more.

'Could the Club Secretary have a word with you m'Lud?'

CHAPTER 11

Miscellany One

DAVID MANN

The Savoir Vivre Club

The Savoir Vivre was founded sometime between 1768 (when they may have organised a masque for the King of Denmark at the Opera House in London) and 1772 at the Star and Garter tavern in Pall Mall. The members' distinctive dress and effete manner led them to being disparagingly referred to as *Maccaroni's*, who wore a 'Uniform of scarlet Cloth, with Velvet Collar and Sleeves of Bleu Celeste'.

In 1774 Horace Walpole wrote to Lady Ossory: 'Methinks an Aesop's fable you relate, as Dryden says in *The Hind and Panther*. A mouse that wraps itself in a French cloak and sleeps on a couch; and a goldfinch that taps at the window and swears it will come in to quadrille at eleven o'clock at night! no, no, these are none of Aesop's cattle; they are too fashionable to have lived so near the creation. The mouse is neither Country Mouse, nor City Mouse; and whatever else he may be, the goldfinch must be a Maccaroni, or at least of the scavoir vivre.'

The Club moved to new premises in March 1776. It was one of the great events of the year. Mrs Hannah More described it as a 'most magnificent hotel in St James's-street was opened last night for the first time, by the name of the 'Scavoir Vivre'; none but people of the very first rank were there, so you may conclude the diversion was cards; and in one night, the very first time the rooms were ever used, the enormous sum of sixty thousand pounds was lost. Heaven reform us!'

The actor and dramatist David Garrick, writing from his home in the Adelphi Terrace wrote of his membership: 'I receive Every honour that a Man can do from all Sorts of people, & I was yesterday enroll'd a member among the first & greatest people in this Kingdom – We have a New house built in the best Taste in ye middle of St James's Street, & it is furnish'd like a palace – Each Member pays 12 Guineas at Entrance – It is ye first Society for titles & property in the known world – I need not tell You that with all this & 14 Dukes at the head of us, that I never was duller in all my Life.'

That same month, on 28 March 1776, Christie's offered for sale the freehold of the old premises 'late in the occupation of the Scavoir Vivre Club' situated on the opposite side of St James's Street.

One of the founders and possible financer of the Savoir Vivre was General Richard Smith. The son of a retail cheesemonger in St James's Market, he went to India, where he 'shook the pagoda tree' and returned with a fortune estimated at £200,000 to £300,000. Described by Horace Walpole as 'the deepest of all deep gamesters'; the man who set up this new Club having been 'excluded from the fashionable young club of men of quality at Almack's, and wishing to plunder them like the Indies, he and a set of sharpers had formed a plan for a new club, which, by the excess of play, should draw all the young extravagants thither. They built a magnificent house in St James's Street, furnished it gorgeously, and enrolled both the clubs at White's, and that of Almack's. The titular master of the house the first night acquainted the richest and most wasteful of the members that they might be furnished in the house with loans of ready money, even as far as forty thousand pounds.'

In 1774 Smith was convicted of extensive bribery in the Hindon bye-election and sentenced to a year in the King's Bench prison. On 4 June 1779 Smith, the 'nabob of nabobs', was elected to Brooks's where he and his son were notorious at the gambling tables.

Little is also known about the members of the Savoir Vivre. John Wilkes was unanimously elected an honorary member. Edward Smith Stanley, 12th Earl of Derby informed his uncle, General John Burgoyne, of this, who

Members of the Savoir Vivre wore a scarlet coat with contrasting azure-blue cuffs and collar as shown in this 1772 print, one of a series of *Macaronies, Characters, Caricatures...* published by Matthew Darly

remonstrated with him on the glaring impropriety of electing a man so obnoxious to the Court. Lord Derby moved for Wilkes's exclusion from the Club.

Richard Fenton, minor poet in the circles of Samuel Johnson and later Welsh antiquarian, wrote an *Ode addressed to the Savoir Vivre Club* dated 1772:

> Th'exclusive right to 'Know to live'
> Think ye from birth that ye derive?'
> and Call you 'To live?' to yawn supine,
> To quench fair reason's light in wine;
> To waste inglorious in the harlot's bed
> The prime of youth, till health be drained.

Another member was Lord Thomas Lyttelton, known as 'Black Tom' whose drunken brawl over some actress was just one more event in a life marked by fighting, imprisonment and affairs, the last of which was immortalised in *The Vauxhall Affray or the Macaronis Defeated* in 1773. That same year a satirical account of a conversation between a 'Country Gentleman' and the 'Savoir Vivre' appeared in John Cooke's *Macaroni Jester, and Pantheon of Wit* showing just how the members were perceived:

Country Gentleman: Pray Sir, may I presume to know who and what you are?

Savoir Vivre: Me! Sir! Why, Sir, I am, what in Polite Life is called a *Savoir Vivre*; Being very different from a *Bon Vivant*.

CG: Savoir Vivre, I do not understand your Gibberish; if you will speak English, I will talk to you. What do you mean by your Savoir Vivre?

SV: Oh! Sir, it is easily explained. I am upon the *Bon Ton*; entirely upon the *Bon Ton*.

CG: This is explaining a Riddle with a Mystery. I know no more of your *Bon Ton* than I do of your *Savoir Vivre*.

SV: Why, Sir, the Bon Ton is easily defined. It is *Taste*, it is *Elegance*.

It is evident that the Club's reputation was shaped by its members most dissolute behaviour: 'the leading plan of the Scavoir Vivre was intended to patronise men of genius and talent; whereas it soon became notorious as an institution tolerating every species of licentiousness and debauchery'. A nineteenth-century publication tartly notes that 'the savoir vivre was probably dropt because the members were conscious that their vivre was not quite adequate to their savoir'.

The Memorial of Richard Miles

Nicholas Kenney, proprietor of the Savoir Vivre, eventually took on as a partner a Richard Miles. In April 1834, in the throes of bankruptcy and attempting to recoup money owed to him, Miles published The Memorial of Richard Miles, *a remarkable document, transcibed here, whose existence was known, until recently, only from an article quoting from it in* Country Life *in 1916.*

THE
MEMORIAL
OF
RICHARD MILES,
PROPRIETOR OR CONDUCTOR
OF ONE OF THE
PRINCIPAL CLUB HOUSES
IN ST. JAMES'S STREET
FOR UPWARDS OF THIRTY YEARS.

THE
MEMORIAL OR NARRATIVE
OF
RICHARD MILES,
CLUB-HOUSE KEEPER OF ST. JAMES'S
STREET FOR UPWARDS OF THIRTY YEARS.

*Addressed to the Noblemen and Gentlemen constituting
the present Clubs held in St. James's Street.*

It will be first necessary to shew, in what manner I attained so distinguished a situation as that which I so long held.

In the year 1773, I entered in St. James's Street under the auspices of Mr. Kenney, an enterprising young man, who was well known to the Members of the Jockey Club in Newmarket as an assistant to Mr. Longchamp, a German, who then conducted it.

At this period, a party of young Gentlemen of the highest rank wanted to form a Club: a house of course was necessary: Mr. Kenney offered them his services, and was accepted. A house was then taken in St. James's Street, and the Club formed under the designation of the SAVOIR VIVRE CLUB. All the members of it wore a uniform; but the Club was more universally known afterwards by their giving a masquerade at the Pantheon in a style and magnificence unknown to preceding times. In the following year this Club gave a REGATTA at Ranelagh House, Chelsea. Most of the Gentlemen went by water *à la Venetienne*, and a most imposing sight it was. But what fairy tale shall outvie in its description the night scene! The Rotunda, brilliantly illuminated, inclosing all the rank, beauty, and fashion of the beau monde: the Ladies, most in masquerade, wore the richest fancy dresses. The Duchess of Devonshire, the mother of his Grace the present Duke, then in the height of beauty and attraction, accompanied by her sister the Lady Duncannon, with other 'loves and graces,' followed by a train of gentlemen! Among the many attentions and compliments paid to her Grace, I recollect seeing one gentleman, as a harlequin, jump over three or four tables, and run and kneel before the Duchess in an attitude of adoration. The supper was the most splendid description, with all costly wines; and well might the songster sing,

O Ranelagh! O Ranelagh! Sweet Elysian scene!
Am I awake, am I awake, or do I only dream?
Or do I only dream, &c.[1]

THE SAVOIR VIVRE CLUB lasted three years only; Mr Kenney's term being expired and the landlord wanting the house for other purposes.

Nearly opposite, in St. James's Street, stood three old and very low houses, which at this time were to be sold. Mr. Kenney, not wanting in enterprise, purchased them, and built on the site a magnificent house which BOODLE'S CLUB now possess. A new Club was formed by managers of high rank. ALMACK'S and WHITE'S were picked, (if I may use the expression,) with others of equal consequence, to amount of about two hundred Members.[2]

The house was furnished in a style beyond and proceeding Club: classical pictures, sofas, chairs covered in satin, &c. &c. And when opened, I will venture to affirm, that no Club ever did, or ever will, flourish as this Club did for some years.

There have been four or five quinze tables going in the room at the same time, with whist and picquet, after which a full hazard table; I have known two at the same time. Two chests, containing in rouleaus 4000 guineas each, was scarce sufficient for the night's circulation.

I have I known a Gentleman[3] winning a hundred thousand guineas in a season; of course heavy losses: the relating of one I cannot omit. A Kentish Baronet[4] in one night lost 11,000 guineas, and brought it to the house the following day: on that night lost he lost 19,500 guineas, the house giving credit to the winners for their respective shares, which sum was *all* paid in about a fortnight.

About this time there were two houses to be disposed of at the corner of the Park Place, and ALMACK'S being almost now deserted, Mr. Brooks, Mr. Almack's partner, was induced to purchase them and on the site to build the house that now goes by his name BROOKS'S. This house being finished and opened, KENNEY'S CLUB went into a gradual decline, and Brooks's took the lead.

'There is a tide in the affairs of men!!'
BOODLE'S CLUB, then held in Pall Mall, increasing, wanted a larger house. Mr. Kenney understanding it, and fearing he should be quite deserted, was induced to offer his house to Mr. Harding, who then conducted Boodle's. The term were at length agreed on, and Mr. Kenney[5] retired into private life. I had now been his partner for three year, and was consequently left to provide for the future.

There was a house to let near St. James's Place, of considerable magnitude, originally White's Chocolate house,[6] (see Tatler.)

This house I became possessed of. It would be tedious and unnecessary to say by what means (after laying out £2000 in its improvement) a Club of the first importance was established, which flourished for near thirty years under my management.

There now occurred an epoch in Clubs of considerable importance, at least to me. At the union of *Great Britain* with *Ireland*, Mr. Gould, a spirited young Irishman, a Gentleman, though of small fortune, knowing the Irish Gentlemen who came to Parliament would have no place wherein to 'Congregate', took Cumberland House in Pall Mall, then empty, and late the residence of his Royal Highness the Duke of Cumberland: but independently of the Irish Gentlemen, Mr. Gould made out a list from the Red Book, the House of Peers, the House of Commons, the Army and Navy list, amounting to nearly five hundred. The first year's Subscription, viz. 10 guineas, was paid in advance into the house of a banker in Pall Mall, so that on the day of opening Mr. Gould had at his command nearly 5000 Guineas. This Club he designated the UNION, and it flourished for some time; but being of so heterogeneous a nature, the subscribers fell off to about one hundred, which was not sufficient to support the establishment of the house. Mr. Gould, aware of this, quitted the concern, and was much to blamed for it, as leaving the Club in the lurch. After this he became

Proprietor or Manager of the Opera House.

The remaining part of the Club, loth to give it up, particularly the Irish Gentlemen, advised Raggett the Head Waiter to take the Duke of Leeds' house in St. James's Square, then empty and to let, and promised him their support.

Now begin my misfortunes. Play was established at this house, and I lost seven or eight hundred pounds per annum by my house, in keeping my establishment on for as many years: for most of my members became members of the 'New Union', and I was quite deserted, which compelled me to issue the following Circular.

MILES'S CLUB HOUSE

St. James's Street, Dec. 26, 1809

SIR,

The task I am obliged to impose upon myself is most mortifying! For, after residence of thirty-eight years in this street—after being a house-keeper thirty years—and after having had the honour of conducting a Club of the first consequence for twenty-eight years—it is with sensations of the most painful regret I am forced to state, that the *total* desertion I have been doomed to experience—the unavoidable expense of an establishment like mine—the increasing pressure of the times—and the *very heavy losses* I have sustained from *unfortunate confidence*—while now almost worn out with most irksome trials and disappointments—compel me (though *most reluctantly*) to respectfully announce to you, the *absolute necessity of dissolving* that which I have ever been proud and happy to recognize under the designation of MILES'S CLUB! I have therefore to beg, with great deference, that you will have the goodness to understand, that *this Club* will be *dissolved* on and after the 31st December instant.

Should my humble yet zealous exertions ever raise me to management of another Club in this House, I can on entreat a renewal of that Patronage which I *formerly* experienced; and I assure you, Sir, individually, and the Club collectively, that every effort on my part shall be used to prove my sincere and lasting gratitude for past obligations.

With every sentiment of respect,
I have the honour to remain,

Sir,
Your old and very faithful humble Servant,
R. Miles.

After the dissolution of the Club, the latter end of the year 1809, I tried to let the house, but could not. On this I continued in the house, and was assisted in the formation of a new Club. I had just brought it to an opening: I newly furnished the house in an expensive manner, and laid in a fresh stock of wines, &c.[7] at this time I was indebted to my banker about £1200. It is true I had been pressed for it, and he having a judgement on my effects, his attorney put an execution in the house, and Mr. Christie sold all off at three days' notice and one day's advertisement. The consequence of this short notice was, that few persons were present, expecting brokers, who played into each other's hands: and thus £2000 of property, consisting of plate, furniture, wines &c. went for half its value; not one shilling of which ever came into my possession. And, to crown all, one of my card makers arrested me as soon as I came down stairs on the morning of the sale, and I was carried by the bailiffs to a spunging-house; so that I was not present at the sale, nor did I enter the house ever afterwards.

I still thought I had something left; an unexpired term in my lease of fifteen years, with valuable fixtures in kitchen, superior to most, laundry, polished stoves, grates, &c. &c.: but, with the expenses attending the sale, landlord, and some taxes, there was hardly sufficient (which was all they wanted) to pay the banker's demand, attorneys, &c. Sorry was I learn that all this went for about £750, which, on the smallest calculation, ought to have fetched double that sum: when its SITUATION is considered, its MAGNITUDE, its CONVENIENCE, and what was laid out to make it so, the Card Room being 31 feet by 27, there was no other in the street *then* to equal it. I am given to understand, that a Club of the first consequence, inferior to none in the street, having given themselves the designation of Arthur's,[8] is now in possession of this house.

Thus ended all my future prospects, and, I need not say, my COMPLETE RUIN!

It may seem strange that I should owe my banker any sum of money, after the prosperous and flourishing state of my Club, and constant play, for so many years. To make my case plain, I must (which *I do most reluctantly*) give a list of the names of the Members who were in my debt at that time.

From the custom of the house advancing money—from too much confidence in delusive promises—from a disposition to oblige—from the unpleasantness of refusing money when called for at the public table—were occasioned the following (and ever will be) debts UNPAID.

An account of monies paid for, or lent to people, the member of Miles's Club, as taken for his Cash Book, this 15th day of April, 1834. [The full account is not included in this extract. It amounted to £11,303 14s.]

Thus went the labour, care and anxiety, day and night, of nearly forty years. This case of misfortune must be allowed to stand unparalleled in the annals of Club-House keeping, or of any mercantile concerns; and to add the the whole, I have two daughters unprovided for, and one of them an invalid.

It may be asked, how have I lived since I have been in the country for twenty-three years? My reply is, I had a small annuity, which I have been obliged to part with under its value; a small patrimonial inheritance, which I was under the necessity of selling in the worst of times, it being land; and some monies, that were owing me, I received.

GENTLEMEN, I have no patron, no advocate to plead my cause, having outlived my old friends: only intreating and trusting the good people of the House will lay this my narrative on your tables; not doubting that some of your philanthropic Members will open a subscription for my use; and so prevent an old Club-House keeper, afflicted with every infirmity incident to old age, from (O dreadful thought!) coming to want.

I have the honour to be,
GENTLEMEN,
With all due respect and deference,
Your devoted servant,
R. MILES.

Harwell, near Abingdon,
April, 1834.

N B Mr. John Gibbons, No.44, Rathbone Place, Oxford Street, is empowered (as well as the Club Houses in St James's Street) to receive any monies on my account.

POSTSCRIPT.

As this Narrative is only meant for the Club Houses in St. James's Street, with two or three exceptions, but few copies are printed off; but should any Gentlemen want one, it may be had of Mr. Graham, Club, bottom of St. James's Street.

[Graham's Club House, 87 St. James's Street]

1 Although there were five managers, it was chiefly under the directions of the Hon Temple Luttrell, the brother of the Duchess of Cumberland. The device of the ticket of admission was Venus Rising from the sea, with other appropriate emblems.

2 After the House was opened there were never less than twenty or thirty Candidates.

3 Colonel Crawford of the Guards, Equerry to the Queens. I hope I may be excused if I relate an anecdote or two of this Gentleman. I have known him win 10,000 guineas in a night, and, which seems almost incredible, for ten night a season, the same sum each night. In the early part of the following season he began to lose heavily: and fearing he would lose all he had won, he tied himself up to a Gentleman, under a forfeiture of 500 guineas, not to lose more than 1000 guineas in one night, which forfeit was paid more than once.

4 Sir Edward Dering

5 Mr Kenney was the father of Mr Kenney, the Dramatic writer, Author of 'Raising the Wind', &c.

6 This house was burnt down; after which the Club removed to the top of the east side of the Street. It was rebuilt about the year 1800.

7 Since writing the above, I have been looking over my expence book, and find I paid for insurance of stock to the Sun Fire Office 6l. 19s. per ann. which will prove to Gentlemen the value of what the house contained.

8 I believe this house was originally known as 'Arthur's Club House,' before it was called 'White's Chocolate House.'

An Extract from Boodles's Betting Book, 1783–1812

1783 Jan 26 Lord Berkeley bets Mr Steele twenty guineas that Sir Jacob Wheate is above forty five years old from this day

1783 Jul 24 Lord Wentworth bets Mr Harvey fifteen guineas to five that no one of the under-mentioned gentlemen die within the year from the above date: Sir Thomas Skipworth, Mr Shaftoe, Lord Wentworth, Mr Curzon, Lord Milsington, Sir John Blois, Sir William Milner, Mr Harvey, Mr James, Lord Stourton, Mr Aston, Mr Thoroton, Mr Adamson, and Mr E Fawkener

1784 Jul 4 Mr Errington bets Sir Thomas Gascoigne one hundred pounds that the Prince of Wales is alive this day seven years with a rump and dozen in the bargain – Sir Thomas bets he is not.

Signed: Errington, Thomas Gascoigne

1785 Apr 2 Lord Milford bets Mr R Wilbraham that Mr Aston is forty four years of age from this date the sum of five guineas

1785 Jul 23 Mr F Fane bets Mr Tate 20 guineas that the market price of hay never at any one day between this and Christmas reaches seven guineas per load in the Hay Market.

NB a damn'd good dinner with plenty of wine into the bargain of which the following gentlemen are certainly to be partakers Vincent Wentworth, Henry Crathorne, T Rous, W Northy and R Wilbraham

1788 Dec 20 Mr Fleming bets Mr G Isted that Mr Steele is of 36 years of age this day. Mr G I per contra. G I the contrary. Rump and dozen

[1789] Sir W Aston bets Mr Fleming one hundred guineas that the King goes to Hanover before the first of January 1790

Signed: Willoughby Aston, John Fleming

[1789] Mr Stephenson bets Sir W Ashton three hundred guineas to one hundred guineas that the Parliament is not dissolved in the month of April 1789

Signed: Willoughby Aston, J Stephenson

1789 Jun 11   Lord Berkeley bets Sir G Paul 5 guineas and a dinner that there are not four people in the following company, viz. Lord Berkeley, Lord Craven, Sir G Paul, Sir John Rous, Mr Shafto, Mr Morant, Mr Churche, Mr Fleming, Mr Kingsman (all of whom are hereby invited to dine) younger than himself

Signed: Berkeley, G O Paul

I name Sir John Rous, Mr Fleming, Mr Kingsman and myself
Signed: G O Paul

Sir Willoughby Aston bets Mr Warre 150gs that Mr Smith's house in Portman Square is nearer by 1000 yards than Mr Warre's House in Queen's Square to Boodle's

Settled. Sir Willoughby lost

1792 Jan 18   Sir Willoughby Aston bets Mr Kingsman five guineas that Lord Eardley went down to Warwick after Lord Gage's death and before the 10th of November with a visible intention to propose his son to succeed Major Gage

Signed: Willoughby Aston, W L Kingsman

Mr Colhoun bets Sir Willoughby Aston 10 guineas that Mr Sheridan and Mr Fox's health were not drank as specified by Mr Burke

1793 Feb 25   Mr Hardy received five guineas of Mr Capel to return two hundred guineas if he plays at the game of Hazard at Boodle's before the 25th February 1795

Signed: J F Capel, Geo Hardy

[1793] Mar 18   Mr Sturt bets Sir W Aston five guineas that Clairfait has been driven back since the last accounts

Sir John Shelley ditto ditto

[1793 Mar]   Mr Sturt bets Mr Crewe ten guineas that the Spanish fleet was not out on the 13th of March 1793

1793 May 4   Mr Macdowall bets Mr Harvey a rump and dozen that the only days in the year for granting licences to victuallers are the first second or third of November by the Justices of any county in England – Mr Harvey – contra
This bet to be determined by the Acts of Parliament granting powers to the Justices to licence victuallers

Signed: William McDowall, Elias Harvey

1793 May 6   Mr Dymoke bets Mr Forester that he does not weigh seven pounds more than he does this day week (being the 13th) one hundred guineas p p off by consent

Signed: Cecil Forester, Lewis Dymoke

1793 Jun 30   Mr S Owen agrees to run his grey horse Helmot by Mambrino against Mr Dymoke's brown gelding Whipcord by Atlas for 100gs each p p the last mile of Lincoln Course the first day of the ensuing races, Helmet to carry 12 st, Whipcord 11st 9lb

Signed: N Smythe Owen, Lewis Dymoke
Off by consent

[1794]   Mr Dymoke bets Sir W Aston 30gns to 10 that Mr Horne Tooke is not hanged before Xmas 1794
Signed: Lewis Dymoke, Willoughby Aston

1794 May 16 Mr R S Milnes bets Sir W Aston 10gs to 5 that Mr Stone is not hanged before he is liberated

Signed: Willoughby Aston, R S Milnes

1795 Feb 14   Mr Forester bets Mr Gurdon 10gs that if Mr Wyndham vacates his seat for Norwich to accept the office of Secretary of State within three months, he will be re-elected

Signed: Cecil Forester, Th Gurdon

1795 Apr 25   Sir Robert Leighton bets Sir Willoughby ten guineas that their Majesties do not come to Boodle's Fete if given at Ranelagh

[1795]   Sir W W Wynne bets Sir W Aston 10gs that either their Majesties and the Prince and Princess come to Boodle's Fete or that neither of them come

[1795]   Sir W W Wynne bets Sir W Aston 10gs on an event they understand and Mr Leicester 5 gs ditto

1795 Nov 3   Mr R Wilbraham has given Sir Watkin Williams Wynne five guineas to receive one hundred guineas whenever Sir W W W shall be made a peer

1795 Nov 15   Sir Francis Molyneux bets fifteen to five with Mr Harrison that the Earl of Lauderdale does not sit as one of the sixteen peers in the next Parliament

1798 Jun2   Mr R Wilbraham has given Sir Henry St John Mildmay five guineas to receive one hundred guineas from him when he shall be made a peer

1800 Apr 22 Mr Henry Howard bets Mr Tyrwhitt ten guineas that Mr Wyndham is not Secretary at War this day two years

1800 Apr 22 Sir John Shelley bets Mr Lamb 25gs to 5 that the divorce Bill does not pass

[1801]   Mr Western bets Mr Colhoun fifty guineas that the supposed change in administration is a juggle
The decision to be made on the ninth of May 1801 by Mr Pierrepont, Mr Howell, Mr James, Mr Henry Howard and Mr Denison

1801 May 21 Mr Dymoke bets Mr Dickens ten guineas that Mr Addington is not Chancellor of the Exchequer and First Lord of the Treasury the first of May 1802
Signed: Lewis Dymoke, F Dickens

1801 Jun 18 Lord Lorne bets Mr Dymoke 50 guineas that peace is proclaimed this day 6 months

1801 Nov 10 Mr Owen Smith bets Mr Dymoke 50gs that Mr Addington retains his situation as Chancellor of the Exchequer and First Lord of the Treasury this time three years if the King so long lives
                Signed: Owen Smythe Owen, Lewis Dymoke
24 Feb 1804 this bet off Mr S Owen being dead

1803 Apr 11 Mr Dymoke bets Lord Milford 5 guineas Mr Pitt is in office this day three months

1803 May 30 Lord Berkeley has given Mr Dymoke one guinea to receive ten if there is a peace within three months from the above date. Also with Mr T Smith from the 10th of June 2gs for 20

1803 Jun 15 Mr R Wilbraham has given Lord Milford 5 guineas to receive one hundred guineas if Sir John Stepney is now past sixty years old

1804 Jun 28 Sir W W Wynn bets Mr Germain and Mr T Smith twenty five guineas each that Mr Pitt is not in office as Prime Minister this day two years. Mr Pitt's decease bars the bet

1806 May 12 Mr Brummell bets Mr Dymoke that there is no dissolution of Parliament in one year from the above date 25 guineas
                Signed: George Brummell. Lewis Dymoke

1807 Jun 4 Mr Vanneck bets Sir G Wombwell 30gs to 10 Lord Milton beats Mr Lascelles at the final close of the present contest for Yorkshire

[1807]   Mr Vanneck bets Mr Legh 6gs to 4 upon the same event

Two faces of a Boodle's one guinea gaming counter

1808 Jul 3   Mr Mildmay bets Mr Dymoke 10gs that Bounaparte's (sic) cause does prevail in Spain this day twelve months if undecided at that period no bet
                Signed: Henry St John Mildmay. Lewis Dymoke

The latter sentence precludes any doubt which might have arisen on the former. I therefore decide this to be no bet
Jan 4th 1812   signed Dudley North

1809 May 5 Sir John Shelley gives Mr Chester one guinea to receive fifty guineas when Mr Chester marries

1810 Jun 26 Mr Brummell bets Sir W W Wynn 20 guineas that Mr Spencer Percival is First Lord of the Treasury on the 20th February next

1810 Feb 18 Lord Limerick bets Mr Silvertoss and Mr H Williams Wynn 25 guineas each that preliminaries of peace are not signed this day two years between England and France

1810 Mar 23 Mr H Williams Wynn received ten guineas from Mr Craven to return sixty if the definitive treaty is signed before this day two years

1810 Apr 29 Mr Goddard bets Mr Brummell one hundred guineas that Mr Brummell is married before him

1810 Jul 29 Mr Brummell bets Mr G Isted eleven guineas there is no Earl of Effingham after the present Earl
                General Grosvenor stands half of Mr G Isted's bet

1811 Jan 30   Mr Daley bet Lord Limerick 50 guineas that His Majesty George the Third is not an acting King on or before the 4th of July next
                Signed: Limerick, D B Daly
                                                Paid L

1811 Feb 1   Mr Blackford bets Mr Silvertoss one hundred guineas that the preliminaries of peace between Great Britain and France are not signed before the 1st of February 1813

Paid

1811 Mar 23   Lord G H Cavendish bets Mr Thornhill 200gs to 100gs that Parliament is not dissolved before this day twelve months

1811 Apr 12   Mr Brummell bets Mr Coleman 50 guineas that he (Mr Colman) is not in Portugal this day three months

Signed: George Brummell, Francis J Coleman

1811 Jul 20   Sir Harry Mildmay bets Mr Henry Pierrepont 60 guineas to 10 that a certain person understood between them does not marry Miss … between this day and this day two years

Signed: Harry St John Mildmay, Henry Pierrepont

1811 Jul 20   Sir H Mildmay bets Mr Brummell fifty guineas that Lord Granville is First Lord of the Treasury against Mr Spencer Percival this day twelve months

Signed: Harry St John Mildmay, George Brummell

1811 Jul 20   Sir H Mildmay bets Mr Brummell 60gs to 50gs that Lord Holland is in administration this day year agst. Mr Canning's being in administration at the same period

Signed: Harry St John Mildmay, George Brummell

1811 Jan 1   Sir Harry Mildmay bets Mr Dymoke five guineas that the commission on sale at Tattersall's is not 5 per cent supposing no alteration to have been made since January 1st 1811

Signed: Harry St John Mildmay, Lewis Dymoke

Paid by Sir Harry

Lord Limerick bets Mr Silvertoss twenty five guineas that Mr Percival is First Lord of the Treasury on the eighteenth of April 1812

1812 May 8   Colonel Cornewall bets Sir Harry Mildmay 25 guineas that the distance from [Burney] Park to Newstead Abbey is not 25 miles

Signed: Harry St John Mildmay, G Cornewall

1812: A lottery for the Derby of 47 subscribers at 5 guineas each to be drawn as soon as completed should there not be sufficient subscribers on Sunday May 10th some of the horses which do not start to be struck out so that there may be as many tickets as there are subscribers

26 Sir W W Wynn	2 Mr Churchill	19 Mr Watson
34 General Milner	22 Mr Goddard	45 Mr Bell
35 Col Vansittart	38 Lord Althorpe	32 Col Cooper
24 Mr Thomas Thornhill	47 Mr B P Blachford	
31 Mr Egerton	7 Mr D Radcliffe	33 Mr Neave
29 Mr Chaloner	17 Sir R Leighton	9 Lord Ducie
13 Mr Arcedeckne	5 Mr T A Smith jun	15 Lord Eardley
44 Lord Gosford	10 Sir Geo Wombwell	8 Mr R James
46 Sir John Shelley	40 Mr Gooch	42 Mr Lambton
23 Mr Thos Darrien	18 Mr R James	21 Mr Wyndham
27 Mr Hy Pierse	4 Mr D B Daly	39 Mr F Lawley
36 Sir W Bellingham	1 Mr Geo Brummell	43 Mr Sneyd
6 Sir C Haggerston	16 Mr Whitmore	31 Mr W Howard
25 Duke of Rutland	11 Mr Edw Davenport	12 Mr Chester
3 Mr Hy Pierrepont	20 Lord Chatham	30 Sir W Milner
14 Mr Edw Wodehouse	28 Mr Thos Heneage	
37 Mr R James		

Won by Col Cooper and settled May 15th 1812

The Trial of John Harvey, otherwise Seagrave
Old Bailey, 10 December 1783

Sir George Onesiphorous Paul, 2nd Bt was having dinner at Boodle's on 25 November 1783 when some of his possessions were stolen from the porter's hall. It is of note that Paul, having been elected in 1770, served on the Management Committee more times than any other member: ten times between 1793 and 1818. His family home was Highgrove House in Gloucestershire, now owned by the Prince of Wales, a patron of the Club. This is an extract from the trial of the accused, John Harvey, who was eventually granted a pardon by His Majesty in 1784 on condition that he would be transported to Africa for seven years.

JOHN HARVEY, otherwise SEAGRAVE, was indicted for feloniously stealing, on the 25th of November last, one gold pin with a diamond set therein value 40l one linen shirt value 10s one pair of leather breeches value 20s one pair of leather boots value 15s one pair of cotton stockings value 3s one woollen cloth dressing gown value 3s one pair of silver knee buckles value 3s the property of Sir George Onesiphorus Paul, Baronet, in the dwelling house of Benjamin Harden [Harding].

JOHN HARDING sworn.
I am butler and valet to Sir George Onesiphorus Paul.

COURT. Does your master live in a house of his own, or does he take lodgings when he comes to town? – He rents a house, and these things were at Mr. Harden's clubhouse, which goes by the name of Boodle's clubhouse, he dined there on the 25th of November, he lost his pin while he was in the house; it was a diamond pin set in gold, a pin he always wore in his bosom when he was dressed; he had it not in his bosom then; he sent there for his things to dress after dinner; he lives in Charles-street, Berkley-square; I carried to Mr. Harden's the things mentioned in the indictment, except the leather breeches and boots, which he changed; he changed the leather breeches for satin ones, and the boots for shoes.

COURT. I suppose these things, exclusive of the pin, are worth more than forty shillings? – Yes, my Lord, for they were almost new; I carried the things to dress my master a little before night, and they were lost between seven and eight; I asked for a room for Sir George to dress in, and I was shown into a room up one pair of stairs, I put the things there, and there he dressed all he did dress; there was fire made on purpose; he only changed the breeches and boots, and the cotton stocking for silk stockings, and put on a clean neckcloth; he was not long dressing himself, and then he went into the room again where he dined: I packed his things up directly after, and put the pin in the coat; I pinned the diamond pin in the coat, and I brought the things all out of that room, and put them into the porter's hall; the boots were dirty, I wrapped them up in paper, and put them inside; I went down the street for some tea, a little lower, which was for my own use; I intended to take the things home myself, I thought I would not take them to the tea warehouse, but call for them as I came back; I was absent about ten minutes, and when I returned, the things were all gone; they were wrapped up in a linen packing-cloth; I immediately enquired after them, and asked the waiter; there is an outward door and a door within that door; all the family of the Hardens lay in the house; when I missed them I immediately informed Sir George. I have seen part of the things since. I first heard of them on the 28th of November; I was at Sir George's own house, and there came a man from the Office in Bow-street, and informed us of them; I do not know his name.

JOHN ATKINS sworn.
I belong to Bow-street; I believe there were hand-bills of these things of Sir George Paul's; I first heard of them on the 28th; when I came to the Brown Bear in Bow-street, I had been home with some prisoners, and I found the prisoner in custody, he was stopped about a pin, we sent to let Sir George know.

COURT. How came you to think of Sir George? – Because the pin answered the description of Sir George's; I took him back and searched him, and he had a ruffled shirt on, and it was marked O.P. No. 14, the same that was in the advertisement; I found nothing else upon him.

COURT to Harding. Look at that shirt. – This is my master's shirt, I marked it myself, I have another of the same set in my pocket.

Can you recollect whether it was the shirt you carried that day to Boodle's? – Yes, I carried it clean, that mark will not wear out.

Mr. Shepherd, Prisoner's Council. As to this pin you pinned in that coat. – Yes, I put the pin in the coat again.

The porter's hall, I believe, is at the entrance of the house? – Yes, there is a door which goes with a spring, any body may open it on the outside.

Was there any porter in the hall when you left it? – There was not.

There are a vast number of waiters and servants in this house? – A good many.

WILLIAM BERRY sworn.

I am a waiter at Boodle's, I know Sir George's servant Mr. Harding, I remember his leaving some things at the Porter's Lodge on Tuesday the 25th of November, I saw the bundle there in the Porter's Lodge, and I saw the servant coming down stairs, as I was coming up stairs, I saw them there about four or five minutes after Harding went away.

COURT. Did you see the prisoner there? – No: there is a little room above the Porter's Lodge for the gentlemen to dress in, the bundle was left behind the door, there is an outside door towards the street which is always open, then there is about that goes into the Porter's room, and generally it shuts of itself.

PATRICK MACMANUS sworn.

I took the prisoner at Mr. Heather's, he said, he had the shirt of one Paterson, who lived at No. 7, Charles Court, in the Strand, and that he took it for seven shillings and sixpence, I went to enquire, and there was such a man lived there near four years back; then he was pressed very hard to know where he lodged, he did not like to tell his lodgings, at last he said at Ratcliffe Cross; I took the directions, I went there the same night, and no such man ever lodged at the place, nor they did not know such a man: Harding went with me, I

think the shirt was tore in struggling to get away from Mr. Heather, and Clarke, and me, in Broad-court.

COURT. Did he endeavour to get away? – Yes.

Prisoner's Council to Harding. Had you examined the shirt before that time? – No, Sir.
Then you do not know it was torn before? – No, I do not.

COURT to Atkins. What account did he give of this shirt? – I took the shirt off his back and I saw it answered; I said to him this will affect you, and he said you need not take it over the way.

COURT to Prisoner. Have you any witnesses to your character? – No.

VERDICT: Guilty

SENTENCE: Death.

Tried by the first Middlesex Jury before Mr Justice WILLES.

An ink stand on one of the Club's desks

Fracas at Boodle's Club in 1863

On Saturday, 3 January 1863, a court-case regarding a 'Fracas at Boodle's Club' was recorded in The Standard. *It describes an encounter between a member, John Calvert Wombwell (1852), who accused William Gainer of assault. Little is known about Wombwell (1821–90) except that he worked as an attaché, unpaid and paid, at the British Embassy in St Petersburg from 1838 to 1851, and the following year was elected a member of Boodle's. In November 1854 he took a five guinea bet with Charles B. Ford (1846) that is recorded in the Club's betting book: 'that Cronstadt (in the Gulf of Finland) is taken or destroyed by the Allies before the end of 1855, provided the present war last up to that period.' (He presumably knew the Baltic island from his time as an attaché in St Petersburg.)*

Wombwell was also well known as a collector of Old Masters paintings, and amassed a fine selection of 'the highest class', possibly during his foreign postings. On 4 June 1850, a collection of pictures from 'a distinguished continental gallery' was sold by Phillips, London. The consignor was not named but the catalogue was later annotated with Wombwell's name. His collection must have been fairly large as even after this sale he had (according to the renowned German art historian Gustave Waagen who was visiting London) examples from the 'Netherlandish Schools; . . . some good specimens of the Italian, French, German, and English Schools are also here'. The collection included Rembrandt's Lucretia, now in Minneapolis, and a Ruisdael landscape in The Frick Collection, New York. Wombwell's estate was valued at £2,839 (present-day value £242,000). His executor was his nephew Sir Henry Herbert Wombwell, 5th Bt, a well-known member of Boodle's. The remainder of John Calvert Wombwell's collection was dispersed in a posthumous sale held by Christie's on 28 February 1891.

William Gainer, manager of Boodle's Club, was summoned before Mr Knox, at Marlborough Street, accused of an assault on Wombwell. Mr Sleigh was acting for the complainant, and Mr Edward Lewis for the defendant.

Mr Knox suggested that the matter be settled in Boodle's 'by the committee or by such machinery as the club was regulated by.' Mr Sleigh explained that the committee 'had excluded Mr Wombwell because he was, as alleged, a defaulter in his subscriptions', which he denied, but that 'the committee insisted on considering him in that light, and if the matter was again referred to them they would adhere to their original decision.' The defense argued that Wombwell was properly excluded. Mr Knox voiced his concern at the precedent of 'letting in magistrates as arbitrators in private questions'.

Mr Sleigh's case was as follows: 'The whole point turned on the construction of the revised rules of 1857, one of which provided that the subscription to the house should be eleven guineas per annum; that if the subscription was not paid by May the name should be put on a board; if not by October a letter was to be sent to the member; if still unpaid the following January the name was to be placed in the morning room; and finally, if not paid before May following, the member was considered to have ceased to belong to the Club.

Now, Mr Wombwell had been elected in 1852, and had paid his subscriptions himself or by Mr Gainer, the manager, up to 1858. A current account was established between Mr Wombwell and Mr Gainer, and Mr Gainer eventually got a judgment for £101, against Mr Wombwell, one item being for his subscription for 1858.

In 1859, and before May, 1860, Mr Wombwell sent a gentleman to pay his subscription. He was told by Mr Gainer that the money could not be received, and that Mr Wombwell was no longer a member. Mr Wombwell went to the Club on Christmas-day, and by Mr Gainer's orders to the servants was forcibly excluded. This was the assault complained of.'

Mr Knox remarked that 'two questions presented themselves. The first was the question of title. It would be pleaded that Mr Wombwell was there in the assertion of his right and title. The next point would be as to the admissibility of the rules. Now, he did not see how he could receive the rules as evidence.' He adjourned the case for one week.

Dispute between Gainer and Members in 1880

Boodle's was founded as a Club, as it still is, of members used to running their own affairs. This was carried forward to the formation in 1856 of the Hunt Committee of the Club for regulating hunting – the MFH Committee, which was the predecessor of the Master of Foxhounds Association and whose main function was resolving disputes about territories of the hunts. What is not clear are the circumstances under which the MFH Committee was dissolved.

Charles Dickens Jr wrote of Boodle's that 'the serious differences of opinions between the members and the proprietor of Boodle's which have recently occurred would seem to make it doubtful whether the Club will long continue to exist in its present form.' According to Roger Fulford, the dispute was over members having to share equally the cost of wine at dinners regardless of how much they had drunk.

The effect of this dispute was the resignation of Henry Somerset, 8th Duke of Beaufort and other members, and a demand from the MFH Committee dated 5 August 1880 that all documents and papers be delivered to John Poynz Spencer, 5th Earl. It may even have been that Gainer's legal background made him concerned about liability because he retained a full manuscript record of the judgments of the MFH sub-committee after the papers were delivered to Earl Spencer. A note in the Club book attests to the change in rules.

Newspaper reports of the meeting held on 18 May 1880 point to a different aspect of the dispute, which was essentially between the members and the arrogance of the proprietor, William Charles Gainer. An excerpt from the 19 May 1880 edition of The Times *appears below:*

Yesterday a meeting of the old members of Boodle's Club was held at Willis's Rooms, St James to consider the steps recently taken by the owner of the house in which the Club is held, whereby it is alleged he has arrogated to himself as the proprietor the right to make laws and regulations, which shall be binding on the members. Among those present were the Duke of Norfolk, the Duke of Rutland, Lord Sefton, Lord Redesdale, Lord Castlereagh, Lord Henry Vane Tempest, Lord Lascelles, Sir William Lethbridge, Sir Hugh Cholmondeley, Mr Brassey MP, Captain Gooch, Colonel Clithero, Captain Phelps, General Price, Mr Portman, Mr Allsopp, Mr Clowes, Mr Gray, Sir Thomas Munroe, Mr R Herbert, Mr Barnett, Mr Bateson, the Hon James Duncan, the Right Hon James Lowther.

Lord Redesdale, who occupied the chair in the temporary absence of the Duke of Norfolk, said that about two years ago the managers of the club tried to make some new rules under which certain things might be done without the consent of the membership of the club being given. The rules of the club set forth distinctly that no new rule could be carried unless two thirds of the members in attendance sanctioned it.

In November last the members received notice from Mr Gainer, who held possession of the club-house, stating that he intended to introduce an entirely new set of rules, which would be submitted to the club, and those members who chose not to accept these rules or abide by them were to be refused admission to the building. Many members objected to having the club subjected to rules so made by the owner of the house; and in consequence many of them have been deprived of the benefits and comforts of the club.

Up to the present Mr Gainer was deaf to all applications made to him for concessions. Under his new rules there was no power to any member to call a meeting of the club, or to propose any alteration in the club rules unless it came from the managers with his sanction. His Lordship thought that no one present would assent to the principle that the owner of the house should make rules to govern the members. Such a thing was contrary to every principle on which clubs were based. [Hear! Hear!]

Mr Lowther explained at length the course which the committee of the club had adopted in order to avert the dissolution of the club. He condemned the course taken by the proprietor as wholly unacceptable to the members and urged, amid applause, that the club should be broken up rather than the new tyrannical element introduced should be submitted to.

The Duke of Norfolk who had just arrived condemned in strong terms the conduct of Mr Gainer and announced that he had withdrawn his name from the club – an example that had been followed by many others and would at once be followed by more. The meaning of the whole of Mr Gainer's conduct was that he and his managers could carry any rule they pleased against the majority of the club [Hear! Hear!]. His Grace said he had done all he could to bring about a settlement, but without avail. He was, he confessed, loath to leave the club of which he had been a member since he was 17 years old, but he did not feel inclined to pay 20 guineas a year for the privilege of writing a letter and dining at Mr Gainer's café and restaurant [Hear! Hear! And laughter]. He certainly shouldn't go back to Boodle's under the present system, and the question was, what was the best thing to do? They had during the last few years made Boodle's a sort of national institution, by making it the club for all masters of foxhounds throughout the country. He thought the meeting ought to appoint some five or six gentlemen to act as a committee in the present emergency [Hear! Hear!].

The Chairman read the following resolution which was put, and carried, *nem con*:

'From the first establishment of Boodle's, one of the oldest clubs in London, and in all similar institutions, the adoption of new and the alteration of old rules have been exclusively under the control of the members, and the claim set up by Mr Gainer, that the owner of the house in which the club meets may make what rules for it he pleases and turn out all members who do not choose to accept them, is one which it is the duty of all members to resist, not only on their own account, but on that of the members of all similar institutions.'

The 4th Earl of Sefton seconded the resolution, and added that he was quite prepared to allow his name and subscription to lapse from the Club if the terms proposed in the resolution were not accepted by Mr Gainer. On the proposal of Mr Herbert a deputation was appointed to wait on Mr Gainer, to formally announce the definite resolutions of the members of the Club, and the meeting formally adjourned to receive the report of the result of the interview.

Evenings at Boodle's

January 14th [1766] – Lord Dunmore [Committee Member 1762] breakfasted here, and went afterwards with Lord Shelburne to the new house in Berkeley Square, and from thence to the House of Lords, the Parliament meeting to-day. Lady Louisa Manners came to us, and Mr Ehret to me, with whom I begun the Chinese plants that blew at Bowood this summer. Mr Sulivan, Lady Louisa, and I dined alone, the House of Lords sitting late, and Lord Shelburne going after-wards to the House of Commons, where Mr Pitt spoke on the repeal of the Stamp Act in America. The Duchess of Bolton, Miss Finches, and Miss Lowther, drank tea here, and Lady Louisa and I were gone to our rooms just as Lord Shelburne returned from Boodle's, where he supped.

Edward Morant, a Jamaican plantation owner, offers one of the rare examples of someone recording his evening at Boodle's. He was a thoroughly independent MP, a cousin of Henry Dawkins (1763) and Richard Pennant (1781?). He did not much attend the House much 1762–74; but did so more after 1774 and still more in the 1780s. His diaries record divisions in the House, and social engagements among other things, including his political results, about which he appears quite insouciant: 3 April 1784: 'Dined at home. Opera and Boodle's. Lost 2 rubbers, 39 guineas. Chose at Yarmouth.' 4 April 1787: 'Dined at home . . . Boodle's. Vacated my seat in Parliament. Easterly wind.'

'I can't wait for the General to get to page three!'

The Royal Family at Boodle's

In 1790, the Prince of Wales, later Prince Regent and then George IV, became a member of Boodle's. HRH Prince of Wales, later Edward VII, was a member of White's, and when prevented from smoking there, formed his own club in Pall Mall, The Marlborough Club, for which he personally vetted the members.

In the decade 1890 to 1900, the Royal Yacht Squadron held their annual meeting in May in London in the drawing room of Boodle's, where HRH the Prince of Wales, Commodore of the Squadron, presided each year. Particularly interesting was the meeting in 1891 when the Prince's cousin, His Imperial Majesty the German Emperor and King of Prussia was elected. This qualified his cutter *Meteor* to compete for Her Majesty's Cup at the Squadron Regatta in August at Cowes.

In May 1921 the Prince of Wales, later Edward VIII, accepted an invitation to honorary membership. Each year he sent a contribution to the staff Christmas fund and in November 1932 attended a dinner to mark the 170th anniversary of Boodle's: 'how honoured both the members and the staff many of whom have been recruited from South Wales would be to see His Royal Highness amongst us'. Upon accession in January 1936, King Edward VIII became Patron of the Club rather than an honorary member. After his abdication in December 1936, came the third change in status in twelve months, and as HRH the Duke of Windsor he was made an Honorary Member until his death in 1972.

At present HRH The Prince Philip, Duke of Edinburgh has been Patron since the death of HM King George VI in 1952. HRH Prince Charles, Prince of Wales has been an Honorary Member since 1975.

Opposite: The Morning Room

ST JAMES'S STREET. 1931

A view of St James's Street showing Boodle's sandwiched between Edwardian Baroque neighbours intended to match the scale of Piccadilly

CHAPTER 12

Miscellany Two

DAVID MANN

What follows is a selection of poems and prose from the last 250 years, in which the Club has been mentioned.

Charles Dibdin, *Patrick Mulrooney*, 1780

Is't my story you'd know? – I was Patrick Mulrooney,
A jolman, and Ireland my nations
To be sure, I was not a tight fellow, too, honey,
Before my transmogrification.
I did not at all talk of flames and of darts,
To conquer the fair, – the dear jewels!
And wid husbands, because why? – I won their wives
    hearts, –
I did not fight plenty of duels.
Then arrah, bodder how you can,
You'll ne'er persuade me, honey,
For I shall always, bull or man,
Be Patrick Mulrooney.

When at Almack's, or White's, or at Brookes' or Boodle's
I've sat up all night in the morning,
'mongst black legs, and coggers, and pigeons and noodles,
The calling to which I was born in:
To be sure, many honest gold guineas it yields;
But, since 'tis a service of danger,
I'm a better man now I'm a bull in the fields,
To popping and tilting a stranger,
Then arrah, &c.

Tim Tartlet, *A Rainy Sunday*, 1802
Published in *The Spirit of the Public Journals for 1802*

The whistling winds tempestuous blow,
The rain descends, good lack!
The *city dame*'s compell'd to stow
Her silk into a hack.

Old Squaretoes, growling, views the glass,
And frets as if on thorns,
Oblig'd to dine at home, alas!
Instead of at *the Horns*!

The spruce *apprentice* angry swears,
And bites his nether lip,
He cannot shew his tonish airs,
Nor sport his *bran new vip*.

The *devotee*, despising mud,
Though splash'd up to the shins,
Demurely walks, in spacious hood,
To *wash away* her sins.

The buck, who scorns the city puts,
And thinks all rich men noodles,
In Hessian boots securely struts
To make his bets at Boodle's.

Ye *raining pow'rs*! Then hear me pray,
And spare! Oh spare us one day!
Throughout the week your fountains play,
And cloudless be each *Sunday*!

Winthrop Mackworth Praed, *Goodnight to the Season*, 1827
Published in *The Museum of Foreign Literature, Science
and Art* (November 1827)

Good-night to the Season! – the buildings
Enough to make Inigo sick;
The paintings, and plastering's, and gildings,
Of stucco, and marble, and brick;
The orders deliciously blended.
From love of effect, into one;
The club-houses only intended,
The palaces only begun;
The hell where the fiend, in his glory,

Sits staring at putty and stones,
And scrambles from story to story,
To rattle at midnight his bones.

Good-night to the Season! – the dances,
The filling of hot little rooms,
The glancing of rapturous glances,
The fancying of fancy costumes;
The pleasures which Fashion makes duties,
The praising of fiddles and flutes,
The luxury of looking at beauties,
The tedium of talking to mutes;
The female diplomatists, planners
Of matches for Laura and Jane,
The ice of her Ladyships manners,
The ice of his Lordship's champagne.

Good-night to the Season! – the rages
Led off by the chiefs of the throng,
The Lady Matilda's new pages,
The Lady Eliza's new song:
Miss Fennel's Macaw, which at Boodle's
Is held to have something to say;
Mrs Splenetic's musical Poodle's
Which bark 'Batti, batti!' all day;
The pony Sir Araby Sported,
As hot and as black as a coal,
And the Lion his mother imported,
In bearskins and grease from the Pole'

Winthrop Mackworth Praed, *School and Schoolfellows*
(from The Poems 1844) or 'Floreat Etona'

Twelve years ago I made a mock
Of filthy trades and traffics:
I wondered what they meant by stock;
I wrote delightful sapphics;
I knew the streets of Rome and Troy,
I supped with Fates and Furies, –
Twelve years ago I was a boy,
A happy boy, at Drury's.
And I am eight-and-twenty now; –
The world's cold chains have bound me;
And darker shades are on my brow,

And sadder scenes around me:
In Parliament I fill my seat,
With many other noodles;
And lay my head in Jermyn Street,
And sip my hock at Boodle's.

Frederick Locker-Lampson, *St James's Street*, 1867

St James's Street, of classic fame,
The finest people throng it.
St James's Street? I know the name,
I think I've pass'd along it!

Why, that's where Sacharissa sigh'd
When Waller read his ditty;
Where Byron lived, and Gibbon died,
And Alvanley was witty.

A famous Street! To yonder Park
Young Churchill stole in class-time;
Come, gaze on fifty men of mark,
And then recall the past time.
The *plats* at White's, the play at Crock's,
The bumpers to Miss Gunning;
The *bonhomie* of Charlie Fox,
And Selwyn's ghastly funning.

The dear old Street of clubs and cribs,
As north and south is stretches
Still seems to smack of Rolliad squibs,
And Gillray's fiercer sketches;
The quaint old dress, the grand old style,
The *mots*, the racy stories;
The wine, the dice, the wit, the bile,
The hate of Whigs and Tories.

Worse times may come. *Bon ton*, indeed,
Will then be quite forgotten,
And all we much revere will speed –
From ripe to worse than rotten:
Let grass then sprout between yon stones,
And owls then roost at Boodle's,
For Echo will hurl back the tones
Of screaming *Yankee Doodle's*.

Theodore Hook, *Clubs*
Published in W D Adams, *Songs of Society from Anne to Victoria*, 1880

If any man loves comfort and has little cash to buy it, he
Should get into a crowded club – a most select society, –
While solitude and mutton cutlets serve *infelix uxor*, he
May have his club, like Hercules, and revel there in luxury,

For country squires the only club in London now is
 Boodle's, sirs,
The Crockford Club for playful men, the Alfred Club, for
 noodle's, sirs:
These are the stages which all men propose to play their
 parts upon,
For Clubs are what the Londoners have clearly set their
 hearts upon.

A Sketch of a Farce, 1779

'Spain, you well know, is the last place where Quixotism flourished; their prejudices in its favour are not entirely rooted out, which may account for their fondness of the expression of the word *honour*; but as to any reserved meaning in it, we may be assured they have none, no more than a modern fine gentleman at Boodle's, or a sailor d___g his eyes in a storm. I therefore think it is for the advantage of the kingdom to accede to the proposals.'

Who's The Dupe? A Farce, by Mrs Cowley, 1806

'You shall confess, my friend, in spite of prejudice, that 'tis possible for a man of letters to become a man of the world. You shall see that he can dress, grow an adept in the science of taste, ogle at the opera, be vociferous at the playhouse, suffer himself to be pigeoned with an easy air at Boodle's, and lose his health for the benefit of his reputation in King's Place.'

O'Doherty on Irish Songs in *Blackwood's Edinburgh Magazine* (March 1825), XVII, no xcviii

Of Dermot and Sheelah, I shall only quote the chorus,
'Beam, bum, boodle, loodle, loodle,

Beam, bum, boodle, oodle, loo.'
Pretty writing that – and very much on a par, in point of sense and interest, with Barry Cornwall's humbugs to Appollor – rather more musical I own.
But is it Irish? *Negatur*. I deny it pos! Boodles! why, Boodle's is a club of good hum-drum gentlemen, kept by Cuddington and Fuller, at 31, St James Street; but not particularly Hibernian. A chorus in the same taste concerning them, would run thus
'Bow, wow, boodle, noodle, doodle,
Bow, wow, boodle, noodle, pooh.'

Oscar Wilde, *An Ideal Husband*, first performed in 1895

Lord Goring, a 'flawless dandy', as a bachelor, the 'result of Boodle's club' who 'reflects every credit on the institution'.

Charles Dickens, *Bleak House*, 1853

In his novel Bleak House, Charles Dickens mocked the class of members who belonged to clubs as 'the great actors for whom the stage is reserved'. He satirised the Boodle's members; referring to Misters 'Doodle's', 'Loodle's', 'Moodle's' and company who only looked out for each other:

'Then there is my Lord Boodle, of considerable reputation with his party, who has known what office is, and who tells Sir Leicester Dedlock with much gravity, after dinner, that he really does not see to what the present age is tending. A debate is not what a debate used to be; the House is not what the House used to be; even a Cabinet is not what it formerly was. He perceives with astonishment, that supposing the present Government to be overthrown, the limited choice of the Crown, in the formation of a new Ministry, would lie between Lord Coodle and Sir Thomas Doodle — supposing it to be impossible for the Duke of Foodle to act with Goodle, which may be assumed to be the case in consequence of the breach arising out of that affair with Hoodle. Then, giving the Home Department and the Leadership of the House of Commons to Joodle, the Exchequer to Koodle, the Colonies to Loodle, and the Foreign Office to Moodle, what are you to do with Noodle? You can't offer him the Presidency of the Council; that is reserved for Poodle. You can't put him in the

Woods and Forests; that is hardly good enough for Quoodle. What follows? That the country is shipwrecked, lost, and gone to pieces (as is made manifest to the patriotism of Sir Leicester Dedlock), because you can't provide for Noodle!'

An extract from *Tremaine – A Novel* published in *Blackwood's Edinburgh Magazine* (May 1825) XVII, no c

'Tremaine felt pushed – but rallying, exclaimed, 'what would you say to Dr Juniper passing up St James's Street, while White's or Boodle's were full of fashionable critics.'
'Why, though fashion is arbitrary enough,' answered Evelyn, 'she yet binds those only who choose to acknowledge her laws ...'

Robert Smith Surtees, 'Ask Mama;' or, *The Richest Commoner in England*, 1926

'The proverbial serenity of Boodles was disturbed one dull winter afternoon by our old friend General Binks banging down the newly-arrived evening paper with a vehemence rarely witnessed in that quiet quarter. Mr Dorford, who was dosing as usual with outstretched legs before the fire, started up, thinking the general was dying. Major Mustard's hat dropped off, Mr Prosper let fall the 'Times Supplement,' Mr Crowsfoot ceased conning the 'Post,' Alemouth, the footman, stood aghast, and altogether there was a general cessation of every thing – Boodle's was paralysed. The General quickly followed up the blow with a tremendous oath, and seizing Colonel Callender's old beaver hat instead of his own new silk one, flung frantically out of the room, through the passage, and into St James's Street, as if bent on immediate destruction.

'We were going to ask for your resignation for presenting a bouncing £1,000 cheque –
but as it was for Arthur Scargill ...!'

Ian Fleming

Ian Fleming, of The Admiralty, Whitehall, Commander RNVR, was proposed as a temporary member of Boodle's in January 1942, by Leonard Ingrams, who had 'something to do with the cloak-and-dagger side of the war'. In 1944 Fleming was elected as a full member of the club 'tired of the relentless socialising and gossiping at White's, he joined the more leisurely Boodle's where occasionally he played bridge, but more often could be seen dining alone in a seat in the window'. Anne Fleming wrote to him: 'I hope Boodle's Club is open again and keeping you away from all the other harpies who desire your black curls and blue eyes'. 'I stump off to Boodles' as he wrote to Alan Ross in 1952 'with *The New Yorker* and the latest US thriller . . . I read through 4 gulls eggs, fried fillets of sole and a half bottle of Chablis . . . forgive telegraphese, but must now play bridge with affronted members'.

In *Moonraker*, published in 1955, James Bond enters Blades and is greeted by Brevett, who is described by Fleming as 'the guardian of Blades and the counsellor and family friend of half the members'. Bond and M. play a little piquet. They have a drink while playing, M. opting for the whisky and soda, while Bond has a dry martini made with vodka and a large slice of lemon peel. Afterwards they decide to go look for Basildon, the Chairman of Blades who is playing Sir Hugo Drax at bridge. They find him at the last table beneath the fine Lawrence of Beau Brummell over the wide Adam fireplace. They make arrangements to play after dinner.

At eight o'clock James Bond and M. head into the beautiful white and gold Regency dining room of Blades. They are given menus, but M. tells Bond he can order anything he likes without having to consult the menu. M. orders first:

'Any of that Beluga caviar left, Porterfield?'
'Yes sir. There was a new delivery last week.'
'Well,' said M. 'Caviar for me, Devilled kidney and a slice of your excellent bacon. Peas and new potatoes. Strawberries in kirsch. What about you James?'
'I've got a mania for really good smoked salmon' said Bond. Then he pointed down the menu. 'Lamb cutlets,

the same vegetables as you, as its May. Asparagus with béarnaise sauce sounds wonderful. And perhaps a slice of pineapple.'

The steward makes a further suggestion 'You wouldn't care for a marrow-bone after the strawberries, sir? We got half a dozen in today from the country.' Now for the drinks. The steward turns to the wine-waiter.

'Ah, Grimley some vodka, please.' M. turns to Bond 'Not the stuff you had in your cocktail. This is the real pre-war Wolfschmidt from Riga. Like some with your smoked salmon?'

'Very much' said Bond

'Then what?' asked M. 'Champagne? Personally I'm going to have a half-bottle of the claret. The Mouton Rothschild '34, please Grimley. But don't pay any attention to me, James. I'm an old man. Champagne's no good for me. We've got some good champagnes, haven't we Grimley? None of that stuff you're always telling me about I'm afraid James. Don't often see it in England. Taittinger, wasn't it?'

Bond agrees that he would like champagne tonight. He asks for a suggestion, and is pointed to the Dom Perignon 46. A waitress appears and puts racks of toast on the table and a silver dish of Jersey butter. As she bends over the table, her black skirt brushes Bond's arm and he looks up into two pert sparkling eyes under a soft fringe of hair. The eyes held his for a fraction of a second and then she whisked away.

Interviewed by *Playboy Magazine* in December 1964, shortly before his death, Fleming stated that 'I have lunch with a friend – always a male friend – I don't like having lunch with women. And perhaps I go to my club, Boodle's or the Turf, where I sit by myself and read in the highly civilised privacy, which is the great thing about some English clubs.'

Smokes

In the first rules of Boodle's in 1762, smoking was not mentioned. The next rules in the archives are those passed at a general meeting of members on 20 May 1857, which state that 'there shall be no smoking in any part of the Club'. The rules agreed on 7 June 1861 allowed smoking 'in the New Room and that room only'. On 13 March 1866, the rules were further eased 'that smoking be permitted after the House Dinner in the Ante-Room next to the Dining Room on the first floor, but not in the Dining Room'. Edward, Prince of Wales, formed the Marlborough Club in 1869 when he was not allowed to smoke a cigar in White's. At Boodle's on 31 March 1870 it was resolved that 'smoking be allowed in the North room on the first floor overlooking St James's Street'.

Further changes were made in 1880 when smoking was 'allowed in the new east Writing Room on the ground floor and in the Billiard Room, also in the Drawing Rooms after 8 pm and in the small Dining Room after a private dinner in that room, but not in the large Dining Room'. Finally, on 12 March 1883 it was voted at another General meeting that 'members be allowed to smoke cigars and cigarettes in the Front and Middle rooms on the ground floor, but not in the Library'.

Smoking is not mentioned in the rules of the members' club in 1899. One hundred and fifty years after the members' ban on smoking, the ban has been re-imposed by Act of Parliament. The passing of the freedom to smoke in Boodle's was commemorated by the Last Cigar Dinner on 6 June 2007 under the chairmanship of Sir Richard Brooke, 11th Bt.

The Cradock Dinner

The Cradock dinner is held each year for members of the Club who serve or served in the Royal Navy. It commemorates the battle of the Coronel, off the coast of Chile, and the death of Rear-Admiral Christopher Cradock, on 1 November 1914, described as 'the most serious British defeat in a naval action in over a century'. Cradock on the armoured cruiser *Good Hope*, together with the *Monmouth* commanded by Philip Francklin were both sunk with all hands by the German East Asiatic squadron under Vice-Admiral von Spee. The responsibilities for this have since been debated, whether Winston Churchill, as first lord of the Admiralty issued ambiguous instructions, or whether Cradock acted in an excessively dashing manner.

The dinner at Boodle's also marks Cradock's last dinner in England, at the Club, before returning to his ships the 4th Cruiser Squadron, based in Jamaica. The exact date is not known, but presumably it was between April 1914 when Cradock was in Veracruz, Mexico saving British and American life and property, and 27 July 1914 when he was again off Veracruz in the *Suffolk*, when the Admiralty issued the warning order for fleet mobilisation. Allowing for sailing times, it might be assumed that he was in England and at his final dinner in May or June 1914.

On 13 August 1914 Cradock reported that the west side of the Atlantic had been cleared of German warships. Thereafter he transferred to the *Good Hope* in Halifax as it was a faster ship. On 14 September 1914 he was ordered to concentrate his squadron at Port Stanley, Falkland Islands, to confront the German East Asiatic squadron heading for the west coast of South America. Before sailing on 7 October, Cradock buried his papers and decorations in the governor's garden.

The dinners seem to have been started in 1961 by Agar and Diggle. They commemorate not so much the defeat at The Coronel as Cradock himself, the only member of Boodle's in the Royal Navy who died in action in the First World War.

Born in 1862 of a well-known Yorkshire family, he entered Dartmouth Naval College in 1875. He served with the Naval brigade in Upper Egypt in 1884, and by 1891 with the Sudan Field Force. He was in China in 1900 for the Boxer Uprising. Cradock was made aide-de-camp to Edward VII between 1909 and 1910 and in 1911 was awarded KCVO by George V for 'personal services', that is rescuing the Princess Royal and her husband the Duke of Fife when the P&O liner *Delhi* was wrecked off Morocco. In February 1913 Cradock assumed command of the America and West Indies station based in Jamaica.

Cradock was described as 'tall, handsome, an athlete and sportsman . . . something of an exquisite . . . another society person not quite up to the mark'. Known for his magnificent hospitality he was also the author of several books, including *Sporting Notes in the Far East*, published in 1889, and *Whispers from the Fleet*, in 1907. Henry Newbolt celebrated the 'gallantry of Sir Christopher Cradock and all the gallant company of the holy order of Knighthood', while Rear-Admiral Sir Robert Arbuthnot, Cradock's friend and contemporary, wrote that 'he always hoped he'd be killed in battle or break his neck on the hunting field'.

Neither Christopher Cradock, nor his brothers Sheldon and Montagu, also members of Boodle's, married. As an acting sub-lieutenant on *HMS Victory*, he was ordered to be retained in the guard ship during the Christmas vacation for taking young women into the rooms of the College.

Among those present at the Memorial Service on 14 November 1914 at Christ Church, Down Street was Maud, Countess Fitzwilliam, said to have worn mourning black for two years thereafter and mentioned as first legatee in Cradock's will. The other woman left 'some little thing' was Mrs Slingsby, perhaps from the well-known family in Yorkshire, widow of a naval officer and unsuccessful litigant in the notorious Slingsby legitimacy case in 1916.

In December 1913 in the US embassy in Mexico City, Mrs O'Shaughnessy met Cradock and wrote in her diary 'Sir Christopher is a singularly handsome man, regular of feature and of distinguished bearing . . . Britannia resplendens'. The following month she visited the *Suffolk*, his flagship, recording that 'we went down to his delightful room. It contains really good things from all parts of the world . . . he really is a connoisseur, but he said that the ladies, God bless them,

had robbed him of his possessions . . . There is something so gallant about him, but with a note of sadness; and I am always conscious of a certain detachment in him from the personal aims of life'.

Cradock is remembered with other members of Boodle's who died in the First World War. There are six other memorials to him and the 1,418 officers and crew. In York Minster, by public subscription, where Lord Balfour gave a controversial address criticising Winston Churchill; in West Gilling Church close to the family house, with a tablet as requested in Cradock's will setting-out all his honours and near to a pair of memorial stained glass windows presented by his family; in the Anglican Church, Concepcion, Chile; in the churchyard of All Saint's Church Catherington, Hampshire

Rear-Admiral Christopher Cradock

presented by Mary C Barnes in 1925 (she was mentioned in Cradock's will); in Christ Church Cathedral, Stanley, Falkland Islands; and in the naval dockyard in Coronel, Chile, erected by the Anglo-Chilean Society in 1989.

One evening, many years after Cradock's death, Sir Anthony Montague-Brown, private secretary to Churchill, escorted the Prime Minister to dinner at Boodle's. Pausing on the stairs to read the Roll of Honour of members who had been killed Churchill 'wept silently and muttered "Coronel"'.

The Military at Boodle's

The lists of members who died in the First and Second World Wars are on the first floor landing. One might notice that in 1914–18 Rear Admiral Sir Christopher Cradock was the only Naval officer to be killed. Of the 650 members in 1914, thirty-eight died, and of the seven hundred in 1939, thirty-five died. In the First World War, ten officers in the Guards Division were killed, in the Second World War, twelve. The most senior officer was killed in April 1916, Thomas Andrew Wight-Boycott DSO, Brigadier General 2nd South Midland Mounted Brigade. The most unexpected were John Julius Jersey de Knoop, Major, Imperial Camel Corps, formerly Cheshire Yeomanry, killed in Cyrenaica in August 1916, and W E Graham Niven in August 1914, father of David Niven, actor and member from 1938.

Also killed, in September 1915, was Frederick Charles Romer. Described as 'a true gentleman with a keen regard for hygiene and fresh air', Lt Colonel Romer (CB 1907) CMG (1900) appears to have joined the Army through the Militia. Commissioned as a lieutenant in the 3rd Battn the Essex Regiment (Essex Rifles Militia) in May 1873, he was made Captain in April 1879 and appointed the Reserve in October 1881. In 1891 he was a captain in the 3rd Battn, Lancashire Fusiliers and would command the Militia battalions of this regiment for thirty years.

He was appointed Lt Colonel in the Militia on 18 December 1895, and commanded the 6th (Militia) Battn in South Africa from February 1900 to October 1901. From 1 July 1904 Romer was assistant-director for militia services at the War Office. He commanded the 4th Battn, Lancashire Fusiliers, a territorial battalion, and thereafter raised the 8th Battn, The Buffs, at Canterbury on 12 September 1914.

Elected a member of Boodle's in 1899, Romer became Honorary Secretary in 1914. Romer 'believed in mature men and wished to have a leavening of the middle-aged among his officers'. He used his influence in the Club to persuade other members to join him in The Buffs. Six members, all aged over forty, joined him. These included Major E M Dansey (1870) formerly 1st Life Guards; Major Sir Philip Crawley (1897), formerly 3rd Battn, Lancashire

ROLL OF MEMBERS OF BOODLE'S WHO FELL IN THE GREAT WAR.

1914

Oswald Bethell Walker,
  Capt: 15th Hussars.
Aug.

Sir Robert George Vivian Duff, Bart.,
  Lieut: 2nd Life Guards.
Oct.

Sir Frank Stanley Di Rose, Bart.,
  Capt: 10th Hussars.
Oct.

Hon. William Richard Wyndham,
  Capt: 1st Life Guards.
Nov.

H.H. Prince Maurice of Battenberg, K.C.V.O.,
  Lieut: King's Royal Rifles.
Nov.

Sir Christopher Cradock, K.C.V.O., C.B.,
  Rear Admiral, Royal Navy.
Nov.

William Joseph Wickham,
  Capt: Scots Guards.
Nov.

Reginald Nigel Gipps,
  Lieut: Scots Guards.
Nov.

Hugh Taylor,
  Capt: Scots Guards.
Dec.

1915

Charles Melville Cottrell-Dormer, D.S.O.,
  Lieut: Coldstream Guards.
Feb.

William Henry Fitzroy Landon,
  Capt: Suffolk Regt.
Feb.

Bertram E. Hambro,
  Lieut: Attached 'A' Battery, R.H.A.
Apl.

John Arnold Cuthbert-Quilter,
  Grenadier Guards,
  Lt. Colonel Commanding Hood Battalion, R.N.D.
May

George Frederick Steele, C.M.G.
  Lt. Colonel Royal Dragoons.
May

J. R. Ewing
  Capt: late 21st Lancers.
June

Edward Charles Stafford-King-Harman,
  Capt: Irish Guards
June

W. E. Graham Niven,
  Lieut: Berkshire Yeomanry.
Aug.

Ashley W. N. Ponsonby,
  Capt: Oxfordshire & Buckinghamshire
    Light Infantry.
Sept.

George Philip Gurney Hoare,
  Troop Sergeant, Essex Yeomanry.
Sept.

Frederick Charles Romer, C.B., C.M.G.,
  Colonel The Buffs.
Sept.

William Howard,
  Capt: The Buffs.
Oct.

1915

James Ogilvie Grant,
  11th Earl of Seafield,
  Capt: Cameron Highlanders.
Nov.

Henry Donald McNeile,
  Lt. Colonel Royal Dragoons.
Dec.

Richard Weld-Blundell
  Lieut: King's Liverpool Regt.
Dec.

1916

Thomas Andrew Wight-Boycott, D.S.O.,
  Brigadier General,
  2nd South Midland Mounted Brigade.
Apl.

John Julius Jersey de Knoop,
  Major Imperial Camel Corps.
Aug.

Edward Lycett-Lyon,
  Major 18th Hussars.
Sep.

Edmond Deacon,
  Lieut: Colonel Essex Yeomanry.
Oct.

1917

Alexander John Fife,
  Lieut: Colonel, 4th Yorkshire Regt.
Feb.

Richard Godolphin Hume Chaloner,
  Capt: Wiltshire Regt.
Apl.

Herbert H. Wilson,
  Capt: Royal Horse Guards.
Apl.

Harold Arthur Gordon Walton,
  Lieut: Royal Field Artillery.
May

Collis George Herbert St. Hill,
  Lieut: Colonel, North Devon Hussars.
July

James Somerled Joseph Silvertop,
  Lieut: Oxfordshire Hussars.
Sep.

Mark Hibbert Philips,
  Lieut: South Staffordshire Regt.
Oct.

Sir John Swinnerton Dyer, Bart., M.C.,
  Capt: Scots Guards.
Oct.

1918

James Bertram Falkner Cartland,
  Lieut: Colonel Worcester Regt.
May

Charles Edward Erroll Hay,
  Lieut: 17th Lancers.
Sept.

HOUSEHOLD

Percival Alford, [Waiter]
  Royal Sussex Regt.
1916

Thomas Missen, [Waiter]
  The Buffs.
,,

ROLL OF MEMBERS OF BOODLE'S WHO FELL IN THE SECOND WORLD WAR.

1940

Lord Frederick Cambridge,
Capt. Coldstream Guards.
— May

The Duke of Northumberland
Lieut. Grenadier Guards.
— May

C. R. Egerton,
Major, Royal Artillery.
— May

Kenneth E. Newton,
Flying Officer, Royal Air Force.
— June

F. W. H. Barnett,
Capt. King's Royal Rifle Corps.
— June

T. H. Rose-Richards,
Lieut. Royal Naval Volunteer Reserve.
— Oct.

1941

G. H. J. Cresswell,
Sub-Lieut. Royal Naval Volunteer Reserve.
— May

David Barnett,
Major, Northumberland Hussars
— May

The Rev. R. J. P. Stewart, M.A.
Chaplain, Royal Navy.
— May

D. Stewart-Clark,
Flt-Lieut. Royal Air Force.
— Sept.

1942

T. G. P. Peyton
Lieut. King's Royal Rifle Corps.
— Mar

E. G. S. Smallwood,
Capt. County of London Yeomanry
(Sharpshooters)
— June

Viscount Garmoyle, D.S.O.
Brigadier, Rifle Brigade.
— July

Henry Wickham-Boynton
Capt. Royal Artillery
— Aug.

J. H. Roberts,
Lieut. Royal Naval Volunteer Reserve.
— Dec.

G. A. Singer
Capt. 10th Royal Hussars, R.A.C.
— Nov.

C. R. Fenwick, T.D.
Major, Warwickshire Yeomanry.
— Nov.

1943

P. Graham,
Capt. Queen's Own Yorkshire Dragoons
— Apl.

G. B. Ismay,
Capt. Irish Guards.
— Apl.

Lord Lyell, V.C.
Capt. Scots Guards.
— Apl.

P. Le R. Shephard
Lieut. Grenadier Guards.
— Apl.

F. C. Boult,
Lieut. Grenadier Guards.
— May

R. J. M. Harley,
Capt. Coldstream Guards.
— Sept.

David Smyth,
Flt-Lieut. Royal Air Force.
— Nov

1944

F. F. A. Heilgers, M.P.
Lt. Colonel, Royal Artillery.
— Jan.

R. V. Pattinson,
Major, Welsh Guards.
— Feb.

G. A. Gillson,
Colonel King's Own Scottish Borderers.
— Mar.

R. W. R. Hely-Hutchinson,
Sgt. Royal Artillery.
— Mar.

H. W. Dods,
Lieut. Scots Guards.
— June

A. Keith-Cameron,
Major, Coldstream Guards.
— July

G. C. Grey, M.P.
Capt. Grenadier Guards.
— July

J. O. Spencer,
Major, Welsh Guards.
— Sept.

1945

D. Cotton-Minchin
Major, Cameronians
— Mar.

Sir G. P. V. Wills, Bart.
Lieut. Coldstream Guards.
— Apl.

C. Scott-Nicholson,
Major, Royal Artillery
— May

Lt Colonel Romer (CB 1907) CMG (1900)

Fusiliers; Captains Edward Hare (1903) and William Howard (1899), who died 8 October 1915, and was buried at Le Treport; and Lt Sir W H Cooke Bt (1897), formerly Yorkshire Dragoons Yeomanry. Two waiters also joined, one of whom, Thomas Missen, died 2 November 1916 aged twenty-five, and was buried at Etretat.

Romer attended all of the Management Committee meetings from April 1914 until August 1915 when, on the 31st of that month, the 8th Battn sailed to Boulogne to join with the 24th Division at Bethune. Three weeks after arriving in France, with no training as to how to handle themselves in the trenches under fire, the battalion was sent into the Battle of Loos on 25 September 1915.

Before the battle Romer spoke to his men: 'I am not going to make a speech but only ask you to remember who you are, The Buffs'. Their objective was the German third line trenches a mile away, which they assaulted in daylight over open country. Of the battalion strength of 1050, twenty-four officers and 610 other ranks were casualties.

Romer was wounded in his shoulder and then received a bullet through his heart: 'what a death for a hero aged sixty-one'. When the battalion was disbanded in February 1918, particular mention was made of the 'gallant Romer'. Romer is commemorated at The Loos Memorial as his body could not be identified.

Among those killed in 1915 was Ashley William Neville Ponsonby. He was appointed Military Secretary to Lord Buxton, Governor General of South Africa and returned to join his battalion in France. After recovering from a wound he went back again and in 1915 was tragically shot through the forehead by a sniper in a fog. Mention of him was made by Henry Newbolt: 'Among those most distinguished by the admiration of their comrades the Regiment will remember Captain Ashley William Neville Ponsonby, a soldier who added to perfect courage, an invaluable coolness and clearness of perception'.

In the Second World War the only man to win a VC when already a member, was Lord Lyell, Captain Scots Guards. Two members of parliament, F F A Heilgers, Lt Colonel Royal Artillery and G C Grey, Capt Grenadier Guards, were killed in 1944.

Members who have been Chairmen of the Club since 1897

T F Kynnersley	1896–1901	J Glyn (later Lord Wolverton)	1964–1967
J D Whitmore	1901–1904	P G Corbett	1967–1970
G A Fenwick	1904–1907	E G E Rayner	1970–1973
The Hon R Parker	1907–1922	P M Barrington	1973–1976
H Allhusen	1922–1925	G E Knight	1976–1979
Hon F G Morgan	1925–1928	Capt A F M Beeley	1979–1982
F R Davenport	1928–1935	J R Ferard	1982–1985
Sir Picton Bagge Bt	1935–1941	I McCorquodale	1985–1988
A Whitworth	1941–1944	R J Shand	1988–1992
D J Robarts	1944–1945	S P Leatham	1992–1995
R V Grimston	1945–1948	S M Corbett	1995–1998
Sir Robert Micklem	1948–1950	Sir Richard Brooke, 11th Bt	1998–2001
H S Mortimer	1950–1953	Charles P Barrington	2001–2004
I D Malcolmson	1953–1956	Patrick H Burgess	2004–2007
Lord Robert Crichton-Stuart	1956–1958	Major Gen Charles G C Vyvyan CB CBE	2007–2010
Lt Col J Chandos-Pole	1958–1961	Alastair Macpherson of Pitmain	2010
Lord Inchyra	1961–1964		

The chairmen of London Clubs gathered for a dinner on 28 March 2012, celebrating Boodle's 250th Anniversary

The Staff

The only records that exist are the censuses taken every ten years from 1841, of those present at each specific address. Over eight censuses, 1841 to 1911, 133 names were recorded, 119 of whom were servants, the balance being members of the Gainer family, particularly 1841 to 1871.

The living-in staff were equally divided between men and women. In the descriptions of occupations, there is no mention of chefs or cooks, as well as other staff who lived outside the Club. The structure seems to have been the proprietor (frequently described as 'The Master'), later the secretary with a butler, under-butler, three waiters plus a female housekeeper with secondary chamber and kitchen maids. In 1901 and 1911 there were two hall boys or page boys.

The surprise is the turnover of staff, as at Brooks's and White's, with merely one name appearing in two census records. In 1880 the average London wages per annum for a butler were £70; for a general servant £12. In 1907 a chef earned £250.

Richard Edmonds, former Boodle's Secretary (1966–98) originated a scheme in the late 1970s to bring in a group of young French women from Angers (a city between Nantes and Tours) to wait tables at the club. In return they got to live in hostels owned by the club, and to study and learn English at a local language school. This scheme, broadened to other countries, continues today.

Andrew Phillips, Club Secretary, checking the wine cellar with Tony Correia, Cellarman

The Secretary with Edward Plunket, House Manager

Magnolia Martin, Assistant Coffee Room Manager, training
two Coffee Room waitresses

Ansereh Anoyke, Club Silverman

Ladies' Side waitresses laying tables

James White, Hall Porter, with
Caesar Caraon Night Porter

David Deeks, Barman, preparing a cocktail

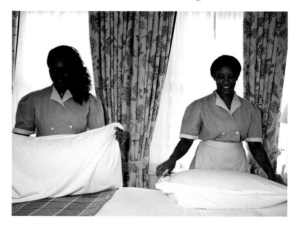

Club chambermaids making beds

David Ryan, Coffee Room Manager, supervising a
Steak Diane

Coffee Room waitresses folding napkins before service

Chef Stephen Carter

Clemence Semensyia, Club Valet

Matthew Abbott-Williams,
Club Pastry Chef

Marcello Dionisi, Ladies' Side Manager

Chefs preparing cold starters from the kitchen larder

Boodle's Original Recipes

Some of the following recipes have a historical connection to the Club and have long disappeared from the menu. Others have become Club standards after being put on the menu by former and current chefs. It is noteworthy that Boodle's is the only club with which a series of recipes is associated, mainly before and after the First World War, in cookery books written by women.

Boodle's Fool

No recipe is more closely associated with Boodle's than the Fool. There are various versions of this signature dish that seem to have originated in the nineteenth century. Keith Podmore, Boodle's Head Chef 1983–2006, dates the use of the recipe at the Club from the 1920s. Below are three versions of the Fool, two of which date from this earlier period. In one the oranges have been substituted with lemons. The third Fool recipe is currently served to members.

Boodle's Orange Fool
From: *Dorothy Allhusen, A Book of Scents and Dishes, 1926.*
The author was married to Henry Allhusen, Boodle's Chairman 1922–25.

INGREDIENTS
4 oranges   2 lemons
570ml cream   sponge cakes

METHOD
Take the juice of the four oranges and the two lemons, and the grated rind of one lemon and two oranges. Sweeten to taste, and add the cream. Fill a bowl with the sponge cakes, cut in four pieces each, and pour the mixture over the cakes. This dish should be made some hours before it is served, to allow the juice of the fruit to penetrate into the cakes.

Boodle's is also known for its signature dish. Rich, comforting and delicious, just like the Club itself, Boodle's Orange Fool – a layer of sponge covered in whipped cream mixed with orange and lemon zest – is more of a Trifle than a Fool, and can now be enjoyed by everyone, regardless of sex or status.

Boodle's Lemon Fool
From: *Agnes Jekyll, Kitchen Essays, 1922*

Serves six.

INGREDIENTS
1 small sponge cake   4 lemons
2 oranges   600ml double cream
25g caster sugar

METHOD
Break up the sponge and scatter it over the bottom of an 18cm soufflé dish. Grate the rind from the fruit and squeeze out the juice. Lightly whip the cream and fold in the rind and juice. Sweeten to taste with sugar, and add more lemon juice of the mixture if not sufficiently tart. Spoon the mixture over the sponge cake. (If you pour it, the sponge will float to the top!). Cover and chill for at least six hours, or overnight. The juice will gradually sink through the cream into the sponge below, leaving a frothy cream on the top. Decorate with twists of lemon before serving.

Boodle's Lemon Fool is a tart version of the famous *Boodle's Orange Fool.*

Chef Carter's Orange Fool
Supplied courtesy of Stephen Carter, Head Chef since 2006.

This recipe includes several separate steps. The important sweetener is honey; this is what sets it apart from other confections. Serves ten.

Step 1: To make the Orange compound:
This makes a relatively large amount but quantity can be easily reduced. The compound will keep for six months.

INGREDIENTS
Juice and zest of 18 oranges, unwaxed (or washed in hot water to clean off wax)   One 454g jar of honey

METHOD
Heat juice, zest and honey until mixture has reduced to a quarter of its volume. Place in a sealed container and chill.

Step 2: To make the Orange Italienne:

INGREDIENTS
100g caster sugar   100ml water   5 oranges

METHOD

Julienne the zest, then peel and slice the oranges. Place caster sugar and water in a pan with the orange zest and slowly heat until zest is tender. Remove zest and continue heating until water and sugar have caramalised. Pour over the orange slices (reserving a small amount to moisten the sponge fingers in the next step).

Step 3: To make the fool:

INGREDIENTS

1 litre double cream   1 orange, juiced
50ml clear blossom honey   200g sponge fingers
80ml of the orange compound (see above for recipe)
The reserved caramel syrup described in the Orange Italienne recipe above.

METHOD

Whisk the double cream, orange compound, orange juice and honey until it has formed firm peaks. Lay the sponge fingers in a single layer in the base of a deep silver dish. Pour the reserved Orange Italienne caramel syrup over the sponge fingers. Pipe the fool mixture on top of this. Garnish with grated dark chocolate.

Serve with the Orange Italienne in a similar dish.
This dish is traditionally silver-served but can be served in a similar earthenware dish or can be packed into individual deep glass dishes.

Boodle's Club Oranges

Boodle's Club, 1922

INGREDIENTS

Oranges   170g sugar   285ml water

METHOD

Peel the number of oranges required – one for each person. Dip the peel in boiling water for a minute or two and remove the pith. Cut the orange peel into very fine julienne and blanch for eight minutes in boiling water. Dissolve the sugar in the water then add the orange peel. Boil until the sugar caramelises and turns golden brown. Cool. When cold, cut the oranges into thin rounds and pour over the syrup and Orange Julienne. Chill.

Devilled Bones

Boodle's Club, 1923

INGREDIENTS

Bones with a little meat on   114g butter
1tsp dry mustard   1tsp ground black pepper
1tsp salt   1tsp curry powder
½ tsp cayenne pepper   1tbs Worcester sauce
A sauce-boat of devil sauce.

METHOD

Work the butter, mustard, pepper, salt, curry powder, cayenne pepper, and Worcester sauce all together, keep on ice. First score the meat, then grill the bones. After grilling, coat with the devilled butter and put under the grill for 2–3 minutes and serve, with or without a devil or grill sauce.

Grouse Stuffed with Bananas

Boodle's Club, 1923

METHOD

Peel and cut up some bananas, mash and mix them with two level teaspoonfuls of black pepper, one of salt, and ten drops of lemon juice. Use this to stuff either grouse or partridges, and roast them as usual.

(This recipe is so unexpected that I have enquired everywhere and advertised to try to determine the origins and culinary logic – without success. RDM)

Boodle's Banana Stuffing

Mashed ripe bananas mixed with an equal volume of wholemeal breadcrumbs, finely chopped onion, chopped tarragon and seasoning. Used to stuff quails, small birds or chicken breasts.

Salad Dressing

From: *Dorothy Allhusen, A Book of Scents and Dishes, Boodle's Club, 1926*

METHOD

Take 1 spoonful of salt. Cover the salt with dry mustard, cover this with pepper ground from the pepper mill. Add 4 tablespoonfuls of olive oil and mix well. Then add not quite 1 tablespoonful of French wine vinegar. Again mix well. Add 1 teaspoonful of very finely chopped onion to this dressing.

Boodle's Fruit Cake

Boodle's Club, 1935
Simple house fruit-cake, served with Port after lunch.

INGREDIENTS

455g flour   227g caster sugar
227g butter   455g stoned raisins
285ml milk   2 eggs
1 dessertspoonful (2 tsp) bicarbonate soda

METHOD
Sift flour and soda in butter, then mix in sugar and raisins, whisk eggs and three-quarters of milk together, and mix in for five minutes.

If too stodgy, add remainder of milk. Bake for 4½–5 hours.

Unsweetened: described as going well with Stilton.

Filets de Sole Jane
Boodle's Club, 1972
Saint-John Harmsworth (elected 1952) and his wife Jane were so popular with the staff that they were always invited to staff parties. Gerry Boriosi created this recipe in Jane's honour.

Fillets of sole stuffed with a crab mousse and finished with a brandy and cream sauce, glazed and dressed with a fleuron.

The two dishes below come from the 1972 Mouton Cadet winning menu. This was the top culinary competition in the United Kingdom at this time.

Supreme of Turbot Beau Brummel

Poached young turbot on a bed of shrimp and lobster purée, coated with a chive soufflé sauce, garnished with truffle and lobster and glazed.

Crepes St James

Pancakes filled with a brandy pastry cream, flambéed and coated with a warm honey and brandy sauce, dressed with warm berries (raspberries or wild strawberries).

Recipes from Victor Ceserani, MBE, Head Chef, Boodle's 1948–1950
The following recipes are taken from Catering for Life: the Autobiography of Victor Ceserani.

Boodle's Cheese

'For the Welsh rarebit we grate or finely slice Cheddar cheese and gently melted it in a little white sauce until smooth. An egg yolk was added and a good measure of ale, which was reduced in a separate pan to a teaspoonful. Two to three drops of Worcestershire sauce, a dash of English mustard and a snuff of cayenne pepper completed the seasoning. The mixture was then poured into the inner part of a small, rectangular double silver dish, the outer part of which contained a heated metal block. The ornate silver lid was put on the dish and sent to the dining room where, in the adjoining pantry, fresh toast was made, buttered, crusts removed and served on a hot plate.'

Crab

'The small legs are pulled off, then the large claws which, after wrenching off into the three joints on each claw, yield the white meat. The carapace is firmly removed with fingers and thumbs and all the soft brown meat is scraped out (the sac behind the eyes and the dead men's fingers (gills)) and discarded. The white meat is shredded between the fingers to ensure there are no fragments of shell and I preferred to serve this plain, accompanied with mayonnaise and vinaigrette. The brown meat is passed through a fine sieve and gently seasoned with a drop or two of Worcester sauce, a spot of cayenne pepper, a touch of mayonnaise and thickened with fresh white breadcrumbs if necessary.'

Stuffed Breast of Pheasant Avyona
From: Graham Rust, The Fine Art of Dining, 1995
Contributed by Chef Keith Podmore.
This recipe is named after Avyona Cripps, wife of a sous-chef.

Breast of pheasant with herb stuffing, wine glaze and garnishes with beetroot and mangetout.

Cold Beetroot and Goats Cheese Soup
Recipe courtesy of Chef Keith Podmore

Serves six.

INGREDIENTS

80g leek	80g onion
65g celery	15g butter
750g raw beetroot	Goat's cheese
1.5 litres chicken or vegetable stock	
150ml double or sour cream	Salt and pepper to taste
Cream to serve	

METHOD
Wash and shred the leek, onion and celery and sweat in the butter until soft. Wash peel and roughly chop beetroot. Add beetroot to

sweated vegetables and mix. Cover with stock and bring to the boil then turn down to simmer for 40 minutes until cooked. Carefully liquidise the soup. Correct the seasoning and chill. Cut the goats cheese into small dice and add to cold soup. Recheck seasoning. Serve in an appropriate bowl or dish. Drizzle the cream in a swirl as decoration and serve.

Cold Cream Germiny
Recipe courtesy of Chef Keith Podmore

Serves six.

INGREDIENTS

14 fresh egg yolks	400ml double cream
150g sorrel	125g fresh butter
Salt and pepper to taste	3 crust ends of bread
Olive oil	1.4 litres good consommé or chicken stock

METHOD

Mix together the egg yolks and cream. Wash and shred the sorrel and then stew in butter until cooked. Place cooked sorrel in a cold pan in an ice bath. Bring the consommé or chicken stock to the boil. Pour the consommé over the cream and egg yolk and mix well with a wooden spoon. The consistency should nearly be that of single cream. If not, carefully return to the heat until it thickens enough to coat the back of a wooden spoon and leaves a line if you run your finger down. When ready, quickly pour over the butter and sorrel in the chilled pan to stop the cooking process. Recheck seasoning. Cut the crusts in half and then into julienne. Place on a tray, sprinkle with olive oil and toast in the oven till golden brown. Serve separately.

Manchester Baked Egg Custard
Recipe courtesy of Chef Keith Podmore

To make the Frangipane
INGREDIENTS

80g caster sugar	8g soft unsalted butter
1 large egg	100g ground almonds
Few drops almond oil (optional)	

Cream all the ingredients together to produce the frangipane.

To make the Egg Custard
INGREDIENTS

4 large eggs	60g caster sugar
Vanilla pod or essence	Raspberry jam
550ml full cream or Jersey milk	

Mix together the eggs, caster sugar and vanilla. Add the milk and mix.

METHOD

Spread some raspberry jam thinly on the bottom of a pie dish (either individual or large). Pipe on the frangipane, and cover with the egg custard mix. Place in a *bain-marie* and heat to nearly boiling point on top of the stove. Place in an oven at 180°C for 30–40 minutes (depends on size of dish) until set and some colour on the surface. Dust lightly with icing sugar. The frangipane will have risen to the top with the custard underneath and the jam settled on the bottom.

Flapjacks with white chocolate, apple and apricot
Recipe courtesy of Chef Stephen Carter

INGREDIENTS (makes 20 bars):

15 Granny Smith apples	150g dried apricots
150g white chocolate	150g porridge oats
2tbs honey	

METHOD

Peel and deseed the apples. Finely grate the apples and squeeze all the liquid through a cloth. Finely chop the apricot and chocolate and mix with the grated apple. Add oats and honey to bind. Roll out on to a baking tray about 2cm thick. Bake at 180°C for 10 minutes then turn over and bake for a further 5 minutes. Leave to cool, then cut into the shapes required. Store in an airtight container. Serve with ice cream

Boodle's Potted Shrimp
Recipe courtesy of Chef Stephen Carter

Serves forty.

INGREDIENTS

500ml USA sauce (recipe below)	1kg Butter Normandy
4g ground mace	4g ground nutmeg
2g pepper (black peppercorns)	4g fine sea salt
50ml brandy	2kg brown shrimp, peeled
60g dill	1kg salad garnish
80g Avruga Cavier	Melba Toast
10 lemons, quartered	

Forty individual small ramekins.

METHOD

Heat USA sauce in a heavy-bottom pan. Whisk the butter carefully into sauce taking care not to split it. Add the mace and nutmeg. Add the salt and pepper to taste, as well as the brandy and shrimps. Stir well. Check for seasoning. You may need to add a little extra lemon juice. Drain the shrimp mixture and reserve the liquid to one side. Pack the shrimp into the forty small ramekins and chill for 10 minutes. Remove from fridge and pour just enough of the reserved liquid to cap each mould. Return to chill. The potted shrimp will keep for seven days.

To serve: Turn potted shrimp out of the ramekins. Garnish with salad, a quarter lemon, the dill and Avruga Cavier. Serve with Melba toast.

To make the USA sauce:
INGREDIENTS (yields 10 litres):

4kg langoustine, size 3	1g bay leaves	400g carrots
250g celery head	250g fennel	100g garlic
5g thyme	250g leeks	
600g onions	10g whole white peppercorns	
200mg tomato puree	200ml brandy for cooking	
8 litres chicken stock	750ml white wine – Catelbello	

METHOD
Wash and remove eyes from langoustines. Smash the langoustines in a large mixer. Sweat all mirepoix and aromates in a large heavy bottom pan. Add langoustines, tomato puree and brandy and cook for 2 minutes. Add chicken stock and simmer for approximately two hours, skimming the scum off the surface of the stock during cooking. Blend in a food processor then pass though a fine sieve.

Boodle's Butter
Recipe supplied courtesy of Chef Stephen Carter
Recipe created by Chef Keith Podmore

Serves eighty.

INGREDIENTS
1kg Butter Normandy, room temperature
2 litres chicken stock   160g chervil
6g ground black peppercorns   8g table salt

METHOD
Reduce chicken stock to a thick glace and cool. Chop the chervil. Place softened butter into food processor along with glace chicken stock, chervil, salt and pepper. Blend, taking care not to let butter mixture split. Place the top of food processor with its contents into fridge for about 10 minutes allowing mixture to set. Remove from fridge and roll butter into logs about 5cm in diameter. Wrap logs in cling film and freeze. Take out and use as needed. The butter can be refrigerated for up to 2 weeks and will keep in freezer for 6 months.

Boodle's Chicken Pie
Recipe courtesy of Chef Stephen Carter

Serves four. *Will need four individual pie dishes.*

INGREDIENTS:

1 litre chicken stock	100g button mushrooms
200g carrots	200g bacon, green streaky
40g thyme	4 chicken breasts (140–150g each)
Butter	500g puff pastry, home made

METHOD
Heat chicken stock until reduced by half. Wash and quarter the mushrooms. Sauté in butter in a heavy bottomed pan for about four minutes. Remove from pan and place to one side. Peel and julienne carrots and sauté using this same pan until softened. Return mushrooms to the pan and add the thyme and stock. Cook for about 4 minutes. Remove the carrots and mushrooms and reduce the stock by half again. Chill carrots and mushrooms as well as the stock. Wrap each chicken breast in a rasher of bacon. Place each breast in their own dish. Sprinkle mushrooms, carrots and just enough of the reduced stock to cover the chicken. Cover entire dish with the rolled out puff pastry and cover with an egg wash. Bake at 190°C for about 35 minutes checking with a skewer or probe that fully cooked.

Above: The bar
Opposite: The Boodle's Christmas puddings in the wine cellar

Notes on further reading

Chapter 2: Edward Boodle and his Successors

There are a number of disparate sources that provided the material for this chapter. Extensive use was made of historical newspapers, correspondence, diaries, census and probate records, as well as sale advertisements, guidebooks and poems.

Richard Samways provided invaluable information about the workings of the Club and its members. He also compiled an index of Boodle's Members 1762–1896 and an index of Club Managers' 1762–1896.

Newspapers included *The Annual Register, Blackwood's Edinburgh Magazine, The Builder, The Gentleman's Magazine, The Graphic, The Gazetteer and New Daily Advertiser, The Morning Post and Daily Advertiser, Notes and Queries, The Observer, The Public Advertiser, The Times*

Select bibliography:

G Birkbeck Hill, ed, *Boswell's Life of Johnson*, III–IV, Clarendon Press, Oxford, 1887; 1934

Francis Bickley, ed, *The Diaries of Sylvester Douglas*, II, Constable & Co., London, 1928

Miscellaneous Works of Edward Gibbon, Esquire. With Memoirs of his life and writings, I, P Wogan, Dublin, 1796

J E Norton, ed, *The Letters of Edward Gibbon*, I, 1750–1773, Macmillan, New York, 1956

L Strachey and Roger Fulford, ed, *The Greville Memoirs* I–IV, Macmillan & Co, London, 1938

J H Jesse, *George Selwyn and His Contemporaries*, I & IV, Scribner and Welford, New York, 1882

Tallis's Illustrated London, London, 1851

W S Lewis, et al, ed, *Horace Walpole's Correspondence*, II, New Haven, Yale University Press and London, Oxford University Press, 1974

W S Lewis, et al, ed, *Horace Walpole's Correspondence with the Countess of Upper Ossory*, I, 1761–1777, XXXII, New Haven, Yale University Press and London, Oxford University Press, 1965

A Francis Steuart, ed, *The Last Journals of Horace Walpole during the reign of George III*, I, J Lane, London, 1910

Peter Cunningham, ed, *The Letters of Horace Walpole, fourth earl of Orford*, IV, John Grant, Edinburgh, 1906

R I Wilberforce & S Wilberforce, *The Life of William Wilberforce*, I, John Murray, London, 1838

Alfred Spencer, ed, *The Memoirs of William Hickey*, I, Hurst and Blackett, London, 1913

The Memorial of Richard Miles, Proprietor or Conductor of one of the Principal Houses in St James's Street for Upwards of Thirty Years, 1834

Pierce Egan, *Sporting Egan, original and selected*, I, New York, 1823

James Grant, *The Great Metropolis*, I, London, Saunders and Otley, 1837

Wyatt Papworth, *John B Papworth, Architect to the King of Wurtemburg*, privately printed, London, 1879

John Bateman, *The Great Landowners of Great Britain and Ireland*, Harrison, London, 1879

Dod's Parliamentary Guide

Arthur Bolton, 'London Clubs: Boodles', *Country Life*, 9 December 1916: 12–20

M Dorothy George, *Hogarth to Cruikshank: A social change in Graphic Satire*, Walker & Co, New York, 1967

Archival material:

Boodle's Club Books at the London Metropolitan Archives (property of Boodle's)

Christie's Archives, King Street

Crown Estate Office: Crown Record Atlas

The Fusilier Museum

Lincolnshire Archives

PRO Kew, The National Archives: probate records

Correspondence with St Paul's School, St James's Church, Piccadilly

For earlier accounts of Boodle's:

F H W Sheppard, ed, 'St James's Street, East Side', *Survey of London: volumes 29 & 30: The Parish of St James Westminster, Part One. South of Piccadilly*, 1960

Roger Fulford, *Boodle's 1762–1962. A short history*, privately printed, London, 1962

Duncan Couper, *A History of Boodle's from 1762: Architectural significance, management and members*, 2007 (not published)

Stephen R Hill, *Boodle's Apocrypha: A Story of Men and their Club in London*, privately printed, London, 2009

For further history of Boodle's and its neighbours see:

London Clubs: their anecdotes and history, London, 1853

Henry S Eeles and Earl Spencer, *Brooks's, 1764–1964*, *Country Life*, London, 1964

T H S Escott, *Club Makers and Club Members*, Sturgis and Walton, New York, 1914

Charles Graves, *Leather Armchairs*, Cassell, London, 1963

Major A Griffiths, *Clubs and Clubmen*, Hutchinson & Co, London, 1907

Anthony Lejeune, *The Gentlemen's Clubs of London*, London, 1979

Anthony Lejeune, *White's. The first three hundred years*, A & C Black, London, 1993

Ralph Nevill, *London Clubs*, Chatto & Windus, London, 1911

Henry C Shelley, *Inns and taverns of Old London*, L C Page & Co, Boston, 1909

J Summerson, *Georgian London*, New Haven and London, Yale University Press, 1945; later edition 2003

Peter Thorold, *The London Rich*, Viking, London, 1999

John Timbs, *Club Life of London*, London, 1866

R S Surtees, 'Ask Mama;' or, The Richest Commoner in England, George Bayntun, Bath, 1926

The Spirit of Public Journals for 1802, IV, 1803

For information on the Savoir Vivre Club see the list of newspapers as well as the following publications:

[R. Fenton], *Ode to the Scavoir Vivre Club*, 1772

The Macaroni and Theatrical Magazine for October, 1772

John Cooke, *The macaroni jester, and pantheon of wit;…* London [1773?]

William Roberts, *Memoirs of the life and correspondence of Mrs Hannah More*, I, Seeley, London, 1834

David M Little and George M Kahrl, eds, *The Letters of David Garrick*, III (Letters 816–1362), The Belknap Press of Harvard University Press, Cambridge, Mass, 1963

F H W Sheppard, ed, 'St James's Street, East Side', *Survey of London: volumes 29 & 30: The Parish of St. James Westminster, Part One. South of Piccadilly*, 1960

Chapter 4: Masquerades and Fetes

For the 3 May 1774 ball at the Pantheon see notices published in *The Gazetteer and New Daily Advertiser, The London Evening Post, The London Magazine, The Morning Chronicle and London Advertiser, The Morning Post Gazetteer, The Public Advertiser.*

For the 18 May 1775 masquerade at the Pantheon see notices published in *The London Chronicle, The Morning Chronicle, The Public Advertiser.*

For the 23 June 1775 regatta and fete at Ranelagh see notices published in *The Craftsman, or Say's Weekly Journal, The Gentleman's Magazine, The London Chronicle, The Public Advertiser, St James's Chronicle, Universal Magazine, Westminster Magazine.*

For the 26 May 1789 ball at Ranelagh see notices published in *St James's Chronicle, The London Chronicle, The Morning Post and Daily Advertiser, The Times.*

For the 2 June 1802 ball at Ranelagh see notices published in *Bell's Weekly Messenger, Caledonian Mercury, The Derby Mercury, The European Magazine, Jackson's Oxford Journal, The Morning Chronicle, The Morning Post, The Observer, The Star, The Sun, The Times.*

The letter from Sir George Onesiphorous Paul, 2nd Bt is published in Harriot, Georgiana Mundy, ed, *The Journal of Mary Frampton from the year 1779 until the year 1846*, 1885

Further accounts are published in diaries, letters, London guidebooks including:

W S Lewis, et al, ed, *Horace Walpole's Correspondence with the Countess of Upper Ossory, I, 1761–1777*, XXXII, New Haven, Yale University Press and London, Oxford University Press, 1965

W S Lewis, et al, ed, *Horace Walpole's Correspondence with Sir Horace Mann, VIII*, XXIV, New Haven, Yale University Press and London, Oxford University Press, 1967

W S Lewis, et al, ed, *Horace Walpole's Correspondence with Henry Seymour Conway, Lady Ailesbury, Lord and Lady Hertford, Lord Beauchamp and Lord Hugh Seymour, III, 1 July 1765–7 July 1795*, XXXIX, New Haven, Yale University Press and London, Oxford University Press, 1974

A Francis Steuart, ed, *The Last Journals of Horace Walpole during the reign of George III, I*, J Lane, London, 1910

Joseph Farington, *The Diary of Joseph Farington, V, August 1801 – March 1803*, Yale University Press, New Haven and London, 1979–85

Jane H Adeane and Maud Grenfell, eds, *Before and After Waterloo. Letters from Edward Stanley*, T Fisher Unwin, London, 1907

James L Clifford, ed, *Dr Campbell's Diary of a visit to England in 1775*, Cambridge University Press, Cambridge, 1947

Alfred Spencer, ed, *Memoirs of William Hickey 1749–1775, I*, Hurst and Blackett, London, 1913

John Feltham, *The picture of London, for 1803 : being a correct guide to all the curiosities, amusements, exhibitions, public establishments, and remarkable objects, in and near London*, 1803

Miscellaneous Works of Edward Gibbon, Esquire. With Memoirs of his life and writings, I, Dublin, 1796

J E Norton, *The Letters of Edward Gibbon, II, 1774–1784*, Cassell & Co, London, 1956

K Balderston, ed, *Thraliana. The Diary of Mrs Hester Lynch Thrale (later Mrs Piozzi) 1776–1809, II, 1784–1809*, Oxford, Clarendon Press, 1942

Letters to and from the Late Samuel Johnson … by Hester Lynch Piozzi, I, London, 1788

A Circumstantial Account of the Ensuing Regatta; comprehending the Plan, Arrangement, Directions, &c. relating to the Entertainment, London, [1775]

Castalia, Countess Granville, ed, *Lord Granville Leveson Gower, 1st Earl of Granville, Private Correspondence 1781 to 1821, I*, John Murray, London, 1916

Gleanings from an Old Portfolio: Containing Some Correspondence Between Lady Louisa Stuart and Her Sister Caroline, Countess of Portarlington, and Other Friends and Relations, by Alice Georgina Caroline Strong Clark, Louisa Stuart, Caroline Stuart Dawson Portarlington, private publication, 1896

Constance Hill, *Fanny Burney at the Court of Queen Charlotte*, John Lane, London, New York, 1912

William Le Fanu, ed, *Betsy Sheridan's Journal. Letters from Sheridan's sister 1784–1786 and 1788–1790*, Rutgers University Press, 1960

Slight Reminiscences of a Septugenarian from 1802 to 1815, Emma Sophia Countess Brownlow, London, 1867

Lewis, Lady Theresa, ed, *Extracts of the Journals and Correspondence of Miss Berry from the year 1783 to 1852*, II, Longmans & Co, London, 1865

Archival material:

Bedfordshire County Council, L30/14/140/8 (Letter from Earl Fitzwilliam [?William Wentworth Fitzwilliam, 2nd Earl Fitzwilliam to Thomas Robinson, 2nd Baron Grantham)

Royal Academy of Arts, London

Guildhall, City of London

The main source for biographical material was the Oxford Dictionary of National Biography which appears both in print and is available online at www.oxforddnb.com. Burke's Peerage and Debrett's were also consulted.

Secondary sources:

Aileen Ribeiro, *The Dress Worn at Masquerades in England, 1730 to 1790*, Garland Publishing, 1984, thesis to University of London, Courtauld, 1975

Charles H Gibbs-Smith, *The Fashionable Lady in the 19th Century*, London, V&A, 1960

F H W Sheppard, 'An Eighteenth-century regatta on the Thames', *History Today*, IX, no 12, December 1959, 823–829

Edward Walford, *Old and New London*, V, 1878

Mollie Sands, *Invitation to Ranelagh 1742–1803*, John Westhouse, London, 1946

H Noel Williams, *Madame Recamier and Her Friends*, C Scribner's Sons, New York, 1907

Beckford Society Newsletter, October 2009 (Arnold Wilson)

Osbert Sitwell, intro, *The Studio*, London, 1929

Sharon H Laudermilk and Teresa L Hamlin, *The Regency Companion*, Garland, New York, 1989

Annette M B Meakin, *Hannah More a Biographical Study*, Smith, Elder & Co, London, 1911

Curtis Price, Judith Milhous and Robert D Hume, 'A Plan of the Pantheon Opera House (1790–92)', *Cambridge Opera Journal* 3, 3: 213–246

Royal Collection's website at www.royalcollection.org.uk

Thomas Rowlandson's watercolour:

The full provenance of the watercolour is incomplete. Despite his name not being on any of the published lists of guests, Rowlandson may well have attended the ball at Ranelagh in 1802, making on-the-spot studies of the setting, guests and architecture. It is also not known whether he was painting this for himself or whether it was commissioned for one of the attendees (James Payne has suggested that this would have been a member of the Club, almost certainly one of the gentlemen depicted prominently). By the last quarter of the nineteenth century the picture was in the possession of Sir John Crampton, 2nd Bt (1805–1886) and was sold posthumously as coming from his collection, at Christie's London, on 16 April 1923, lot 1. It was again sold by Christie's on 22 November 1929, lot 59, as part of the collection of Rowlandson drawings accumulated by Captain Desmond Coke. It was bought by the dealer, Frank Sabin.

I would like to thank James Payne for his help.

John Baskett and Dudley Snelgrove, *The Drawings of Thomas Rowlandson in the Paul Mellon Collection*, Brandywine Press, New York, 1978

Desmond Coke, *Confessions of an Incurable Collector*, Chapman & Hall, 1928

Osbert Sitwell, *Famous Water Painters: Thomas Rowlandson*, The Studio, London, 1929

Robert R Wark, *Drawings by Thomas Rowlandson in the Huntington Collection*, Huntington Library, San Marino, 1975

Charles H Gibbs-Smith, *The Fashionable Lady in the 19th Century*, London, V&A, 1960

Chapter 6: St James's Street

Historical newspapers consulted:

The Aberdeen Journal, The Bristol Mercury, The Builder, The Court Journal: Gazette of the Fashionable Word, Freeman's Journal and Daily Commercial Advertiser, The Graphic, The Hull Packet, Lady's Weekly Miscellany, Lloyd's Weekly Newspaper, The Morning Chronicle, New Monthly Magazine and Literary Journal, Observer, The Times

Select Bibliography: primary sources:

A Companion to all the Principal Places of Entertainment in and About London and Westminster …, 8th edition, J Drew, London, 1795

New Pictorial and Practical Guide to London, Ward, Lock and Bowden, London, 1896

Thomas Allen, *History and Antiquities of London*, IV, London, 1839

Boyle's. The Fashionable Court Guide, or town visiting directory, for the year 1793, considerably enlarged, and carefully corrected.

Karl Baedeker, *London and its environs; handbook for travellers by Karl Baedeker*, 16th rev ed, Leipzig, New York, 1911

John Britton, ed, *The Original Picture of London, enlarged and improved*, 24th edition, London, [1826]

E J Burford, *Royal St James's: being a story of kings, clubmen and courtesans*, Hale, London, 1988

E B Chancellor, *Memorials of St James's Street*, Grant Richards, London, 1922

E B Chancellor, *The XVIIIth Century in London. An Account of its social life and arts*, B T Batsford, London, 1920

George Hamilton Cunningham, *London, being a comprehensive survey of the history, tradition & historical associations of buildings & monuments*, London and Toronto, J M Dent and sons, Ltd, E P Dutton & Co., 1927

George Frederick Cruchley, *Cruchley's Picture of London*, [London] 1851

Joseph Farington, *The Diary of Joseph Farington*, 17 vols, Yale University Press, New Haven and London, 1979–85

John Feltham, *The picture of London, enlarged and improved: being a correct guide for the stranger, and useful compendium for the inhabitant . . .*, 22nd ed London, Longman, Hurst, Rees, Orme, and Brown, [1821]

Augustus J C Hare, *Walks in London*, 5th ed, Smith, Elder & Co, London, 1883

Samuel Leigh, *Leigh's New Picture of London*, London, 1820

Edward Mogg, *Mogg's New Picture of London and Visitor's Guide to its Sites*, London, 1847

Joseph Nightingale, *London and Middlesex; or, an Historical, Commercial, & Descriptive Survey of the Metropolis of Great Britain. Vol III, pt II*, London, 1815

Thomas Malton, *A picturesque tour through the cities of London and Westminster, II*, London, 1792

Thomas Pennant, *Being a Complete Guide to the British Capital*, London, 1814

Flora Brenann, trans, *Puckler's Progress, The Adventures of Prince Pückler-Muskau in England, Wales and Ireland as told in letters to his former wife, 1826–9*, Collins, London, 1987

Peter Gordon, ed., *The Red Earl, papers of the 5th Earl Spencer*, Northamptonshire Record Society, Northampton, 1986

Thomas Moore, *Memoirs of the Life of Richard Brinsley Sheridan, I*, London, 1825

Louis Simond, *Journal of a Tour and Residence in Great Britain during the years 1810 and 1811, I*, 2nd ed, Longman, Hurst, Rees, Orme, and Brown, London, 1816

John Timbs, *Curiosities of London*, London, 1855

Friedrich Von Raumer, *England in 1835: Being a Series of Letters Written to friends in Germany during a residence in London and Excursions into the Provinces*, Carey, Lea, and Blanchard, Philadelphia, 1836

Secondary sources:

F H W Sheppard, ed, 'St James's Street, East Side', *Survey of London: volumes 29 and 30: St James Westminster, Part 1*, 1960

Oxford Dictionary of National Biography

Celina Fox, ed, *London, World City 1800–1840*, Yale University Press, New Haven and London, 1992

Marmaduke Milton, *St James's Street, A Poem, in Blank Verse*, London, 1790

T S Eliot, *Old Possum's Book of Practical Cats*, Faber & Faber, London, 1983

Frederick Locker, *London Lyrics*, London, 1885

Chapter 8: Boodle's Food

This chapter could not have been written without the assistance of Boodle's employees, past and present. Richard Edmonds, Boodle's Secretary 1966 until 1998, whose recollections of his time at the Club are published herein. Conversations with, and the written recollections of, Chef Keith Podmore, who was Head Chef between 1983 and 2006, have been reproduced. He has also generously supplied some of his recipes. Chef Stephen Carter has kindly allowed us to publish some of his recipes, as well as providing guidance.

Victor Ceserani's account of his time in the kitchen, originally published in *Catering for life: the Autobiography of Victor Ceserani*, 1989.

Archival material:

Boodle's own records have been an important source of information including *Boodle's Club's General Committee Minutes* and the record in an extant Club book of the 'The Attorney General's dinner April 23rd 1828 for the Kings Counsel.'

Pierpont Morgan Library, New York: Complete Pocketbook of Edward Gibbon for 1776 [PML 19089]

Historical newspapers including the *Bristol Mercury, Caledonian Mercury, The Morning Chronicle, The Times*

Select Bibliography:

Duff Hart-Davis, ed., *End of an Era: letters and journals of Sir Alan Lascelles, 1887–1920*, Hamish Hamilton, 1986

The Epicure's Almanack; or, Calendar of Good Living, London, Longman, Hurst, Rees, Orme and Brown, 1815

Charles Ritchie, *The Siren Years*, Macmillan, 1974

H B Wheatley, *London, Past and Present*, London and New York, 1891

Bibliographical material is supplied courtesy of the *Oxford Dictionary of National Biography*.

Chapter 10: A Ladies' Boodle's in the 18th Century

Historical newspapers include:

The Gentleman's Magazine, The Oxford Magazine; The Town and Country Magazine, or Universal Repository

Select primary sources include:

Charles Duke Yonge, Letters of Horace Walpole, II, G P Putnam, New York, 1890

W S Lewis, et al, ed, *Horace Walpole's Correspondence with the Countess of Upper Ossory, I, 1761–1777*, XXXII, New Haven, Yale University Press and London, Oxford University Press, 1965

W S Lewis, et al, ed, *Horace Walpole's Correspondence with Sir Horace Mann, VIII*, XXIV, New Haven, Yale University Press and London, Oxford University Press, 1967

James Harris, Earl of Malmesbury, ed, *A series of Letters of the 1st Earl of Malmesbury, His Family and Friends*, I, Richard Bentley, London, 1870

Lady Llanover, *The Autobiography and Correspondence of Mary Granville, Mrs Delaney: with interesting reminiscences of King George the third and Queen Charlotte*, I, Richard Bentley, London, 1862

Sarah Chauncey Woolsey, ed, *The Autobiography and Correspondence of Mrs Delany*, Roberts Brothers, Boston, 1878

George Paston (Emily Morse Symonds), *Mrs Delaney (Mary Granville) A Memoir 1700–1788*, E P Dutton & Co and G Richards, New York and London, 1900

Sidney Herbert, ed, *Henry, Elizabeth and George, 1734–1780: letters and diaries of Henry, Tenth Earl of Pembroke and his circle*, Jonathan Cape, London, 1939

Court Case: Case 50. Queensbury (Duke of) v. Cullen (23 March 1787)

Select secondary sources:

F H W Sheppard, ed. 'St James's Street, East Side', *Survey of London: volumes 29 & 30: The Parish of St James Westminster, Part One. South of Piccadilly*, 1960

The *Oxford Dictionary of National Biography*, print edition, and also online at www.oxforddnb.com.

'A Georgian Ladies' Club', *The Times Literary Supplement*, no 1593, 11 August 1932

Lewis Melville (Lewis Saul Benjamin), *The Beaux of the Regency*, Hutchinson & Co, London, 1908

Lewis Melville (Lewis Saul Benjamin), *Regency Ladies*, Hutchinson & Co, London [1927]

Jane Rendell, 'Almack's Assembly Rooms – A Site of Sexual Pleasure', *Journal of Architectural Education*, February 2002: 136–149

Arthur Friedman, ed., *Collected Works of Oliver Goldsmith*, V, Clarendon Press, Oxford, 1966

Chef Carter and Matthew Abbott-Williams, Pastry Chef, add the finishing touches to Grand Marnier soufflés

Notes

CHAPTER 1

1   In the order they were entered into the 'Club Book' of 1762–1764, original now housed at the London Metropolitan Archives

2   Peter Clark, *British Clubs and Societies, 1580–1800: The Origins of an Associational World* (Oxford, Oxford University Press, 2001), p 37

3   *London Evening Post*, November 18, 1760

4   Horace Walpole, *Memoirs of the Reign of King George II*, vol 2 (New Haven, 1985), p 279

5   Lady Sarah Bunbury to Marchioness of Kildare, September 30, 1762, in *Correspondence of Emily, Duchess of Leinster (1731–1814)*, ed. Brian Fitzgerald, vol 2 (Dublin, 1953), p 114

6   Lady Caroline Fox to Marchioness of Kildare, February 16, 1762, in *Correspondence of Emily, Duchess of Leinster*, vol 1 (Dublin, 1949), p 317

7   Horace Walpole, *Memoirs of the Reign of King George III*, vol 1 (New Haven, 1985), p 110

8   Clark, *British Clubs and Societies*, pp 16, 37, 41, 60, 94, 128

9   *St. James' Chronicle or the British Evening Post*, March 16–18, 1762

10 *London Evening Post*, April 20–22, 1762

11 *St. James' Chronicle or the British Evening Post*, March 31–April 3, 1764

12 Richard Rigby to Duke of Bedford, August 18, 1761, in *Correspondence of John, Fourth Duke of Bedford*, vol 3 (London, 1846), pp 39–40

13 Lady Caroline Fox to Marchioness of Kildare, February 4, 1762, *Correspondence of Emily, Duchess of Leinster*, vol 1, pp 312–13

CHAPTER 3

1   Joseph Harris, King's Assay Master of the Mint, and author of *An Essay upon Money and Coins* (1757 and 1758), which some claim to be one of the best studies of monetary analysis in the 18th century. Harris's book was one of five or six principal guides to his fellow Club member Adam Smith on the subject of money. He was an original member but not a Committee Member. He appears to have had some administrative role in the club, based on the evidence of his handwriting in the manuscript subscription book in 1762–63, according to Jenny Stanesby Moody, who is editing Harris's letters. It seems likely that the evidence of Harris's annotations have led earlier historians of the club to conclude that Boodle's and Brooks's separated in 1764. But a simpler explanation is that Harris died around this time and the handwriting in the subscription book therefore changed

2   Survey of London

3   Survey of London

4   Selwyn to Carlilse, 7 December 1775. Namier and Brooke, *History of Parliament: The Commons, 1754–1790*. Hereafter, Namier and Brooke

5   *Memoirs of William Hickey*, ed. Alfred Spencer, 1913, vol i, pp 236–37

6   *Last Journals of Horace Walpole during the Reign of George III from 1771–1783*, ed. A. Francis Stewart, 1910, vol i, pp 545–46

7   G E Cockayne, *Complete Peerage*, 2nd ed. (1910–40)

8   Survey of London

9   Namier and Brooke

10 E Fitzmaurice, *Life of Shelburne* (London, 1876), vol 1

11 Fitzmaurice, *Life of Shelburne*, vol 1, p 142

12 Formerly Lady Sarah Lennox, who was now married to Sir Thomas Bunbury, MP

13 'Thomas Bunbury', Namier and Brooke

14 Unidentified, but surely a relation

15 27 Jan 1762 letter. See 'Thomas Bunbury', Namier and Brooke

16 E de Champs, 'Jeremy Bentham at Bowood', *An Enlightenment statesman in Whig Britain. Lord Shelburne in context, 1737–1805*, N Aston and C Campbell Orr, (eds), p 233–48

17 Fitzmaurice, *Life of Shelburne*, vol 1, p 142

18 For all of the above see Namier and Brooke

19 Created Earl Talbot, March 1761

20 The 3rd Duke of Portland (succeeded 1762), elected MP for Weobley, the family seat, 1761

21 Later 3rd baronet

22 Succeeded as 2nd Earl Cornwallis, 1762

23 KNOWN=92; UNK=30; N=122. The names on the list which are crossed out or recorded as not paying subscriptions are included as an indication of the initial social profile of the club

24 *Public Ledger* (1779)

25 R Pares, *A West India Fortune* (New York, 1968), p 280–92

26 *A Letter to a Noble Member of the Club in Albemarle Street from John Wilkes, Esq, at Paris* (1764)

27 Survey of London

28 Namier and Brooke

29 Fitzmaurice, *Life of Shelburne*, vol 1, p 143

30 Fitzmaurice, *Life of Shelburne*, vol 2, p 181

31 Fitzmaurice, *Life of Shelburne*, vol 1, p 144

32 Greville was even on the Management Committee in 1762

33 N Phillipson, *Adam Smith. An Enlightened Life* (2010), p 166–70

34 Namier and Brooke

35 Succeeded as Viscount Howe, 1758

36 Later General Lord Amherst

37 Elected 1764

38 Wolfe's ADC (elected 1770)

39 Later the 1st Earl Grey (elected 1789)

40 C P Stacey, 'Benjamin West and the Death of Wolfe', *Bulletin of the National Gallery of Canada*, 7 (iv.1) 1966

41 Fitzmaurice, *Life of Shelburne*

42 Discussions with Jenny Moody have been valuable on some of these points

43 Survey of London

44 Camden to Frances Stewart, 7 February 1781 (Camden MSS); *English Chronicle* 1781; quoted in Namier and Brooke

45 Namier demonstrated the limited power of the nobility over the Commons decades ago, however. Namier, *Structure of Politics*, p 144

46 *Enlightenment Statesman* Aston and Campbell Orr, p 117

47 B Simms, *Three Victories and a Defeat: The Rise and Fall of the First British Empire* (Penguin, 2008), p 520

48 P Whiteley, *Lord North. The Prime Minister who lost America* (London, 1996), p 103–14

49 Namier, *Structure of Politics*, p 144

50 D E Ginter, 'The financing of the Whig party organisation, 1783–1793', American Historical Review (vol 71:2, Jan 1966)

51 Namier and Brooke

52 Namier and Brooke

53 Fitzmaurice, *Life of Shelburne*

54 N Phillipson, *Adam Smith. An Enlightened Life*

55 F O'Gorman, 'Shelburne: a Chathamite in Opposition and in Government, 1760–82?', *Enlightenment statesman*, Aston and Campbell Orr, p 117–40

56 Namier and Brooke

57 Namier and Brooke

58 N Wraxall, *Memoirs*

59 Namier and Brooke

60 Cockayne, *Complete Peerage*

61 Fitzmaurice, *Life of Shelburne*, I, vol 1, p 79

CHAPTER 5
1 *The Clubs of London* (Anon) 1828 p 15

2 T Malton, *Picturesque Tour through the Cities of London and Westminster* (1792)

3 *London Clubs: Their History and Treasures* by Ralph Nevill (London 1911, reprinted 1969)

4 Survey of London xxx, 441–9

5 Memoir of Richard Miles April 1834

6 Christopher Hussey, 'Boodle's Club, London' in *Country Life* December 24, 1932

7 Alison Kelly, *Mrs Coade's Stone* (1990), pp 164–167

8 Robert Adam, *Ruins of the palace of the Emperor Diocletian at Spalatro in Dalmatia* (1764), pl xlix

9 Crunden's birthdate is given as *c*.1741 in Howard Colvin's *Dictionary of British Architects 1600–1840*, 4th ed, 2008 but Eileen Harris gives a date of *c*.1745 in her *British Architectural Books and Writers 1556–1785* (1990)

10 H Colvin, *Dictionary of British Architects 1600–1840*, 4th ed (2008), p288

11 Cited in description accompanying Grade II listing in February 1958

12 *The Southampton Guide* 1787 and *Architectural Review*, xlv, Feb 1919, 33

13 *Survey of London* xxxix, pl 13c, xl, 174

14 Charles Welsh, *A Bookseller of the Last Century*, 1885, 143–4

15 G D Squibb, *Belfield and the Buxtons*, privately printed 1954, 2; RCHM Dorset, ii (2) 340 and plates

16 Cited in Grade II* Listing description of 1953

17 Survey of London xxx, 441–9

18 Howard Colvin, *Dictionary of British Architects 1600–1840*, 4th ed, (2008)

19 Henry Luttrell, *Advice to Julia. A Letter in Rhyme* (1820)

20 Amy Milne-Smith, *London Clubland: A Cultural History of Gender and Class in Late Victorian Britain* (2011)

21 National Archives CRES 35/3791

22 National Archives CRES 35/3793

23 'London Clubs: Boodle's *Country Life*, December 9, 1916

24 Humphry Repton, *Fragments on the theory and practice of landscape gardening* (1816) on the 'Ancient Cedar Parlour and the Modern Living Room'

25 Photographs in English Heritage Archive, Swindon (former National Monuments Record)

26 *Survey of London*, xxxix

27 This was taken from The Memorial of Richard Miles

28 'Clubbable Colours' by John Martin Robinson in *Country Life*, April 17, 1997

29 'Boodle's Club London' in *Country Life*, December 24, 1932

30 http://www.apter-fredericks.com/blades/636.htm

31 *The Survey of London* notes that the dimensions of a 'capacious dining room' on the first floor, mentioned in the sale particulars of 1802 corresponded closely with those of Papworth's dining room. He may therefore have been remodeling an earlier room (ref 73)

32 *Country Life*, December 24 ,1932

33 'Great Social Clubs-III. Boodle's', *The Field*, July 22, 1939

34 Information from Stefa Hart

35 National Archives CRES 35/3791

36 National Archives CRES 35/3791

37 National Archives CRES 35/3792

38 National Archives LRRO/4208

39 National Archives CRES 35/3792

40 *The Economist*, July 15, 1961

Postscript

MARCUS BINNEY

This book has grown to include fresh, exciting and substantial research and contributions on the history on the Club and its early members. These provide a new window on the role of London clubs in 18th-century social and political life. The Club is privileged to have such distinguished historians and authors illuminating its history.

A second point to emerge from this book and its illustrations is that the architecture, interiors and furnishings of Boodle's are of a quality and interest greater than has been apparent, and that the Regency remodelling in particular is an exceptional survival of a wonderful era.

This book already substantial, evidently does not carry a detailed examination of the Club's history and members in the 19th and 20th century, though there is entertaining material on this in Stephen Hill's *A Boodle's Apocrypha* which is not duplicated here. For the Club's next major anniversary I venture the hope that present or future members may wish to take the story forward in the context of unfolding historical research and writing on London clubs and their members, who were, and are, far from the Noodle's engagingly caricatured in the cartoons and verse in these pages.

I hope too this book will stir the memories of members and staff to provide further thoughts and insights, and hopefully some ephemera too in the form of menus, letters and the like, which will lend further colour to the story of the Club.

It is very sad that David Mann is not here to enjoy the fruit of his enthusiasms and labours but I hope that members will find the book is the handsome and intriguing memoir on the Club he hoped to produce.

MARCUS BINNEY
November 2012

Acknowledgements

Richard Edmonds, Keith Podmore, Andrew Phillips and Stephen
    Carter as well as current and former staff of Boodle's
Alexandra Aslett, St Paul's School, London
Stephen Astley, Sir John Soane's Museum
Shawn De Clair
Andrea Gilbert, Wallace Collection
Philip Hewat-Jaboor
Amanda Ingram, McGowin Library, Pembroke College, Oxford
Anne Kriken Mann
Jeremy Linton, The Crown Estate
Lynda McLeod, Christie's Archive
Marie Murphy
Lord Northbook
Bryan Oates
James Payne
Richard Samways
Robin Darwall Smith, Magdalen College, Oxford
Miriam Stewart, Harvard Art Museum
Sir Nigel Thompson KCMG CBE
James Collett White, Bedfordshire County Records Office
Scott Wilcox, Yale Center for British Art
Hon Georgina Stonor
Lord Shuttleworth of Gawthorpe
Francis Shepherd
John Nicoll, Jessica Halliwell, and all staff at Frances Lincoln
And individuals who wished to remain anonymous.

The Baring Archive, London
Department of Special Collections, Bodleian Libraries, University
    of Oxford
British Library
British Library Manuscript Collections
British Museum
Centre for Buckinghamshire Studies

Christie's London
Country Life Picture Library
Coutts Bank
Durham County Record Office
Fusilier Museum, Bury
Guildhall Library
Heinz Archive & Library at the National Portrait Gallery
Hertfordshire Archives and Local Studies
Hoare's Bank
Isle of Wight Record Office
Kensington Central Library
Lincolnshire Archive
London Library
London Metropolitan Archive
Morgan Library, New York
National Art Library
The National Library of Wales, Aberystwyth
National Monuments Record Office, Swindon
New York Public Library
Newport City Library
Royal Institute of British Architects
Royal Academy of Arts
The Royal Bank of Scotland Group plc, Group Archives
Royal Collection
Shropshire County Council
Sotheby's London and New York
Surrey History Centre
Topfoto
Thomas J Watson Library, New York
The University of Nottingham, Manuscripts and Special
    Collections
Victoria and Albert Museum Theatre Collections
Wiltshire and Swindon History Centre

My warmest thanks to the following: John Hardy, formerly of the V&A Museum and Christie's, who has provided me with numerous insights as we have walked round Boodle's on successive occasions discussing the interiors and furniture: Calder Loth, formerly senior architectural historian to the State of Virginia, for his expertise on the classical Orders; Professor David Watkin for his suggestions of sources for Papworth's designs; Philip Hewat-Jaboor, fellow member of Boodle's, and a fount of knowledge on neo-classical interiors; Michael Snodin, formerly of the V&A, who suggested Bacchus and Ariadne as the possible subject for the mural over the saloon chimneypiece; James Knox and William Zachs for their ideas on Boodle's and the 18th-century Scottish enlightenment; John Harris, Tim Knox and Richard Garnier for thoughts on Crunden and the Adamesque decoration in the Saloon; Seth Alexander Thévoz at the History of Parliament for information about facilities in the Lords and Commons in the 18th and early 19th century; to Jeremy Linton for information on the archives of the Crown Commissioners; Veronica Hitchcock for information about *Blow-Up*; Simon Smithson, son of Alison and Peter Smithson, who gave me his observations on the design of the Economist Plaza; Andrew Knight former Editor of *The Economist* for further enlightenment; and also David Gordon, former CEO of *The Economist* and Robert Turner of SOM who worked on the Economist Tower and Plaza in 1987–89; Stuart Richmond Watson who has overseen so much of the work on the Club; Stefa Hart who has walked round the Club explaining her many contributions; and Peregrine Bryant the Club architect who provided details of his recent work; David Brook for his speed and efficiency in taking photographs of the Club and its furnishings including many fine details of furniture, clocks and candelabra; John Goodall of *Country Life* for allowing the excellent photographs taken by William Pryce for my article in *Country Life* to be used in this book; and Justin Hobson for his repeated help in supplying images from the *Country Life* archive taken for successive articles in the magazine; Sue Palmer at the Soane Museum for help with illustrations; Francis Russell at Christie's for the same; Lindsay Jones, Ian Leith, Charlotte Wiberg and Nigel Wilkins of English Heritage in supplying historic photographs.

I wish to thank Neil Hitchin for detailed and fascinating analysis of the early members of Boodle's, and Professor David Hancock for finding time, at short notice, amidst his major research on a monograph on Lord Shelburne, to write a thrilling and wholly new account of the 25 founding members of the Club.

At Boodle's thanks to Andrew Phillips, Club Secretary, for help of many kinds, including the documents and photographs kept at the Club; to his tireless assistant Jeanette Davies for ordering photographs and supplying print outs and photocopies and also Edward Plunket House Manager; Montse Ruiz for transcribing The Memorial of Richard Miles and other documents; Chef Stephen Carter for his contribution to the section on recipes; Anne Kriken Mann for hospitality in Basel; Daniella Ben-Arie who suggested many of the historic illustrations in the book including portraits, caricatures, prints and engravings. Three successive chairmen of Boodle's have played an important role in the evolution of the book – Patrick Burgess, Charles Vyvyan and Alastair Macpherson; John Nicoll of Frances Lincoln for publishing advice; my wife Anne and sons Francis and Christopher who have lived with this book rather longer than intended.

The design of the book is the work of Michael Mitchell of Libanus Press and his colleague Susan Wightman who have undertaken every aspect of layout and production with unswerving patience and skill giving us the benefit of their unrivalled expertise in typography.

MARCUS BINNEY

229

Picture credits

Published in Great Britain in 2012 by

Boodle's
28 St James's Street
London SW1A 1HJ

ISBN 978-0-9574617-0-3

Designed by Libanus Press, Marlborough
Printed and bound in Great Britain by Hampton Printing (Bristol) Ltd

New London Almanack for the Year 1777.

The ALMANACK
EXPLAINED.

Note *that under the Title of every Month is the change of the Moon & every Month contains three Columns.*
1 *Days of the Month.*
2 *Saints Days, &c.*
3 *The Time of high Water at London Bridge*

Printed for G. Robinson Nº. 25. Paternoster Row.

The SÇAVOIR VIVRE,

JANUARY XXXI

◐ Last 1 day 9 at night
● New 9 day 4 afternoon
◑ First 16 day at noon
○ Full 23 day 4 afternoon
◐ Last 31 day 6 at night

1	Circumcision	8 M 45
2	☉ rises 8.4	9	6
3	☉ sets 3.57	9	39
		10	63
E	S. aft. Circum. Old Christ. Day	
6	Epiphany	0 A 31
7	Clock fast 7 m	1	25
8		2	31
9	Day inc. 0.20	3	18
10	☉ rises 7.57	4	14
11		5	9
E	1. S. aft Epiph.	6	2
13	Camb. Term beg.	6	53
14	Oxf. Term. beg.	7	43
15	Clock fast. 10 m.	8	34
16		9	25
17		10	17
18	Q. Char. Birth day kept	
E	2. S. aft. Epiph.	Morn
20		Oct. Hill.
21		1	1
22		1	55
23	Term begins	2	47
24	Day inc. 2.58	3	37
25	Conv. St. Paul	4	23
E	Septuagesi. S.	5	9
27	Pr. Aug. Fred. bo.	Qui Hill.
28		6	31
29	☉ sets 4.29	7	12
30	K. Cha. I. mart.	7	54
31	Clock fast. 14 m.	8	37

FEBRUARY XXVIII

● New 8 day 5 morning
◑ First 14 day 8 at night
○ Full 22 day 9 morning

1	Day inc. 1.24	9 M 23
E	Sexage l. Sund. Pur. Vir. Ma.	
3		Cras Pu.
4		11	58
5		0 A 55
6	☉ rises 7.28	1	53
7	☉ sets 4.45	2	50
8		3	46
E	Shrove Sund.	Oct. Pu.
10	Clock fast 15 m.	5	34
11	Shrove Tues.	5	26
12	Ash Wednesd. Term ends	
13		8	11
14		9	4
15		9	58
E	1 S in Lent	10	53
17	☉ rises 6.58	11	47
18	☉ sets 5.5	Morn
19	Ember Week	0	39
20	Clock fast 14 m.	1	29
21	Day inc. 2.37	2	17
22		3	2
E	2 S. in Lent	3	46
24	St. Matthias Pr. Adol. Fre. bo.	
25		5	9
26	☉ rises 6.41	5	51
27	☉ sets 5.22	6	33
28		7	17

MARCH XXXI

◐ Last 2 day 2 afternoon
● New 9 day 3 afternoon
◑ First 16 day 6 morning
○ Full 24 day 3 morning

1		8 M
E	3. S. in Lent	8	5
3	☉ rises 6.27	10	4
4	☉ sets 5.36	11	4
5		0 A
6		1	
7		2	
8	Clock fast. 11 m.	3	
E	4. S. in Lent	4	
10	Day inc. 3.47	5	
11		6	
12		6	
13	☉ rises 6.9	7	
14	☉ sets 5.54	8	
15		9	
E	5. S. in Lent	9	
17		10	
18		11	
19	Clock fast. 8 m.	Morn
20	Equal. D. & N.	0	
21	Camb. T. ends	1	
22	Oxf. T. ends	2	
E	Palm. Sunday	3	
24	☉ rises 5.47	4	
25	Lady-Day	5	
26	☉ sets 6.18	5	
27		6	
28	Good-Friday	6	
29	Day inc. 5.3	7	
E	Easter-Day	8	
31	Easter Mond.		